A Publication of the Egon-Sohmen-Foundation

Herbert Giersch (Ed.)
for the Egon-Sohmen-Foundation

Economic Progress and Environmental Concerns

With 34 Figures

Springer-Verlag

Berlin Heidelberg New York
London Paris Tokyo
Hong Kong Barcelona
Budapest

Prof. Dr. Herbert Giersch
Past President
Kiel Institute of World Economics
D-24100 Kiel

This book was produced with financial support of the Egon-Sohmen-Foundation

ISBN 3-540-56466-7 Springer-Verlag Berlin Heidelberg New York Tokyo
ISBN 0-387-56466-7 Springer-Verlag New York Berlin Heidelberg Tokyo

42/7130-543210 - Printed on acid-free paper

Preface

This is the third volume in the series of books emanating from the activities of the Egon-Sohmen-Foundation, established by Helmut Sohmen in memory of his late brother. Egon Sohmen (1930–1976) was a highly respected international economist who studied and worked in Vienna, Lawrence (Univ. of Kansas), Tübingen, Cambridge (MIT), New Haven (Yale), Saarbrücken (Univ. of the Saar), Heidelberg, Minneapolis (Univ. of Minnesota).

The first two books, published in 1991 and 1992 by the Springer-Verlag, contain essays on *The Economic Transformation of Central and Eastern Europe* and on *Money, Trade, and Competition.* The essays were discussed at conferences held at Laxenburg near Vienna and at Tegernsee in the Bavarian Alps. The Tegernsee Conference was organized in 1990 to commemorate Egon Sohmen's 60th birthday and assembled scholars eager to pay tribute to his major achievements.

At the end of the Tegernsee discussions Regine Sohmen, Egon's widow, suggested holding a symposium on environmental issues relevant to present-day economists. Linz in Austria, Egon's birthplace, was chosen as the conference venue.

In preparing the conference we adopted as a working title "Economic Evolution and Environmental Concerns." The emphasis on evolution was to serve several purposes. We wanted to avoid "growth" for the reason that the term is often misunderstood to describe an essentially quantitative phenomenon. Moreover, it seemed useful to direct attention to the role that innovation plays in advanced countries, notably innovation for quality improvement and resource saving. Innovations are like mutations in evolutionary biology; some of them are viable, others are not. The selection mechanism of competition could perhaps be biased in favor of what has been termed "sustainable development." But we also wanted to avoid the word "development," as many economists and others have become used to associating it with the problems of poor countries in what was once called "the Third World." Finally, "economic evolution" was chosen, as a challenge to those scholars who are working towards an evolutionary approach in economics. It was our hope that we could enlist more than one author to show that evolutionary economics is particularly suitable to meeting environmental concerns.

As we failed on the last account, we decided to reserve "evolution" for another occasion and to use the word "progress" in the title of this book. It reflects the editor's belief that progress in meeting environmental concerns – as they arise when people endeavor to overcome scarcities – will essentially come from the growth of knowledge, a growth we can expect from the increasing division of labor among brains in a market for ideas that becomes ever larger as communication costs continue to shrink. This optimism is in tune with the nonalarmist nature of most of the papers in this volume. It should, however, not be misunderstood to imply that environmental concerns are unwarranted. They remain a great challenge to the natural sciences as well as to economics.

There is no need to summarize the papers or the discussions or to make more detailed comments. The titles speak for themselves, and the major points made during the conference, which was held in late August 1991, were taken account of in the versions revised for publication. One paper was withdrawn by its author after the conference. During the conference, the discussions were quite relaxed, though from time to time opposing views were brought forward and harsh criticism was applied.

As at previous conferences, members of the Sohmen family who were present attended all of the sessions and took an active part in discussions. The whole atmosphere was pleasant, not in small part due to their involvement. Presiding over the meetings was an enjoyable experience.

If all participants went home with good feelings, despite the seriousness of the issues raised, generous credit has to be given also to the Raiffeisenlandesbank in Linz and to its Director-General, Mag. Dr. Ludwig Scharinger, and his aides. Their hospitality and support greatly added to the quality of the conference. The participants all enjoyed the beauty of Linz and its surrounding countryside.

The conference and the present volume owe a great deal to the considerable advice and help I received from Joachim Fels before and after the event. Thanks are also due to Torsten Amelung and Johannes Heister for their valuable advice on the choice of topics and speakers for the conference. We are also indebted to Prof. Friedrich Schneider of the University in Linz who not only contributed a paper to the volume but also assisted with the organization locally.

Contents

Part I
General Aspects

The Environmental Limits to Growth: A Fresh Look

Wilfred Beckerman

Introduction

A The Limits to Growth

The proposition that there must be limits on the feasibility or desirability of economic growth set by the adverse impact of economic activity on the environment has always been just one strand in the frequently encountered arguments to the effect that continued economic growth is fraught with many dangers to the human race. Just over twenty years ago many people in developed countries began to express grave doubts as to the desirability of continued economic growth. The main reasons for this concern were first set out brilliantly by E.J. Mishan (1967), who enumerated various alleged shortcomings of economic growth. Pollution of the environment was only one of them. Others included congestion of travel facilities and holiday resorts, and other forms of externality, as well as less tangible effects, such as the subordination of nobler social values to the pursuit of commercial objectives and the consequent deterioration in society's moral standards. Similar concerns were set out in well-known books by Fred Hirsch (1977) and E.F. Schumacher (1973).

Paradoxically, at the same time as the undesirability of continued economic growth was being proclaimed it was also often maintained – usually by the same people – that continued economic growth was also impossible on account of an impending shortage of raw materials or food supplies, or of environmental catastrophe. It was never clear why such groups of people were so alarmed at the prospect that economic growth was both undesirable and impossible, for it would have presumably been much more alarming if it had been either undesirable but inevitable, or desirable but impossible. A situation in which something was both undesirable but impossible would seem, on the face of it, to be highly satisfactory.

Nevertheless, much attention was given to the warnings about the inevitable constraints on growth that were formulated precisely in *The Limits to Growth*, a study commissioned by the "Club of Rome" (Meodows et al., 1972). This study purported to show that (i) on any reasonable assumptions, continued economic growth would mean that the world would run out of resources of key materials within a time period that ought to be of concern to current generations; (ii) population growth would outrun the world's capacity to increase food supply, and (iii) increasing environmental damage would make this planet uninhabitable. This paper is primarily concerned with the last of these three alleged consequences of economic growth, but the two others require some brief mention, particularly since the environmental effects of economic growth are often defined widely to include its effects on supplies of natural resources.

B Economic Growth and Resources

Whilst the basic methodology used in the *Limits to Growth* was derived from that developed by Jay Forrester (1968), in that it employed a computerized "systems dynamics" model that enabled the emphasis to be placed on the interrelationships and "feedbacks" between different parts of a complex model, serious defects in its particular application of the Forrester techniques were immediately apparent, and as soon as it appeared the main assumptions and methodological procedures adopted in *The Limits to Growth* and similar doomladen predictions were subjected to sharp criticism by expert commentators.[1] One of the main criticisms was of the failure to allow for crucial economic feedbacks between rising prices of any resource that seems to be becoming in short supply and the numerous mechanisms that would be brought into play to alleviate the shortage. These would include substitution of other materials for the material in question, increased prospecting for further supplies, technological progress in extracting and pro-

---

Footnotes appear on pp. 20–22

cessing supplies, or economizing in their end-use, and so on. Such feedback mechanisms seemed to have operated successfully throughout history, so that numerous predictions made at least as far back as Ancient Greece to the effect that the human race was about to exhaust available supplies of some key material have always turned out to have been wrong.

For example, a 1972 World Bank report on *The Limits to Growth*, pointed out that a major 1929 study had concluded that "... the known resources of tin do not seem to satisfy the ever increasing demand of the industrial nations for more than 10 years."[2] But over forty-three years later the authors of *The Limits to Growth* were worried because existing "known" reserves of tin were only enough to last for another fifteen years. Still, that was better than in 1929 when tin reserves were believed to be only enough to last for ten years. At this rate we shall have to wait millions of years before we have identified enough tin reserves to last us forever. Meanwhile, we shall just have to go on using up that ten years' supply which was all we had back in 1929.

During the roughly two decades that have passed since *The Limits to Growth* and similar doomsday pronouncements were published the story is essentially the same. For example, in *The Limits to Growth*, 1970 world supplies of lead were put at 91 million metric tons. Between 1970 and 1989 the world consumed 98.5 million metric tons. Yet by 1989 total known reserves of lead instead of being negative were actually 125 million tons. Exactly the same applies to natural gas and zinc, in that cumulative world consumption during the period 1970–89 equaled or exceeded the 1970 "known reserves," yet the known reserves at the end of the period were greater than at the outset.[3]

Similarly, the balance between world supply and demand for food has not developed along the lines of the doomsday predictions. World food output over the last twenty years – as, indeed, over the preceding twenty years as well – has continued to rise faster than world population. Food output per head, therefore, has continued to grow (UNCTAD, 1989, p. 456, Table 6.5) It is true that this does not apply to every area of the globe and that this has not prevented human factors – such as civil wars, blatant discrimination, and so on – from leading to massive food shortages in particular regions. But the fact that human stupidity and evil is capable of leading to disasters is nothing new and has nothing to do with the "Limits to Growth" thesis.

However, as indicated above, limits to growth arising out of constraints on supplies of food or raw materials – like the problem of whether economic growth does really add to human welfare in some sense – are not the central theme of this paper, which is one of the other alleged reasons why economic growth was either impossible or undesirable or both, namely the harm done to the environment. Here, at first sight, the "Limits to Growth" school of thought appeared to be on safer ground, since evidence of environmental deterioration accompanying economic growth was not difficult to find.

I The General Nature of the Growth/Environment Relationship

Although there is ample evidence of the manner in which economic activity can harm the environment, there is often a confusion between the problem of the misallocation of resources at any moment in time and the problem of the misallocation of resources over time. The debate over the impact of economic growth on the environment is a clear example of this. The crucial feature of environmental damage is not that it takes place, but that at any point in time it tends to be excessive. Some pollution of the environment may be perfectly optimal in the sense that, at the margin, the costs to society of the environmental damage are just matched by the social benefits of the particular use of the environment involved. Unfortunately, certain characteristics of the environment – notably the absence, usually, of clearly defined property rights – means that it is used to excess. This is a well-known type of market failure caused by externalities. Insofar as policies to correct the market failure are not adopted, so that certain economic activities lead to excessive pollution of the environment, then it is true that, *other things being equal*, a rise in the scale of the economic activity in question will tend to make the pollution even more excessive.

But, of course, stopping economic growth will not bring excessive pollution to an end. Resources can be misallocated at any moment in time with or without economic growth. The key issue concerning the relationship between the environmental pollution problem and economic growth is how far do other things remain equal. More precisely, the real question is how far economic growth is conducive to changes in preferences, technologies, or governmental policies that reduce the pollution intensity of economic activity at any moment in time. And there is ample evidence that, in the longer run, economic growth does lead to such favorable changes, so that "other things" do not remain equal.

The prima facie reasons for expecting economic growth to be good for the environment, on the whole, as well as bad for it in specific instances and particular time periods, hardly need elaboration. A casual glance at the state of the environment in the major cities of the world shows that the environment that matters most to human beings – notably access to water and sanitation, housing, social infrastructure and the more traditional types of air pollution such as SO_2 and smoke – is much better in the richer countries than in the poorer. And although the data are more fragmentary, the disparity between developed and developing countries is even greater in rural areas.

Nor is the reason for this difficult to see. As people get richer their priorities change and the environment moves up in the hierachy of human needs. When their basic needs for food, water, clothing and shelter are satisfied they can begin to attach importance to other ingredients in total welfare, including, eventually, the environment. As public perceptions and concerns move in the environmental direction, so communities will be more willing to allocate resources to this purpose. And this shift in expenditure priorities is easier insofar as richer countries will be more able to afford them.

For example, U.S. public and private expenditures on pollution abatement and control ("PAC" expenditures) represent nearly 2 percent of GNP, which is a higher share than for any other country for which comparative data are available. And the share is still rising (OECD, 1990, p. 40, Table 2). PAC expenditures in the U.S.A. rose at an average annual rate of 3.2% over the period 1972–1987, during which period total real GNP rose by 2.6% (Farber and Rutledge, 1989, p. 19–23). The only other country for which comparable data are available for any length of time is

Germany, where, too, total private and public PAC expenditures rose (at constant prices) at an annual average rate of 3.4% during the period 1975 to 1985, raising the share of these expenditures in GNP from 1.37% to 1.52%. In Japan, data are available for a long run of years for pollution control expenditures only in the public sector, and these show an average annual rise (at constant prices), from 1975 through 1986, of 6.1%, which outstripped even Japan's fast rate of growth and so raised the share of these expenditures in GNP from 0.95% to 1.17%.

These increases in expenditures have done more than just keep pace with the increasing burden that, in principle, higher levels of economic activity can impose on the environment. This is partly because the pattern of output in advanced countries has been changing in a direction that tends to impose less of a burden on the environment than was the case at earlier stages of their development. At higher levels of income, industry accounts for a smaller share of GDP, and services, which are relatively nonpolluting, account for an increasing share. Even within industry there has tended to be a shift away from the highly polluting heavy industries, including metallurgy and heavy engineering, towards high-tech, high value-added industries employing large amounts of very skilled human capital and with smaller inputs of energy or raw materials.[4] In addition, policies to combat pollution have been introduced mainly in richer countries, of course, since they have the resources to implement their shift in priorities.

A striking example of the complexity of the growth/environment relationship and the role of policies is the incidence of automotive air pollution in large cities. The largest reductions in automotive pollution have been achieved in Germany, Japan, and the U.S.A. as a result of their relatively early introduction of stringent controls on motor vehicles. There has also been a move in this direction in most Western European countries, although such policies as have been adopted so far seem to have been offset, in some cases, by increases in numbers of the vehicles. By contrast, although similar regulatory measures have also been introduced recently in some developing countries, with one or two exceptions they have had little effect.

The reasons for this are basically related to their level of development. For example, a recent World Bank report states that "motor vehicles in many developing countries are not as fuel efficient as in industrialized countries. Many of the vehicles are old and poorly maintained because of lack of spare parts and other resources. For example, in India a major portion of the vehicle fleet is older than ten years ... Two-stroke engine motorcycles are also a major source of air contaminants ... Moreover, the gasoline used in most developing countries still has a high percentage of lead" (Faiz et al., 1990, p. 40). The same report points out that, for example, in Mexico City, more than 40% of the cars are over 12 years old and, of these, most have engines in major need of repairs (Faiz et al., 1990, p. 17) In addition to the poor quality of old cars and the backward technology associated with low income levels, where controls have been introduced the conditions in most developing countries have made it very difficult to monitor them effectively.

Thus the effect of rising incomes and the commonly associated changes in policy demonstrate that the scope for changes in the growth-environment relationship must not be neglected. It is a crude fallacy to suppose the technical relationship between any particular activity and its impact on the environment is fixed and not amenable to major changes in response to incentives of one kind or another. Even back in the late 1960s and early 1970s, before many countries had introduced significant disincentives to pollution, there were numerous striking instances of massive reductions in the pollution intensity of various important and highly polluting forms of economic activity, such as in oil refining, or pulp and paper production, and many metal using processes (Beckerman, 1974).

One of the main changes that has taken place over the last decade has been the greatly increased acceptance of economic incentives to reduce pollution. In the past, government policies to reduce the pollution intensity of economic activities have been mainly of the "command and control" variety, and little use has been made of price mechanism incentives, such as pollution charges. It is true that, as far back as February 8, 1972, the imposition of a charge on sulphur oxide emissions was announced in the U.S. President's Message to Congress, and a "Coalition to Tax Pollution" was set up by some environmentalist groups in the U.S.A. Numerous studies were also produced both by academics and by the OECD to strengthen the case for pollution charges.[5] But bureaucratic traditions die hard, and it is probably no coincidence that it needed the worldwide shift towards more market-oriented policies for the use of pollution charges, or "tradeable permits" to become more acceptable in most countries.

Thus for one reason or another – rising incomes and changes in priorities in favor of more expenditure to reduce pollution, or increasing awareness of the rise in pollution, or increasing understanding of the market failure nature of excessive pollution and hence of the scope for appropriate policies to remedy the market failure – higher incomes seem to be associated with measures that can bring about drastic favorable changes in the relationship between economic activity and environmental pollution. Some of the highlights of this changing relationship are surveyed briefly in the next section of this paper.

II The Empirical Relationship between Growth and the Environment

A Longer-Run Historical Trends

When concern about the environmental consequences of economic growth began to become widespread, towards the end of the 1960s and the early 1970s, data on environmental pollution were fragmentary and limited to recent years except for very few countries, mainly the U.K. and, to a lesser extent, the U.S.A. Nevertheless, descriptions of the environment in British cities in earlier times made it perfectly clear that however much one might complain about the air pollution, say, in the center of London it was incomparably better than in the 19th Century.[6]

But less it be thought that the comparison with the more distant past is irrelevant, it should be noted that even in the more recent past such evidence as was available in the early 1970s already pointed to an improvement in the environment in the more advanced countries. For example, in Britain, the dramatic reduction in air pollution was well documented by the late 1960s. The total smoke produced in Britain had fallen from 2.3 million tons in 1953 to 0.9 million in 1968; the total quantity of sulphur oxides emitted in the air in Britain had been falling since 1962, and there had been a sharper fall in ground-level concentrations of sulphur oxides. Over the 1960s average smoke concentrations in urban areas in Britain fell by 60 percent, and SO_2 (sulphur dioxide) concentrations fell by 30 percent, despite increasing population and industrial output.[7] In Greater London, smoke emissions decreased by over 80 percent in the 12-year period 1958–70, even though output must have risen by at least 30 percent over the same period, implying a fall in the pollution/output ratio of about 85 percent.[8] And similar improvements were being achieved in other cities in advanced countries where environmental controls were at last being introduced.[9]

But these results related only to advanced countries. This was partly because, for the reasons given above, it would be the advanced countries that first began to attach importance to measures to protect the environment. But it was also because data were only available for a handful of countries, these being, of course, countries that were motivated to take action to protect their environment. The developing countries of the world were not very interested in giving any priority to environmental protection – for very legitimate reasons – and so would not be prepared to devote the resources necessary to monitor their environments, even if they had possessed the resources necessary to do the job. But in the last few years, of course, many developing countries have become aware of the extent to which their economic development has damaged their environments and the focus of world attention has been shifted far more in the direction of the environmental threat in the third world countries.

As a result a body of data describing environmental conditions in many countries is beginning to be built up, largely under the impetus of the GEMS program.[10] Whilst these data do make it possible to demonstrate that, in the longer run, economic growth still has a favorable impact on the environment – as in the earlier periods referred to above – they do not permit precise estimates of the relationship between economic growth and the environment. This is because environmental data are subject to numerous practical and conceptual limitations a discussion of which is precluded here on account of space limitations.

B Environment and Development: The Recent Experience

Given the many constraints on environmental data any comparison of environmental conditions in countries at different income levels has to be limited to comparisons between broad groupings of countries. However, even such broad comparisons demonstrate clearly that:

(i) in the long run, economic growth has a favorable impact on those components of the environment that are of most concern to the population of the developing countries. And, it should be remembered, these are generally defined in such a way as to comprise about 75 percent of the world's population; and

(ii) the main environmental problems of developing countries are not those that are fashionable in the media discussions of the developed world, such as the ozone layer, or global warming. The most important environmental issues for developing countries are access to safe drinking water and adequate sanitation, and, in many large cities, urban air quality.

The following data are consequently limited to water access and quality and urban air quality. This does not mean that other components of the environment – such as biodiversity, soil erosion and so on – are not regarded as being important. But it is even more difficult to pin down reliable data on what exactly is happening in these particular environmental media. Nor does it mean that no importance is attached to influences on the global environment. But my views on this have been set out elsewhere (see Beckerman, 1991), and, in any case, the contribution by William Nordhaus to this volume deals with global warming.

1 Water

Table 1 below shows the percentage of the population with access to safe drinking water in countries with different income levels, in 1975 and 1985. As one would expect, higher incomes tend to be associated with a higher proportion of the population having access to safe drinking water.[11] There has also been some progress in almost all countries over the period 1975 to 1985, in spite of the rapid growth of the population of most developing countries

Table 1. Income Levels and Access to Safe Drinking Water, 1975 and 1985

	1975		1985	
Quintile	Average Income	Water Access	Average Income	Water Access
1	$206	25%	$224	39%
2	$342	25%	$373	48%
3	$692	35%	$746	48%
4	$1,094	48%	$1,209	60%
5	$2,381	75%	$3,372	87%

Notes: Quintiles are based on income ranking for 1985 in 1987 $US and all income figures are in 1987 $US. Water access refers to the percent of the total population of the countries in question having access to safe drinking water. For definitions and sources, see World Resources Institute (1990, Table 16.4 and pp. 265–266).

during this period. It can be seen that there is both a generally much higher percentage of the population with access to safe drinking water in the top two quintiles, and that in all quintiles, the rise in incomes between 1975 and 1985 was accompanied by a rise in this percentage.

Although satisfactory sewerage and sanitation arrangements are more difficult to define and hence to represent in a simple number, Table 2 below also confirms what one would expect, namely that an increase in incomes is the best way of increasing access to the sanitation facilities that most people in advanced countries would take for granted as normal attributes of a minimum standard of living.[12] Of course, in many countries, the pace of urbanization has meant that sanitation and waste disposal arrangements have been totally unable to cope with the additional demands and bring the services up to the levels normally associated with even medium income level countries. For example, even in Thailand, where the growth of prosperity has been remarkably sustained, it is estimated that in Bangkok only 2% of the population is connected to sewers.[13]

In the longer run, when incomes approach the levels enjoyed currently by advanced countries, one must assume that similar

Table 2. Income Levels and Access to Sanitation, 1980 and 1985

	1980			1985		
Quintile	Average Income	Urban Access	Rural Access	Average Income	Urban Access	Rural Access
1	\$211	33%	9%	\$236	51%	11%
2	\$404	52%	28%	\$420	55%	28%
3	\$785	53%	15%	\$790	68%	41%
4	\$1,178	78%	35%	\$1,313	85%	50%
5	\$2,814	85%	49%	\$3,140	87%	57%

Notes: Incomes in same units as in Table 1. Numbers relate to percentage of the population with access to sanitation. For definitions and sources, see World Resources Institute (1990, Table 16.4 and pp. 265–266).

degrees of access to sanitation will be achieved. But it is clear that very rapid urbanization poses special problems, even if average incomes are rising, so that in the short-to-medium run the conflict between economic growth and the environment can be more pronounced. And, rapid urbanization – which seems inevitable whatever is happening to incomes per head – means that the medium-run conflict might be quite extended.

2 *Air*

As far as SO_2 and suspended particulate matter (SPM) or smoke are concerned, if cities are grouped into broad bands corresponding to the income levels of the countries in which they are located an interesting pattern emerges. Data for the earlier years (between 1977 and 1981 depending on the cities in question) show that cities for which data are available and that are in countries classified by the World Bank in its World Development Reports as "low income countries" had lower ambient concentrations of SO_2 than cities in "middle income countries", which, in turn, had lower concentrations than cities in "high income countries".[14] But about ten years later (usually mid or late 1980s) the position had been reversed. This corresponded to a decline in SO_2 concentrations of about 8.9% per annum in the high income countries and a rise of about 3.7% in the low income countries. Taking all the 33 cities covered in the GEMS data on SO_2 ambient air quality, "27 have downward (at least 3% per year) or stationary trends and 6 have upward trends (at least 3% per year) with most improvements noted in cities of developed countries" (UNEP, WHO and GEMS, 1988, p. 15). Whilst the trends over time are similar for SPM (suspended particulate matter) or smoke, in that they were more sharply downwards in the richer countries, and upwards in the poorest countries, even in the earlier years the cities in low income countries had far higher urban concentrations of SPM and smoke than the middle or high income countries did.

The picture is slightly more confused when one turns to two other pollutants, namely carbon monoxide (CO) and (nitrous oxides) NO_xs, since emissions of these, particularly the CO, are heavily influenced by the automobile – both the numbers and the speeds at which they are able to circulate.[15] Furthermore, the limitations on inter-city comparability of measures of these pollutants are particularly severe. Hence, in terms of ambient air concentrations of, say, NO_xs, "cities of the developing and developed countries are found at both ends of the concentration range ... some of the lowest NO_2 values are reported from the two Indian cities Bombay and New Delhi, presumably because traffic levels are relatively low" (UNEP, WHO and GEMS, 1988, p. 44).

Nevertheless, some overall difference can be observed between poor and rich country cities. For example, although there are some exceptions – notably London, Frankfurt and Amsterdam – trends in ambient NO_2 concentrations in most other developed countries' cities are now stable or declining, in spite of sustained increases in automobile numbers. By contrast, although data are scarce it appears that trends are generally rising in cities in developing countries (UNEP, WHO and GEMS, 1988, p. 43).[16] The picture is roughly the same for ambient CO concentrations. Data are only available for cities in eleven countries and CO concentrations are declining in all of them. With one exception – Santiago – the cities are all in high income countries. By contrast, fragmentary data on a few individual cities in developing countries confirm the rise in concentrations of these pollutants.

Another important pollutant from mobile sources has been lead. Relatively accurate indicators are available of the amounts of lead in gasoline in individual countries and it can be seen that in recent years almost all industrialized countries have taken effective measures of one kind or another to reduce lead emissions from automobiles, often with striking results. For example, the total quantity of lead used in gasoline in the U.S.A. was cut from 170,000 tons in 1975 to 40,000 tons in 1984, and Japan has made even greater progress. By contrast, "few developing countries have yet made significant reductions in petrol lead content ..." (UNEP and WHO, GEMS, 1988, p. 60). There have been no or negligible falls in lead levels in petrol in Africa and South and Central America and the Caribbean, whereas there has been a big fall in Europe and North America, and quite a big fall in Asia, even without taking account of the consumption of unleaded petrol in these countries (UNEP, WHO and GEMS, 1988, p. 60).

In general, therefore, although one cannot say precisely how overall "air quality" should be defined, or at exactly what income level individual aspects of air quality begin to improve with further growth, it is fairly clear that it does so sooner or later. How much sooner or later – i.e., at what point in time or level of income – urban air conditions reach a point when effective policies are introduced will depend on a host of variables, including technical, social and political variables. It is not surprising, therefore, that the record of individual countries shows a reversal in the trend in the traditional pollutants (SO_2 and SPM or smoke) at very different stages in their history. In Britain, for which country data on these two basic pollutants go back several decades, a considerable improvement began in the late 1950s.[17] In the United States the

Table 3. Ranges of Lead Levels in Petrol in Different Regions of the World, 1974 and 1984[a]

	1974	1984
Africa	0.63–0.84	0.63–0.84
Asia	0.31–0.84	0.17–0.56
South and Central America and Caribbean	0.64–0.84	0.64–0.84
North America	0.58–0.95	0.22–0.77
Europe	0.40–0.84	0.15–0.40

[a] Data indicate ranges of grams of lead per liter of petrol.

Source: UNEP and WHO, GEMS (1988, Table 7.1, p. 60).

reversal of trends in emissions and then in ambient concentrations began in the early 1970s. In cities in some other countries – including some in developing countries – the improvement has started even more recently.

In recent years there has been a shift in emphasis in the environmental debate towards issues such as global warming and climate change, which is alleged to be inevitable given the increasing emissions of various "greenhouse gases," the most important of which being carbon dioxide. How far this threat is serious enough to justify costly action to prevent it or moderate it or adapt to it is outside the scope of this paper, but there is little doubt that, like the other new pollutants mentioned above, carbon dioxide emissions have not followed the same steep downward trends in the developed countries that have been followed by the most traditional "old" pollutants, such as SO_x.

For example, in six developed countries for which adequate data are available emissions of SO_x have been following steeply declining trends over the period 1975 through 1985, whereas their emissions of CO_2 were either stationary or increasing (OECD, 1991, pp. 17 and 21).

Nevertheless, even these latter trends are consistent with the proposition that, on the whole and in the end, the richer countries are able to reduce their pollution levels, for there is a sharp contrast between the trends in CO_2 emissions of the developed countries, as represented by the OECD totals, and those of the rest of the world, as can be seen in Table 4 below.

Table 4. Comparative Changes in CO_2 Emissions. OECD and Non-OCED Countries, 1975 to 1985 (levels in millions of tons and annual average percent growth rates)

	1975	1985	% Growth
World	4,811	5,802	1.89
OECD	2,522	2,648	0.49
Non-OECD	2,289	3,154	3.26

Source: United Nations Environment Program (1991).

III The Poverty-Environment Nexus

In addition to the generally favorable relationship between higher incomes and the environment postulated above and demonstrated with respect to air quality and to water supply and sanitation, there are, of course, numerous particular instances of the way that low incomes cause environmental degradation. Space permits only one or two well-known examples here. One of these is the poverty-deforestation-poverty cycle. For example, in Thailand, it is reported that "poverty and deforestation are locked in a vicious circle of mutual reinforcement" (Phantumvanit and Panayoton, 1990, p. 27). A typical sequence is where poverty and lack of any other employment alternative drives people to cut down trees and cultivate the land often with damaging longer term effects on either soil productivity or water supplies, or both. In Thailand it is also reported that

> landless and small-scale farmers, among others, encroach on forest reserves in search of a better livelihood. They either clear the land themselves usually following legal or illegal loggers, or they purchase the land from influential persons who claim control over large areas of forest reserves. During the first few years after encroachment, crop yields are relatively high because of the nutrients in the slashed-and-burned forest land. Once these nutrients are exhausted yields begin to drop ... Except in areas where off-farm employment is abundant, farmers sooner or later are forced by declining productivity to move deeper into the forest in search of new, more productive land. (Tongpan et al., 1990, p. 6)[18]

The harmful effects of the deforestation in Thailand had become so serious by 1989 that the Thai government banned commercial logging activities, although it is reported that the ban is difficult to enforce.

In Brazil, the "pull" exercised by certain government policies, including road construction, tax exemptions, fiscal and credit subsidies for investment programs and so on, was probably a major force behind the rapid pace of "frontier settlement" and its associated deforestation. But there was also some "push" coming from landless peasants for whom "migration is basically motivated by the possibility of accumulating wealth (and, with luck, becoming a landowner) through the clearing of lands in a frontier area where property rights are still undefined"(Reis and Margulis, 1990).

Deforestation, then, is caused partly, if not largely, by poverty – aggravated in some cases by policies. Another such poverty-environment-poverty cycle is often found in coastal areas, such as those in the Philippines, where

> like the uplands, coastal and near-shore fisheries are a public resource, the open-access nature of which has attracted the most impoverished elements from adjacent agricultural and coastal areas and induced them to use non-sustainable extraction techniques. Destruction of coastal mangrove forests opens interior areas to increased typhoon damage, creating a backward linkage.

A similar vicious circle in the Philippines is reported to affect the roughly one million poor people employed in the fishing industry, who tend to fish beyond the sustainable yield.

In short, a major cause of many forms of environmental degradation is the combination of rising population with the lack of alternative ways of making a living other than those that degrade the environment. Most developing countries share the problem of, say, the Philippines, of which it is reported that

> improved management of natural resources requires an attack on underlying causes of degradation and depletion, specifically excessive population growth and poverty, which are the main sources of migratory "push" into the uplands and coastal areas ... A strong program to reduce population growth rates ... and measures to create jobs for unemployed and underemployed rural residents ... will be crucial to the long-run prospects for reducing the rate of environmental degradation ... This is needed in order to reduce pressure to clear forests, especially in upland areas, or to overfish limited water resources. (World Bank, 1989, p. XVI)

IV Conclusions

The main conclusion emerging from the above is that although in the course of their development developing countries may have to experience a period of deterioration in some features of their environment – notably on account of rapid urbanization – in the longer run they are able to reverse trends in the more common forms of air pollution, and attain levels of water supply and sanitation that are essential components of an acceptable, decent and healthy standard of living. For on the whole there is a strong relationship between income levels and the quality of the environment – at least, as measured by these particular ingredients of the environment This can be seen across broad income bands, and also in the context of particular country situations that demonstrate the various ways that low incomes lead to environmental damage, even if, in many cases, economic progress can harm the environment.

Exactly when countries adopt policies to reduce excessive pollution depends on a variety of influences – technological developments, changes in tastes, public pressures, and so on. These are all correlated with rising incomes. Rising incomes also enable countries to be able to afford the diversion of resources into environmental protection that is necessary for the implementation of such policies. Exactly when individual countries adopt policies to protect the environment will thus differ considerably from one country to another and progress is often erratic. Favorable trends can easily be disrupted by other disturbances – such as oil shocks, or recessions, or counterinflationary policies that include cutbacks on "nonessential" expenditures, and so on. But as long as incomes rise, in the end all countries seem to move towards the goal of optimal protection for the environment – though it is most unlikely that any actually reach it, or, indeed, that optimal protection of the environment could be precisely identified in any operational manner.

Notes

[1] See, for example, Sir (now Lord) Eric Ashby, "Pollution in Perspective," Lecture to The Times 1000 Conference, *The Spectator*, 27th May 1972; Professor K. Mellanby "The Phoney Crisis," *Minerva*, July, 1972; Cole et al. (1973), for the Science Policy Research Unit of Sussex University; the World Bank *Report on the Limits to Growth*, Report by a Special Task Force of the World Bank; and Solow (1973). A survey of the main criticisms was given in Beckerman (1974), and these were summarized in "The Limits to Growth" in Eatwell, Milgate and Newman (1987, Vol. 3, pp. 192–193).

[2] The World Bank, *Report on the Limits to Growth* op. cit., pp. 38–39.

[3] 1970 reserve estimates in Meadows et. al. (1972, pp. 56–59); consumption data from *Metal Bulletin's Prices and Data* (Surrey, U.K.), 1990, pp. 255 and passim; 1989 known reserves from *The World Almanac*, 1990, p. 130 (derived from U.S. Bureau of Mines data).

[4] Gordon Hughes argues, in "Are the Costs of Cleaning up Eastern Europe Exaggerated? (draft of paper for the World Bank and the Commission of the European Communities, Nov. 1990, page ii), that insofar as Eastern European economies develop along the lines of the currently advanced Western economies their pollution intensities, and possibly levels, will decline precisely on account of this shift in economic structure that seems to characterize economic growth in almost all countries of the world.

[5] One of the most distinguished of these was the study by Baumol and Oates (1975). The OECD published a set of papers on the main principles involved in *The Polluter Pays Principle*, (Paris, 1975), and in 1989 it published a survey of the main price incentives introduced in *Economic Instruments for Environmental Protection*. For an up-to-date assessment of the operation of tradable permits in the U.S.A., see Tietenberg (1990). A survey of some of the pros and cons of economic incentives as against the "command and control" approach is given in Beckerman (1990).

[6] For some details, see Beckerman (1974, pp. 65–67).

[7] See *First Report of the Royal Commission on Environmental Pollution* (1972), and Warren Spring Laboratory (1972).

[8] Details of this and other sharp falls in the pollution/output ratios in many key industries were given in a speech by Mr Eldon Griffiths, then a Minister in the Department of the Environment (*House of Commons Debates*, Hansard, 22 Dec. 1972, Col. 1794).

[9] For details see, Beckerman, (1974, pp. 122–135).

[10] The Global Environment Monitoring System, set up under the auspices of the United Nations Environment Program in collaboration with the World Health Organization.

[11] For the reasons given above, figures for individual countries are not strictly comparable, so that a more reasonable picture of the income/water supply relationship is provided by grouping countries into broad income bands.

[12] World Bank report on the Dominican Republic.

[13] Internal World Bank memo: *Thailand*: *Environment Fact Sheet*, 9 May 1991, p. 5.

[14] In the 1990 World Development Report a high income countrie is one with a per capita GDP of over $6000, and a low income country is one with a per capita income of less than $700. Air quality data have been taken from GEMS, *Air Quality in Selected Urban Areas*, (WHO, Geneva,) various issues, and United Nations Environment Program, *Environment Data Report*, 3rd edition.

[15] Up to a point the emission of pollutants from automobiles falls off rapidly as their speed increases, so that a major cause of urban air pollution from automobiles is traffic congestion. See Faiz, (1990, Tables 19, 20, and 21, pp. 42, 43, and 46).

[16] Even here, however, there are notable exceptions, namely Singapore.

[17] See evidence in Beckerman (1974, p. 123–124). This source also documents

improvements in air and water quality in the 1960s and early 1970s in a number of developed countries as well as the pollution abatement policies being introduced around that time in the countries in question, (pp. 124–140).

[18] Tongpan, S. et al. (1990, page 6). See also Phantumvanit and Panayotou (1990, Chapter 3).

Bibliography

Baumol, W.J. and Oates W.E. 1975. *The Theory of Environmental Policy*. New Jersey: Prentice-Hall.

Beckerman, W. 1974. *In Defence of Economic Growth*. London: Cape. (U.S. edition: *Two Cheers for the Affluent Society*. St. Martin's Press, 1975.)

———. 1990. "Pricing for Pollution." Hobart Paper 66 (Second Edition). London: Institute of Economic Affairs.

———. 1991. "Global Warming: A Sceptical Economic Assessment." In: D. Helm (ed.), *Economic Policies for the Environment*. Oxford: Blackwells.

Cole, H.S.D. et al., (eds.). 1973. *Thinking about the Future: A Critique of the Limits of Growth*. London: Chatto and Windus.

Eatwell, J., M. Milgate and P. Newman. 1987. *The New Palgrave: A Dictionary of Economics*. Vol. 3. New York and London: Macmillan.

Faiz, A. et al. 1990. "Automotive Air Pollution." Working Paper, Transport, WPS 492. Policy, Research and External Affairs, The World Bank (August).

First Report of the Royal Commission on Environmental Pollution. 1972. London: H.M.S.O.

Forrester, J.W. et al. 1968. *Principles of Systems*. Cambridge, Mass.: Wright Allen Press.

Global Environment Monitoring System (GEMS). *Air Quality in Selected Urban Areas*. Geneva: WHO (various issues).

Hirsch, F. 1977. *Social Limits to Growth*. London: Routledge and Kegan Paul.

Farber, Kit D. and G. Rutledge. 1989. "Pollution Abatement and Control Expenditures, 1984–87." *Survey of Current Business* (June): 19–23.

Meadows, D.H. et al. 1972. *The Limits to Growth*. New York: Universe.

Mishan, E.J. 1967. *The Costs of Economic Growth*. London: Staples Press.

OECD. 1990. *Pollution Abatement and Control Expenditure in OECD Member Countries*. Paris.

———. 1991. *Environmental Indicators*. Paris.

Phantumvanit, D. and T. Panayotou. 1990. "Natural Resources for a Sustainable Future: Spreading the Benefits." Synthesis Paper 1, presented at the 1990 TDRI Year-End Conference.

Reis, E.J. and S. Margulis. 1990. "Options for Slowing Amazon Jungle-Clearing." Paper presented at the Conference on Economic Policy Responses to Global Warming, Rome, October.

Schumacher, E.F. 1973. *Small is Beautiful*. London: Blond and Briggs.

Solow, R.M. 1973. "Is the End of the World at Hand?" In: A. Weintraub, E. Schwartz and J.R. Aronson (eds.), *The Economic Growth Controversy*. London: Macmillan.

Tietenberg, T.H. 1990. "Economic Instruments for Environmental Regulation." *Oxford Review of Economic Policy* 6(1).

Tongpan, S. et al. 1990. "Deforestation and Poverty: Can commercial and Social Forestry Break the Vicious Cycle?" Research Report 2, presented at the 1990 TDRI Year-End Conference.

UNCTAD. 1989. *Handbook of International Trade and Development Statistics*.

United Nations Environment Program (UNEP). *Environment Data Report*. Third Edition.

United Nations Environment Program (UNEP), World Health Organization (WHO) and Global Environment Monitoring System (GEMS). 1988. *Assessment of Urban Air Quality*.

Warren Spring Laboratory (Department of Trade and Industry). 1972. *National Survey of Air Pollution 1961–1971*. London: H.M.S.O.

World Bank. 1989. *Philippines: Environment and Natural Resource Management Study*.

World Resources Institute. 1990. *World Resources 1990–91*. Washington, D.C.

"Ecological Concerns in a Market Economy: On Ethics, Accounting and Sustainability"*

Johannes Heister and Friedrich Schneider

Introduction

Today it is becoming increasingly clear that economic and environmental problems emerge as two sides of the same coin. The threat of heating up our planet by the massive burning of fossil fuels is but the most recent and widely discussed example.[1] This leads to the question whether we should modify and/or widen our models of market economies in order to incorporate environmental concerns and to provide solutions to environmental problems within the market economies.

One obvious difficulty in dealing with environmental issues is that environmental quality is a typical public good that cannot be so easily incorporated into our economic models. This essay tackles three important questions that have been discussed for quite some time by economists concerned with the environment and for which no clear answers have emerged yet. These questions are:

(1) Do we need (new) environmental ethics?
(2) Do we need a modification of the national income accounting system?
(3) Should we switch to sustainable economic development?

---

* This paper is a synthesis of the original conference contribution by Friedrich Schneider and the extensive comments made by Johannes Heister during the conference.

[1] Compare, for instance, the contributions of Cline (1991), Nordhaus (1991a) and Pearce (1991).

We will treat these three questions simultaneously in this paper, since it appears that values (ethics), information (the accounting system) and tools or operational guidelines (sustainability) are indispensable elements of rational economic planning and activities. Moreover, these elements are interdependent to some extent: new values require a new information system and new tools with which these values can be implemented.

The development of a comprehensive system that gives full reasons for establishing new environmental ethics and describes possible realizations of the related values should be the ultimate goal. However, this task cannot be mastered in a short paper. Therefore, the present contribution summarizes possible solutions to the problems raised and evaluates their advantages and disadvantages before arriving at a preliminary answer. Sections 2 to 4 analyze and discuss the above-mentioned questions; section 5 draws some conclusions.

I Do We Need (New) Environmental Ethics?

Activists in the environmental debate have raised a growing sense of unease in industrial societies about the current relationship between man and nature. It appears that there is a lack of normative insight into this relationship.[2] Environmental activists seem to be strongly in favor of some new kind of (intuitive) environmental ethics, as strict rules seem to be required to prohibit current behavior that has a negative effect upon the long-range future as well as on the present. They argue that humans must become generally more aware of nature's regulatory mechanisms and must devise new evaluation strategies in the use of natural resources. The "exploitationist" viewpoint, which is constrained only by the current rate of discounting future benefits, ought to be replaced by a "conservationist" or even an "eco-preservationist" world view. The

[2] Compare, for example, Daly (1980), the last issues of the Worldwatch Report (1989/90, 1990/91) and Global 2000. For a critical discussion of the relationship between ethics and economics, see Gäfgen (1968, 1985 and 1991).

conservationist viewpoint stresses the notion of a growth process constrained by the criterion of sustainability of resource productivity over time. The viewpoint of the preservationists covers the entire ecosystem and requires additional constraints on the production of all goods and services.[3]

According to Turner (1988a,b) there is little consensus among philosophers as to whether these rather "intuitive ethics" can be derived from rational and theoretical arguments, or what the content of such new ethics should be. In fact, quite a number of authors (e.g., Reagan, 1981; Turner, 1988a,c; Norton, 1984) have argued that conventional forms of ethical reasoning should be broadened. Most of them are convinced that there should be some extension of the moral reference spectrum, but the limits of this process are disputed. Three essential questions lie at the heart of this theoretical controversy:

(1) Should the "new normative world view" be essentially ecocentric or can it be established along the lines of the traditional anthropocentric view?
(2) Should individualism or collectivism be the focus of environmental values?
(3) Should distributional issues, which come up as intergenerational equity problems due to environmental degradation, be decided on the grounds of utilitarian, libertarian or contractarian (value) judgements?

As concerns question (1), at the basis of ecocentrism as a normative theory lies the belief that moral values exist that are external to and independent of man and his interests and which man can nevertheless recognize and acknowledge: ecocentric ethics are, by definition, nonanthropocentric. This belief entails as a consequence that nature is assumed to be endowed with (quasi) rights of its own that would require a particular treatment of nature by humans.

It is doubtful, however, whether the ecocentric postulation is a reasonable and feasible normative concept. Moreover, ecocentrism

---

[3] For a more detailed description of the three positions, compare Norton (1982, 1984), Parfit (1984), Edwards (1987) and Turner (1988b).

is not necessary for establishing new environmental ethics. One could rather argue that environmental ethics is a question of deeper insight into humanity's own place in the universe, of more human self-respect, and, derived from that, of more respect for all of creation. Then, however, environmental ethics is anthropocentric: man's (moral) behavior with respect to nature can (and should) be developed further on the basis of conventional ethical reasoning. Such an approach may very well provide us with all the moral guidelines that we may need in order to cope with our ecological problems.

As concerns question (2), individualism as an idea and many different individual values lie at the basis of our liberal market economies. But, as was noticed above, the quality of the environment is a public good and, this being so, environmental problems demand collective decisions on environmental values. Hence, could collectivism as the focus of such value judgements contribute to a better environment? The experience of large collective economies (the former COMECON countries) advise us to the contrary. Moreover, collectivism plus ecocentrism are the ingredients of an eco-dictatorial regime – and, hence, are out of line with liberal economics.

Rather, in the framework of a market economy, the question of collectivism versus individualism is a "technical" matter: how should individual values be aggregated to maximize social welfare. Framing the question in such a way leads us astray of philosophy and into the fields of collective choice theory and environmental policy design. There, we find a rich tool chest of instruments which are based on individual value judgements and which still await application.

As concerns question (3), another central issue of the environmental ethicists is the demand for a new theory of compensatory and distributive justice. Neither utilitarianism nor libertarianism can support an ethical basis for principles of intra- or intergenerational equity. For example, Parfit (1984), Norton (1982) and Broom (1988) argue that current policy cannot be governed by reference to harm to the interests of future individuals because today's policies determine who those individuals will be and what interests they will have.

The contractarian approach and Rawls's decision model have been cited as possible sources of intergenerational equity criteria.[4] However, the Rawlsian framework has its weaknesses, too, as soon as the analysis moves away from the self-contained society of contemporary, rational and self-interested individuals. If all generations are represented in the original position, then the representatives themselves could work out how many actual generations there will be. However, this is one of the issues that are supposed to depend on their deliberations. If only some generations have representatives, then all possible rights of people might not be taken into account. Most egalitarians (like Norton, 1984) do not restrict their conception of human nature to that characterized by a rational economic human being. They also emphasize the social and communal aspects of human nature and the possibility of some sort of social contract. Using such an approach, the concept of generalized obligations developed by Norton means that the obligations of the current generation have to preserve a continuous stock of resources into the future in order to guarantee the continuation of human life rather than just meeting individual requirements on a short-term basis.

Intergenerational equity is interpreted by Page (1983) in terms of a "justice as opportunity" argument. Page proposes that future generations should receive compensation for any reduction in the availability of natural resources due to the activities of the current generation. So the future's loss of productive potential must be compensated for "if justice is to prevail" – so Page's argument. The current generation pays some compensation via improved technology and increased capital investment designed to offset the impacts of depletion, but whether this is enough is a highly disputed question. The passing-on of the basic resources needed for human life in an undamaged condition over the next few generations is central to the concept of sustainable economic development. Such a managed growth policy could also improve the chances of the survival for the majority of nonhuman species and their natural habitats.

---

[4] Compare Rawls (1971), and in the context of the environmental debate, Kirchgässner (1990).

The problem of intergenerational equity has, even conceptually, not yet been solved. However, many policy decisions would become easier if policymakers could rely on a simple rule that would tell them how to respect future generations in their decisions. But one can have severe doubts whether such a rule could be constructed. Instead, a reasonable alternative approach could be to base public decisions that severely affect future generations more on the care and provisions that parents (ought to) take for the future well-being of their children. Hence, the question would be how parents' (and perhaps young people's) preferences can better be reflected in the political decision-making process. This would provide a more pragmatic answer to the questions of intergenerational equity, one that does not rely on fixed ethical standards but is open to changes of individual values.

II Do We Need a Modification of the National Income Accounting System?

It seems obvious that the environment can be seen as the victim of misconceptions of economic growth and welfare, since economic policy issues are usually measured in terms of national income. Since the establishment of the system of national accounts in the early 1940s, proposals for counterbalancing this weakness have quite often been made in the literature. Much has been written about the necessity of correcting traditional GNP accounting to include environmental damage and declining natural resources.[5] Moreover, quite a number of institutions (e.g., the German Office of Statistics) are currently working on new accounting frameworks to reflect the state of the environment.[6] Hence, it appears that the question is no longer whether an environmentally sensitive national accounting system is desirable, but how it should be designed. The literature proposes four possible approaches:

---

[5] An overview of the methods used can be found in Kneese (1984), Ewers and Schulz (1982), Schulz (1985). These methods have also been criticized; compare, for example, Knapp (1982).

[6] Compare, for example, Ahmad, Serafy and Lutz (1989), Hölder und Mitarbeiter (1991) and Ministry of Finance (1991).

(1) A system of satellite accounts in physical units as a supplement to the traditional accounting system.
(2) An alternative national income figure that is corrected for defensive expenditures.[7]
(3) The above-mentioned corrections including a figure that reflects the willingness-to-pay for the environment.
(4) The above-mentioned defensive corrections plus deductions for the loss of environmental functions that are estimated as expenditures on measures required to meet certain physical standards that ensure the sustainable availability and quality of those environmental functions.

The *first approach* proposes, in principle, leaving unchanged the national accounts as they were constructed. The advocates of this approach favor counterbalancing the one-sided orientation towards the growth of national income by the following two arguments:

(1) The traditional national accounts system has provided more or less exact information on the relative importance of production and its growth.
(2) In the traditional national accounts system, as much as information possible on the consequences of the losses of environmental functions is provided in monetary terms, so that compensation and elimination cost and financial damages can be calculated.

Considering these arguments, Theys (1984) suggests that the information in physical units should be collected in so-called satellite accounts of the national accounts. Theys argues that theoretically this is one of the best solutions. Correction of the national income for environmental losses is possible only partially because shadow prices for environmental functions, which are directly comparable with the market prices of goods and services, can be constructed only in very rare cases. Carrying out a correction on this quite small basis leads to the following problem: The information from

[7] Defensive expenditures are expenditures that are induced by environmental deterioration in the areas of transportation, housing, security, health, etc. For further explanations compare, for example, Leipert (1986a).

only some environmental problems is quite often interpreted as the total environmental effect. Moreover, such corrected figures may give the impression of being an indicator of the "true" national welfare, which they by far are not. However, information on the environment (in physical units) can only be provided by means of a great number of figures, because of the tremendously differing and almost incomparable effects of activities burdening the environment – like the discharge of all kinds of harmful substances, the felling of woods, and the intensification of agriculture. It seems obvious that environmental quality and the changes in it should be described in a great number of different physical units, which are then extremely difficult to interpret and compare, and only expertly trained scientists are able to do so.

A considerable number of physical units of measure that describe the state of the environment have been developed during the past 15 years. Quite often such information elicits only fractional ad hoc reactions on the part of policymakers. Moreover, it does not lead to an essential change in economic policy with respect to environmental problems.[8] Measures are often taken in response to disastrous events, but not on the basis of information in physical units from which warnings can be derived that such events are likely to occur if no measures are taken; information in physical units is scarcely absorbed by economic policy and the literature. As we are living in a "monetary society," it seems that only monetary terms play a role in economic decision making with respect to our environmental problems. Politicians only deal with monetary numbers that show damages or cost;[9] Hence, they are strongly in need of a macro-environmental indicator in monetary terms as a supplement to the indicator of production.

The *second approach* is also in favor of providing the information (mentioned under point [1] and [2]), but besides the isolation of preventive and compensatory expenditures, an alternative national income figure should be published which is corrected for these environmental "outlays." This could have the great advan-

---

[8] Compare, for example, Wegehenkel (1981, 1983), Frey (1985, 1987), Hahn (1989) and Kirchgässner (1990).

[9] Compare, for example, Bonus (1985), Höffe (1981) and Ryll and Zimmermann (1989).

tage that the attention of politicians and the public, which is now monopolized by one figure (e.g., growth of income), will at least be drawn to the fact that part of the increase of the national income is swallowed by an increase in environmental costs. Leipert (1987, 1986a,b) has done research in this direction and comes to the conclusion that the development of "defensive expenditures" (his term) in the Federal Republic of Germany revealed a strong increase in the share of "defensive outlays" in GNP between 1970 and 1985 from 5 per cent to 10 per cent. These calculations consist not only of the defensive expenditures induced by environmental deterioration, but also the defensive expenditures in the field of transportation, housing, social security and health. The calculations reveal not only a doubling of the ratio of defensive expenditure to GNP, but also show that in the period 1970 to 1985 about 1/5 of the growth of GNP is driven by an increase in defensive expenditures, for example, additional economic costs caused by the same growth. Leipert concludes that all available indicators make it clear that this trend will probably continue and become more pronounced in the next 10 to 20 years.

Both the "expenditure by purpose approach"[10] and the publication of a second national income figure have of course certain advantages and disadvantages. The advantages are:

(1) The isolation of and the correction for the above-mentioned items provide more knowledge of the interaction between production and environmental deterioration.
(2) Both methods could also be used for linking environmental expenditures with the satellite accounts, in which the results of these expenditures are registered in physical terms. Stahmer (1987) argues that this amounts to a (partial) cost effectiveness analysis on the macro level.

The disadvantages are:

(1) It seems obvious that the connection between environmental factors and the system of national accounts, as well as the correction of the national income, can be made only to the extent that measures which can lead to defensive expendi-

[10] This expression is taken from Leipert (1986a).

tures are actually taken. All losses of environmental functions and exploitation of natural resources that do not lead to compensatory financial outlays are not taken into account in the system of national accounts. This is especially relevant in the case of environmental deterioration that may decrease the level of scarce environmental resources available to future generations for production and consumption.

(2) The opportunity costs of shifts in production and consumption patterns that are deliberately made on behalf of the environment can quite often not be counted in national statistics. This has the consequence that opportunity costs are either not reflected or are not visible in the system of national accounts. For example, the opportunity costs involved in a decision *not* to construct a dam in an area that could be used for other purposes (e.g., to promote wildlife and special plants) cannot be explicitly calculated in statistical terms.

Another problem is that it is quite often extremely difficult to determine which expenditures are defensive expenditures, especially in the areas of security and health. Another factor that has to be considered is technical progress. Quite often with the help of technical progress it is possible to overcome environmental problems, but to evaluate today which solutions will be found for environmental (and, of course, all other) problems tomorrow is an extremely difficult task, but also has to be considered here.

The supporters of the *third approach* want to supplement the corrections mentioned under the second approach with the amounts that people are willing to pay to restore the damaged environment. There is much research going on in this field of willingness to pay.[11] As environmental damages are quite often public goods, it is (as Pommerehne, 1987, argues) difficult to find out exactly how much people are willing to pay for the damaged environment. Some of the difficulties in using these methods are listed below:

(1) Information on the importance of environmental systems is in many cases very difficult to calculate. This is especially the

[11] Compare, for example, the work of Pommerehne (1986, 1987, 1988), who provides an excellent overview of the various methods.

case with regard to such systems that are determinants for the future quality of the environment. With respect to these systems, it is often a question of the risks involved in interrupting complicated processes, for instance, of ecosystems, which may lead to either serious overshooting or collapses. Most people will not be able to evaluate such risks, and thus it is very difficult for them to answer on the basis of today's knowledge how much they are prepared to pay to avoid them.

(2) There is a considerable difference between saying that one is willing to spend money on something and later actually paying for it or, to put it in other terms, having the choice between a tax deduction and using the money for one's own private purposes or spending it for environmental purposes.

(3) The questioning method, in fact, tries to approach the value of a collective good as if it were a private marketable good. In the private good case the bidder knows fairly well what quality and quantity can be acquired by different bids. In the public good case the bidder does not, because other bids cannot be predicted.

(4) In order to make the questioning precise enough, considerable research has to be done in the field of environmental accounting, especially because "clean air," "clean water," and "unpoisoned ground" are not homogeneous goods due to the fact that they have quite a number of different functions. If a precise figure has to be given by the persons who are questioned, information must first be given to them on the importance of the different functions, the consequences of their loss, and the measures and costs involved in their restoration. Altogether this is a huge amount of information, which not everybody will be able to evaluate.

(5) Questioning people about how much they are willing to pay for the environment can lead to the impression that conserving the environment always requires extra provisions for which people have to pay. However, in quite a few cases conservation is a matter of refraining from doing things, and sometimes this saves rather than costs money. Thus not building a highway through a mountainous area that is vulnerable to erosion and pollution damage might be cheaper

than constructing it; bicycling might be cheaper than driving; and wearing a sweater and using an extra blanket might be cheaper than increasing the heat.[12] People who realize this may refuse to answer because the questions do not seem to be relevant for them.

(6) A number of people may argue that they have an explicit right to a healthy and safe environment and will probably not make a bid at all, because they may argue that in their view these rights cannot be evaluated in monetary terms at all.

(7) Finally, a number of people might have doubts about the participation of others (these may be the economists who believe in the prisoner's dilemma situation) or prefer to wait and see, or they might react as free riders.

Pommerehne has further arguments against the willingness-to-pay method, but he also argues that if this method is carefully prepared, it might at least provide a scientifically justified base for taking into account what people are willing to pay. This might be extremely useful if special taxes have to be levied in order to restore the environment.[13] Whether or not the willingness-to-pay method is a sound base for correcting the national income for losses of scarce environmental functions is difficult to answer. It may be one method, but it cannot be argued that it is the only method.

Finally the *fourth approach* advocates supplementing the corrections mentioned under the second approach with the estimated expenditure on measures required to meet physical standards for the availability and quality of environmental functions (including natural resources). These physical standards can be based on the prerequisites of health and a sustainable economic development, that is, a development with sustainable yields. This seems to be the most natural guideline for setting standards for environmental

[12] However, this depends crucially on how the opportunity costs of *not* doing such activities are evaluated.

[13] Compare, for example, Kneese (1984), Blankart (1988), Bonus (1985), Leu and Frey 1987), Nutzinger and Zahrnt (1989) and Oates (1986).

functions which are widely accepted as an important norm for national economies. Such standards relate, for instance, to the occupation of space, the use of soil, the availability of stocks of natural resources, the composition of products, the consumption of raw materials, the use of energy, and emissions caused by economic activities.

Relating these standards to the environmental functions allows new standards to be derived which describe, for example, how a forest should be exploited in order to guarantee a sustainable use of its functions as "supplier of wood," "regulator of water management," "preventer of erosion," "buffer of CO_2 and heat," "regulator of the climate," "supplier of natural products for the local population" and "source of income from tourism."[14] The estimated expenditures on the measures required to meet these standards then show how far a nation has drifted away from its standard of sustainable use of its forest resources. In a similar way it is possible to formulate checklists in which surface and ground water reserves should be used in order to arrive at a sustainable use of its functions. Again, the estimated expenditures on measures required to meet the standards (like water as raw material, water for agriculture, water for flushing and transport, water for recreation) show how far a nation has drifted away from a sustainable use of its water resources. Similar measures could be developed for the use of air, soil and space.

If such measures were consistently used and put into practice, they would lead in one way or another to different sustainable production and consumption patterns. The level of welfare of people might not decrease if people prefer sustainable development rather than running the risks of a possible breakdown of the present production and consumption patterns. Whether this is the case cannot be "proved" or "disproved" because of the impossibility in many cases of constructing shadow prices for these environmental functions. But also one has to argue here that (as said above) technical progress might help to overcome some disadvantages of present production. To summarize this approach, the advantages are:

---

[14] These expressions are taken from Leipert (1987).

(1) The method described above is the only way to supplement the national income figures with the losses of environmental functions in monetary terms.
(2) This approach requires an exact definition the term "sustainable economic development." Without such a definition, the term remains vague and not operational in economic policy regarding the environment.[15] The physical data required for comparison with the different standards are the basic environmental statistics, which have to be collected anyhow if a government wants to know something about the state of the environment.

The disadvantages are:

(1) The result of this approach does not represent individual valuations in the typical economic sense, and the intensity of the preferences for a sustainable economic development can hardly be measured.
(2) The method ignores the loss of welfare suffered by those people who have a strong preference for the survival of plant and animal species apart from their role in the maintenance of the life-support functions of our planet. The same holds true for species which might not be considered indispensable for a sustainable economic development. This, too, should be mentioned in the presentation of the current results.

On the basis of these four approaches, it is concluded that one can recommend a correction of the national income figures for the losses of environmental functions (including resources) on the basis of standards for health and sustainable economic development. Indeed, this solution has some appeal, since it evaluates environmental functions in terms of money saved for producing yields that nature supplies free of charge. Thus, to some degree the environmental costs of, for instance, a forest development project are incorporated in the national income system, independent of whether compensatory investments are made or not. Of course, this is not an adequate procedure for maximizing national wealth,

---

[15] Compare, for example, Bishop (1978), Edwards (1987), Redclift (1987), Pearce (1988), Turner (1988a,c), and Pearce, Barbier and Markandya (1990).

since this would require adding a figure that reflects the willingness-to-pay for environmental functions instead of the costs for compensatory measures, which may be higher.[16]

III Should We Switch to Sustainable Economic Development?

The precise damages that are most likely to result, for example, from the destruction of the ozone layer, acid rain or the "greenhouse effect" are currently only vaguely known. Further, the timescale over which ecosystem degradation may stretch before thresholds are irreversibly reached is unknown.[17] In the policymaking area, the belief in infinite substitutability, the high positive rates of discount and a strong belief in a long-lasting resilience of the ecosystem quite often lead to strong resistance to any radical restructuring of economic growth or resource pricing policies. It is obvious that in a number of developing economies severe ecosystem losses have accumulated in a matter of decades (Turner, 1988a,b). Furthermore, Turner argues that neglect of sustainability constraints could also result in irreversibility for future generations in both developed and developing economies. Algorithms should be developed that demonstrate that the likely occurrence of irreversibility (for example, a permanent loss of unique wilderness areas and other valuable environmental resources, such as wetlands, productive soils, etc.) almost always favors at least the postponement of the development options and strong support for resource conservation options. Reinterpretations of cost-benefit analysis (CBA) are also thought necessary. Supporters of extended CBA have adopted a "value sensitivity" approach and try to incorporate nonefficiency decision criteria into their analysis. It is argued

[16] A major problem, however, arises with this approach when it comes to setting the necessary baseline standards. The requirements on the environment to provide sustainable functions may change in the course of time. Functions may become obsolete and new, yet unknown functions may emerge if preferences, income or technology change.

[17] Compare, for example, the challenging contributions by Nordhaus (1977, 1991a,b) and Schneider (1989).

that actual decision makers require advice on both their objectives and on their means of achievement. In any case the attack against such an extended CBA is based on the argument that the standard value judgements that underlie the concept of a Pareto optimum are widely accepted. Obviously, a multicriteria analysis does involve a trade-off of greater comprehensiveness against a loss of precision.[18]

To maintain the services of a natural capital stock is of course not the same thing as to maintain some physical measure of the stock itself. It is possible to maintain the value of the services at an approximately constant level and to allow the stock of exhaustible resources to decline. Such a focus involves giving more regard to ways in which technological change can enhance environmental quality and the level of environmental services, and to the incentives to deplete resources in a nonsustainable fashion. In such a way a sustainable development path keeps open as many options for future choice as possible. Such a strategy does not imply that no options should be closed. Nevertheless, it does mean considerable caution when undertaking economic policies that do possibly lead to irreversible costs. Increased attention should be given to approaches for dealing with irreversibility and for valuing the benefits that are lost by reducing the natural capital stock in such a way that its flow of services is reduced. While it is the case that a loss of natural capital can be supplemented in many instances in the form of human-made capital, advocates of sustainability would clearly point to limits of such a process. The relationship between economic development and natural resource maintenance is twofold:

(1) Up to some level of resource base utilization there is unlikely to be a trade-off between development and the services of the natural resource base. Development and environment can be seen as true complements.
(2) Beyond this level, economic development is likely to involve reductions in one or more of the functions of the natural environment – as input to economic production, as a waste deposit service or as a provider of other ecological services.

[18] Compare Mishan (1982, 1984) and Pearce (1986).

> Taking this trade-off into account, the multifunctionality of natural resources is a critical concept. Trade-offs occur between the various functions of the environment and between the environment and economic development. Economic development in one geographical area can affect environmental functions in another area. Development in one period of time affects environmental functions in another period of time. In determining the trade-offs, it is critically important to value environmental functions accurately. Recent economic research has succeeded in revealing the broad order of magnitude of the value of some environmental resources, and has begun to uncover the relative importance of the types of values, e.g., user and nonuser values.

Due to the above-mentioned accumulation of environmental hazards and on the grounds of new information on the environmental impact of economic development (e.g., the greenhouse effect), it seems that our present development pattern can destroy the basis of our existence unless significant adjustments are made. Hence, a shift toward sustainability seems to be inevitable. In democratic market-oriented societies adjustments to a changing environment take place consistently, at least if adequate incentive structures are provided by the political process. Hence, under normal conditions pursuing sustainability is equivalent to setting the correct incentives.

Of course, increased public awareness is required if risk and uncertainty play a growing role and irreversible damage is possible. In these cases, sustainability, if interpreted as the preservation of environmental functions, may have a meaning as a rule of precaution. But even then it can be argued that the prevailing security-biased preference patterns in well-informed, rich industrial societies will inevitably press for the necessary nature-preserving political decisions.

The situation may be different in developing countries,

- where poverty and hence very short-sighted preferences prevail, and current survival may, in extreme cases, even depend on the overexploitation of natural resources,
- and where incentive structures favor a rapid exploitation of natural riches with enormous external costs, whilst the ruling

political establishment is, for some reason, incapable or unwilling to take the required corrective measures.

In such circumstances the notion of sustainability may be a reasonable fallback position if it can be made sufficiently operational. In a recent book, Pearce, Barbier and Markandya (1990) try to do just this. They suggest that the constancy of the natural capital stock (in physical or monetary terms) is the key necessary condition for sustainability. Furthermore, they show that this approach can be made operational in traditional cost-benefit analysis if cost-benefit analysis is applied subject to keeping the natural capital endowment constant. This is possible by evaluating a portfolio of investment projects that includes shadow projects whose aim is to compensate for the environmental degradation that is caused by the target project. It is interesting to see that this idea is similar to making corrections in national income accounting for the loss of environmental functions as estimated on the basis of hypothetical compensatory expenditures.

IV Conclusions

Many of the environmental problems we are facing today are a result of an important lack of understanding of the interdependences between the environment and economic development. But equally important, environmental problems are the result of a wrong perception of the role of nature in the economic process. Nature is not unlimited. It is not only a resource that may be exploited, but also a factor of production that requires proper maintenance, as does any other factor of production. But proper maintenance, in turn, requires that the services that nature provides be paid for by those who use them once these services become scarce.

Which conclusions can we draw from our deliberations? It is obvious that we have to take environmental problems much more seriously in the economic discipline. Traditional neoclassical analysis has made much progress in terms of the valuation of environmental goods and services. However, it has just begun to incorporate the notion of the environment as an amalgam of assets requiring careful management. It has always been argued that the neoclassical assumptions about human behavior are only a partial reflection of the complex reality with respect to environmental problems.[19] Humans do not merely receive a given environment but actively seek alternatives or change the environment. Moreover, they create, destroy and modify aspects of the environment by their own activities. Economic development can therefore be viewed as a process of adaptation to a changing environment, while itself being a source of environmental change, as argued by Wilkinson (1973) and Common (1988).

Turner (1988a) states that evolutionary development should be treated as a process of moving through a succession of ecological niches, but that environmental costs increase if economic development does not take care of the environment. Even when conventional analysis remains optimistic about technological arrangements, which are necessary to maintain economic development, economic progress should be in line with nature. Moreover, technical progress induces social transformation, and human preferences are neither static nor independent; they are interdependent, and do change over time.

Quite often it is argued that severe ecological problems can only be overcome if new institutions are founded; for example, Uexkull and Braungart (1991) suggest creating a democratically elected, environmental authority for the European Community. The authors propose that this EC authority should act in a very wide sense, intervene into member-state affairs and have the power to set up new standards and guidelines for environmental policies. The idea that rules concerning the environment should be part of the constitution is often brought forward, and implicitly the proponents think that environmental problems can only be solved with the help of law. As an economist one has to ask whether this will not lead to a new dirigism, which does not help to overcome the environmental problems but weakens the market economy. To build new institutions on the European or even on the world level may be a challenging task. But who is willing to

[19] Compare here the stimulating work by Kirchgässner (1988, 1989) and Gäfgen (1985).

give enough power to such institutions to allow them to operate and who will control them? Where are the rigorous studies that check whether such institutions are at all needed and whether they will be able to deal with environmental problems better than the alternative procedures discussed in this paper?

Obviously, cooperation between reseachers in environmental economics, other social sciences, and, natural sciences needs to be strongly supported in the coming years if society is to successfully face the multidimensional challenges posed by an expanding range of environment-related problems.

To conclude, this paper has pointed to the necessity of developing improved methods that ensure that economic activities lead to the desired outcome of increased wealth in a broad sense, even in the presence of critical environmental impacts. The point this paper has tried to make can be summarized in three propositions:

(1) Ecological objectives will become increasingly important and have to be incorporated into the economic analysis.
(2) We have to think much more in terms of a model of a sustainable economy. This model should be based on individual values and employ improved market-based instruments in order to bring ecological needs in line with a developing economy.
(3) We have to modify our national accounting system so that we have better information and an early warning system for environmental damages.

Bibliography

Ahmad, Y.J., S.E. Serafy and E. Lutz (eds.). 1989. *Environmental Accounting for Sustainable Development: A UNEP – World Bank Symposium.*

Bishop, R.C. 1978. "Endangered Species and Uncertainty: The Economics of a Save Minimum Standard." *American Journal of Agriculture and Economics* 60(1): 10–18.

Blankart, Ch.B. 1988. "Umweltschutzorientierte Sonderabgaben und ihre Alternativen: Teil B: Besteuerung und Haftung im Sondermüllbereich. Eine ökonomische Analyse." In: K. Schmidt (ed.), *Öffentliche Finanzen und Umweltpolitik I*, p. 67–89. Berlin: Duncker & Humblot.

Bonus, H. 1985. *Marktwirtschaftliche Konzepte im Umweltschutz: Auswertung amerikanischer Erfahrungen.* Stuttgart: Kohlhammer.

Broom, J. 1988. "Some Principles of Population." In: B. Colard et al. (eds.), *Economics, Growth, and Sustainable Environment*, p. 126–151. London: MacMillan.

Cline, W.R. 1991. "Scientific Basis for the Greenhouse Effect." *The Economic Journal* 101(407):904–919.

Common, M. 1988. "Poverty and Progress Revisited." In: B. Colard, D. et al. (eds.), *Economics, Growth, and Sustainable Environment*, p. 201–223. London: MacMillan.

Daly, H.E. 1980. *Economics, Ecology, Ethics.* San Francisco: Josey Bass.

Edwards, S. 1987. "In Defense of Environmental Economics." *Environmental Ethics* 9(1):73–85.

Ewers, H.-J. and W. Schulz. 1982. "Die monetären Nutzen gewässergüteverbessernder Maßnahmen - dargestellt am Beispiel des Tegeler Sees in Berlin." Mimeo, Berlin.

Frey, R.L. 1987. "Wirtschaftswachstum und Umweltqualität: Auf der Suche nach einer neuen Wachstumspolitik." *Schweizerische Zeitschrift für Volkswirtschaft und Statistik* 123(2):289–315.

———. 1985. *Energie, Umweltschäden und Umweltpolitik in der Schweiz.* Zürich: Grüsch.

Gäfgen, G. 1968. "Wissenschaftliche und ethische Methodenfragen des Zielkonfliktes in der Wirtschaftspolitik." In: Katholisch-Soziales Institut (ed.), *Wirtschaftspolitischer Zielkonflikt und katholische Soziallehre*, p. 9–37. Köln: Arche.

———. 1985. "Ökonomie und Ökologie: Gegensätze und Vereinbarkeiten." Diskussionsbeiträge der Fakultät für WW und Statistik, Nr. 212. Universität Konstanz.

———. 1991. "Wechselbeziehungen zwischen Wirtschaftswissenschaft und Ethik." Diskussionsbeiträge der Fakultät für WW und Statistik, Nr. 253. Universität Konstanz.

Global 2000 Report to the President. 1980. Washington: United States Government Printing Office (edited by the Council of Economic Quality).

Hahn, R.W. 1989. "Economic Prescriptions for Environmental Problems: How the Patients follow the Doctors Orders." *Journal of Economic Perspectives* 3(1):95–114.

Höffe, O. 1981. "Umweltschutz als Staatsausgabe." In: O. Höffe (ed.), *Sittlich-politische Diskurse*, p. 135–159. Frankfurt: Surkamp.

Hölder, E. und Mitarbeiter. 1991. *Wege zu einer umweltökonomischen Gesamtrechnung: Ein Diskussionsbeitrag des statistischen Bundesamtes.* Stuttgart.

Kirchgässner, G. 1988. "Ökonomie als imperial(istisch)e Wissenschaft." *Jahrbuch für Neue Politische Ökonomie* 7, p. 128–145.

———. 1989. "Homo Oeconomicus: Das ökonomische Modell individuellen Verhaltens und seine Anwendung in den Wirtschafts-und Sozialwissenschaften." Mimeo, Universität Osnabrück.

———. 1990. "Umweltschutz als Staatsaufgabe: Einige Überlegungen aus ökonomischer Perspektive." Beiträge des Fachbereichs Wirtschaftswissenschaften der Universität Osnabrück, Nr. 56.

Knapp, K.W. 1982 "The Social Costs, Neoclassical Economics, and Environmental Planning: A Reply." *Social Science Information* 11(1):17–28.

Kneese, A.V. 1984. *Measuring the Benefits of Clean Air and Water.* Washington, D.C.: Resources for the Future, INC.

Leipert, C. 1986a. "Social Costs of Economic Growth." *Journal of Economic Issues* 20(1): 109–131.

———. 1986b. "What the GNP Does Not Account For." *Development: Seeds of Change* 3(1):58–65.

———. 1987. "Defensive Ausgaben in der Bundesrepublik Deutschland 1970 bis 1985: Absolute Werte und Relationszahlen mit dem BSP." Unpublished paper, WZB/IIUG, Berlin.

Leu, R. and L.R. Frey. 1987. "Umweltpolitik mit marktwirtschaftlichen Elementen." In: H. Buchhofer (ed.), *Liberalismus als Verjüngungskur*, p. 104–114. Zürich: Orell-Füssl.

Ministry of Finance. 1991 . *Taking Nature into Account – Proposed Scheme of Resource and Environmental Accounting.* A Report by the Commission for Environmental Accounting, Stockholm (published in Sweden as Swedish Government Official Reports, 1991:37).

Mishan, E.J. 1982. "The New Controversy about the Rationale of Economic Evaluation." *Journal of Economics Issues* 16(1):29–47.

———. 1984. "GNP - Measurement or Mirage?" *National Westminster Bank Quarterly Review* 4(1):3–27.

Nordhaus, W.D. 1977. "Strategies for the Control of Carbon Dioxide." Discussion Paper No. 443. Cowles Foundation

———. 1991a. "To Slow or not to Slow: The Economics of the Greenhouse Effect." *The Economic Journal* 101(407):920–937.

———. 1991b. "The Cost of Slowing Climate: A Survey." *The Energy Journal* 12(1):37–65.

Norton, B.G. 1982. "Environmental Ethics and the Rights of Future Generations." *Environmental Ethics* 4(3):131–148.

———. 1984. "Environmental Ethics and Weak Anthropocentrism." *Environmental Ethics* 6(2):319–337.

Nutzinger, H. and A. Zahrnt (eds.). 1989. *Ökosteuern, Umweltsteuern und -abgaben in der Diskussion.* Karlsruhe: C.S. Müller.

Oates, W.E. 1986. "Market Incentives for Environmental Protection: A Survey of Some Recent Developments." In: M. Peston und R. Quandt (eds.), *Prices, Competition and Equilibrium*, p. 256–281. Cambridge: Cambridge University Press.

Page, T. 1983. "Intergeneral Justice as Opportunity." In: P.G. Brown and D. MacLean (eds.), *Energy and the Future*, p. 68–93. New Jersey: Rowan Littlefield.

Parfit, D. 1984. *Reasons and Persons.* Oxford: Oxford University Press.

Pearce, D.W. 1986. *Cost Benefit Analysis.* Second edition. London: MacMillan.

———. 1988. "Optimal Prices for Sustainable Development." In: D. Colard et al. (eds.), *Economics, Growth, and Sustainable Environments*, p. 250–269. London: MacMillan.

———. 1991. "The Role of Carbon Taxes in Adjusting to Globing Warming." *The Economic Journal* 101(407):938–948.

Pearce, D.W., E. Barbier and A. Markandya. 1990. *Sustainable Development: Economics and Environment in the Third World.* Hants: Brookfield.

Pommerehne, W.W. 1986. "Der monetäre Wert einer Flug- und Straßenlärmreduktion: Eine empirische Analyse auf Grundlage individueller Präferenzen." In: Umweltbundesamt (ed.), *Kosten der Umweltverschmutzung*, p.199–213. Berlin: Erich Schmidt.

———. 1987. *Präferenzen für öffentliche Güter: Ansätze zu ihrer Erfassung.* Tübingen: Mohr (P. Siebeck).

———. 1988. "Measuring Environmental Benefits: A Comparison of Hedonic Technique and Contingent Valuation." In: D. Bös und K. Rose (eds.), *Measuring Welfare Change of Economies*, p. 308–336. Heidelberg: Springer.

Rawls, J. 1971. *A Theory of Justice.* Cambridge, Mass.: Harvard University Press.

Reagan, T. 1981. "The Nature and the Possibility of an Environmental Ethic." *Environmental Ethics* 3(1):19–34.

Redclift, M. 1987. *Sustainable Development: Exploring the Contradictions.* London: Methuen.

Ryll, A. and K. Zimmermann. 1989. "Der rationierte Umweltschutz oder der diskrete Charme des Profitinteresses." *Jahrbuch für Sozialwissenschaften* 40(1):45–64.

Schneider, S.H. 1989. "The Greenhouse-Effect: Science and Policy." *Science* 243(4):771–781.

Schulz, W. 1985. "Bessere Luft: Was ist sie uns wert? Eine gesellschaftliche Bedarfsanalyse auf der Basis individueller Zahlungsbereitschaft." Mimeo, Berlin.

Stahmer, C. 1987. "Umweltberichterstattung im Rahmen der Volkswirtschaftlichen Gesamtrechnungen." In: Statistisches Bundesamt (ed.), *Statistische Umweltberichterstattung*, p. 120–127. Stuttgart/Mainz: W. Kohlhammer.

Theys, J. 1984. "Environmental Accounting and its Use in Developing Policy." Discussion Paper (Mimeo). Washington, D.C.: The World Bank.

Turner, R.K. (ed.). 1988a. *Sustainable Environmental Management, Principles and Practice.* Boulder: West View Press.

———. 1988b. "Wetland Conservation: Economics and Ethics." In: Colard, D. et al. (eds.), *Economics, Growth, and Sustainable Environment*, p. 221–248. London: MacMillan.

———. 1988c. "Pluralism in Environmental Economics: A Survey of the Sustainable Economic Development Debate." *Journal of Agriculture and Economics* 39(3):352–359.

Uexkuell, J. and M. Braungart. 1991. "Getting our European Priorities Right." Unpublished paper, London.

Wegehenkel, L. (ed.). 1983. *Umweltprobleme als Herausforderung der Marktwirtschaft – Neue Ideen jenseits des Dirigismus.* Stuttgart: Kohlhammer, p. 9–44.

———. 1981. *Gleichgewicht, Transaktionskosten und Evolution.* Tübingen: Mohr (P. Siebeck).

Wilkinson, R.G. 1973. *Poverty and Progress: An Ecological Model of Economic Development*. London: Methuen.
Worldwatch Institute. 1989/90. *Zur Lage der Welt 89/90, Daten für das Überleben unseres Planeten*. Frankfurt: Fischer.
Worldwatch Institute. 1990/91. *Zur Lage der Welt 90/91, Daten für das Überleben unseres Planeten*. Frankfurt: Fischer.

Philosophical Aspects of Intergenerational Justice

Joanna Pasek

Introduction

In his Introduction to an anthology entitled *Responsibility to Future Generations* Ernest Partridge (1981) puts some rather challenging questions to the reader. "What do we owe posterity?" he asks, and he goes on to say that "the question is unavoidable, for the course of human events has forced the issue upon us. We of this generation have in our hands unprecedented power to affect the future – forever." And further, he says: "... it appears that we are not morally permitted simply to let the future be, for our responsibility is forced upon us."

These somewhat dramatic statements, which suggest that modern civilization has reached a very dangerous stage and that our generation will play a historical role in either saving the human race from a catastrophe or allowing it happen, arise from a reflection on the state of the world with its continuing destruction of the environment, depletion of natural resources, problems of overpopulation, and the development of nuclear weapons.

To what extent these problems – and others related to them – put the existence and the welfare of human race in jeopardy, is a subject of controversy. The optimists, as they are often referred to, believe that the developments enumerated above can be handled and that the progress of scientific knowledge will make it possible to solve hitherto insoluble problems. The pessimists, such as Meadows et al. (1972), the authors of the Club of Rome report on *The Limits to Growth*, warn us that the very existence of our civilization is in grave danger.

Leaving aside the question of whether the gloomy predictions are well founded or not, they have had an impact on recent philosophical discussion addressed to the ethical aspects of the problem of the futurity of the human race. The problem is usually formulated as follows: Do "future people" have rights such as a fundamental right to come into existence? And do they have "rights" such as the right to live in tolerable conditions? Conversely, insofar as it is assumed that the existence and welfare of the future people is at least to some extent dependent on the policies of the presently living people, do we have any obligations to future generations and, if we do, what are these obligations. In particular, are we obliged to make certain sacrifices for the sake of their welfare? At this point the concept of intergenerational justice becomes a major philosophical issue.

Is this a new issue in philosophy? In a certain sense it is. For although philosophers have often expressed views about the future, the very existence and welfare of posterity has rarely been presented as a major ethical challenge to the present generation. Today, however, when many people are worried that our civilization has entered a self-destructive stage, this problem has become more than an academic issue. Reaching conclusions about intergenerational justice would have a bearing on our choice between alternative policies that have implications for the future.

Against a background of about twenty-five centuries of philosophical speculation, the problem of intergenerational justice seems a newborn baby. The literature on the subject has been growing only from about the beginning of the 1970s, being closely correlated with the growing concern with the negative implications of economic growth. An expression of that concern is the alleged need to distinguish a new area of philosophical inquiry called "environmental philosophy" or "environmental ethics."

I Intergenerational Justice and the General Theory of Justice

As indicated above, this paper is addressed to the question of what our obligations to future generations are. One of the important things we would like to know about this question is whether it differs in any significant way from the question of what our obligations are to other people in general. In other words, is there anything special about the notion of intergenerational justice as opposed to justice as such? To put it in more general terms, can we discuss the question of our moral obligations to posterity within the framework of the ethical theories we already possess or does the question pose a special problem for these theories and – perhaps in some cases – call for their revision?

The possibility that the problem of intergenerational justice may not just be a straightforward application of a general theory of justice arises on account of certain special characteristics of future generations that make them different from the present ones and which may have implications for moral consideration (Kavka, 1978). The three most important appear to be:

1. Futurity It may sound trivially obvious, but the essential quality of the future people is their futurity – i.e., the fact that they do not presently exist. This has considerable moral significance, since it is by no means certain that nonexisting entities can be treated as moral subjects in the same way that present people can. For example, it is not obvious whether they can be said to have rights and whether we can be said to have duties towards them.

2. Contingency Future people cannot be simply characterized as not yet existing, as if they were separated from us only by time. For their existence in, say, 500 years time is not the same sort of fact as that the sun will rise in 500 years time. Their existence is possible in the sense of being contingent on us. In the extreme case, our present course of action could mean that they will not come into existence at all. In the less extreme case, our present policy will have a significant impact on the size of the future population. And the size of the population obviously plays an essential role in the discussion of intergenerational justice. If we decide to adopt the view that we do have responsibilities for the welfare of future people, then these responsibilities grow as the predicted size of the population grows.

3. Our ignorance of future generations' needs, values, and technological possibilities Many of the authors who have written about intergenerational justice have drawn attention to the fact that our knowledge of the remote future is very limited. As Jan Narveson

(1978) points out, "differences likely to be made by the next couple of hundred years' growth in knowledge are literally unimaginable. Only mystics will engage in futurology over even that time span, short as it is by historical standards" (p. 41). On the one hand, we do not know what technological possibilities will be open to future generations, and, on the other hand, we do not know how their needs and preferences will differ from ours. This lack of knowledge makes an important moral difference in our discussion of intergenerational justice. For if we adopt the view that we do have some obligations to future generations, then we would like to know what they are, and in order to decide what they are we ought to be able to predict – with some reasonable probability – what the future people will need. Otherwise, our sacrifices may turn out to be pointless. As Passmore (1974) puts it:

> We cannot be certain that posterity will need what we save – or on the other side that it will not need what we should not think of saving. There is always the risk, too, that our well-intentioned sacrifices will have the long-term effect of making the situation of posterity worse than it would otherwise be. This is the case for simply ignoring posterity and doing what we can to repair present evils. (p. 98)

To be sure Passmore's view is not that we should neglect the future or be indifferent to it. His view is that from a purely *rational* perspective our ignorance of the future would justify our ignoring posterity on the grounds that we cannot make any rational prediction. In other words, our ignorance of the future would remove the question of intergenerational justice from the agenda. But as Passmore suggests, we are not really capable of being ruthlessly rational and, despite all uncertainties, we are prepared to make sacrifices even if it means making mistakes. Our source of concern for posterity lies, according to Passmore, in the emotional – as distinct from the rational – part of our nature, a view to which we shall return later in this paper.

As will be seen, the three salient characteristics of future generations mentioned above – futurity, contingency, and our ignorance of their tastes and technological possibilities – have an important bearing on most of the issues encountered in the problem of intergenerational justice.

Let us consider first the view that is often discussed in the literature and that may be called – in deference to Derek Parfit – the "person-affecting view" (or "the person-regarding view"). According to this view, "duties must always be duties to someone or other; if no person is affected by an action, then that action (or inaction) cannot be a violation or fulfillment of a duty" (Narveson, 1978, p. 43). As Narveson rightly shows, the view that we can have duties only to existing identifiable people implies that we cannot say their coming into existence is something that we owe to future generations, for "if there is no subject of obligation, then, given the person-regarding view, there is no obligation" (1978, pp. 43–44). In other words, on that view, we cannot say that we owe it to future generations to ensure the perpetuation of the human race or that we have failed to fulfill some obligation to them if the human race does not survive as a result of some particular policy that we have adopted. In general we cannot say that we owe them anything, since they are not persons.

Derek Parfit (1983) explains the way that the adoption of the person-affecting view would affect our choice between alternative policies in the following manner:

> Suppose that, as a community, we must chose whether to deplete or to conserve certain kinds of resources. If we chose Depletion, the quality of life over the next two centuries would be slightly higher than it would have been if we had chosen Conservation, but it may later be much lower ... If we choose Depletion rather than Conservation, this will lower the quality of life more than two centuries from now. But the particular people who will then be living would never have existed if instead we had chosen Conservation. So our choice of depletion is not worse for any of these people.

Here Parfit assumes that the two policies will produce two different sets of people of which only one will come into existence as a result of the depletion policy. Then, for these particular, people the choice of the depletion policy will seem to have been the desirable one, since they will have owed their existence to it, even if some other set of people would have been happier had the Conservation policy been chosen instead.

Thus once we adopt the person-affecting view, it does not matter which policy we adopt as long as each produced different moral subjects and as long as the life of each group is not miserable enough to be not worth living. But does this conclusion correspond to our moral intuitions? Most of us would say that it does not and that "it is bad if those who live are worse off than those who might have lived" (Parfit, 1983, p. 175). We would like to choose a policy that it more likely to lead to a happier life irrespective of whose life it is, and this conclusion – which Parfit subscribes to – means that we ought to abandon the person-affecting principle.

A different approach from the one that denies attributing rights to future generations on account of their nonexistence is the approach that claims that they are to be treated seriously as moral subjects and that we ought to take their interests into account. Certainly it would not be possible to point to any ultimate, universally acceptable principles providing grounds for that claim, and hardly anybody hopes to identify them. But perhaps here we are not in a much worse situation than we would have been if we had tried to say whether or why we have any obligations to other existing people, such as our own children or needy people whom we do not know and who may live in distant lands. Different approaches are possible that start from different premises or different hierarchies of values. This is characteristic of ethical theory in general, which probably does not contain a single proposition that would command universal assent amongst philosophers.

Arguments purporting to show that we do have obligations to future generations include some that appeal to religious principles, others that emphasize the intrinsic value of human life, which commands respect for future people, or others that stress the virtue of humanity or those that stress solidarity between generations. Still others are built around the notion of utility or happiness, and there are others that are built around the notion of justice, and others that are based on the notion of love. Here I shall limit myself to brief sketches of two or three of the most common approaches.

II The Utilitarian Approach

As was indicated earlier the contingency of future people means that, to some extent, it is the present generation that determines how many of them will exist, or even whether they will exist at all. The moral question related to this is how to decide how many people there "ought" to be. The question is essential, since – as most people would agree – the size of the future population will be one of the most important factors determining the level of welfare that future generations will enjoy and the scale of the sacrifices that the present generation may need to make. The problem of the optimum population level is often discussed within the framework of utilitarian theory. In its classical version – sometimes called "total utilitarianism" – developed by Bentham, John Stuart Mill and Sidgwick, the utilitarian principle states that it is our moral duty to maximize the total amount of happiness (or utility) of all persons. This could be achieved in various ways, including, for example, making present generations better off than they already are or, alternatively, allowing an increase in population, or both.

Critics of total utilitarianism point out that "the main difficulty with the objective of maximizing total utility is that it would justify any increase in population – even if, as a result, the lives of most people were not very happy – so long as some increase in total utility were produced" (Sterba, 1981, p. 108).

The alternative version of utilitarianism is "average utilitarianism," according to which the objective is to maximize average utility (per head). (Of course, for a given population the two theories coincide). The implication of average utilitarianism for population policy is that population growth is only desirable if average utility is not reduced. Narveson (1978, p. 46) claims that such a conclu sion is counter to our moral intuition. For example, other things being equal, should one abstain from having a child if it were believed that the child in question would be less happy than the average person? On the other hand, should one feel morally obliged to produce a child if it is believed that the child's happiness will be greater than average?

A different sort of criticism of average utilitarianism in the context of optimal population policy comes from Sumner (1978), who argues that average utilitarianism is not so faithful as is claimed to the principle of impartiality in taking account of peoples' utilities. For it tends to favor the living over the unborn. In his example, let us imagine a population of size 'P' which can increase its utility to the level 'U' either by making just one person,

Smith, better off or by adding one person, Jones, to the population. According to the classical (i.e., "total utilitarianism") theory, both policies are equally desirable, since the same total utility is attained in each case. But "average utilitarianism" would prefer increasing Smith's utility rather than creating Jones's utility.

> In favouring steady state over expansion it is difficult to avoid the conclusion that the average theory favors Smith over Jones *simply because he already exists.* But that is to favor a person simply on the grounds of his temporal location and that contradicts utilitarian impartiality ... The preference which the average theory exhibits is a pure (and arbitrary) preference for the living over the yet unborn. (Sumner, 1978, p. 103)

Of course, Sumner's point only arises in the context of optimal population policy. In other contexts average utilitarianism does not seem to be open to the same objection of having a bias against future generations. For example, in a model with two generations, if it can be shown that a sacrifice in average utility by the first generation will lead to a more than commensurate rise in average utility of the second generation (after appropriate discounting), then, other things being equal, average utilitarianism would favor the sacrifice by the first generation.

III The Contractarian Approach

Those who believe that justice requires that all generations deserve equal moral treatment and that belonging to one generation rather than another should not have any impact on one's moral rights or obligations may find a contractarian approach to intergenerational justice is a viable alternative to utilitarian models. Contractarian theories of justice are, of course, not new, but John Rawls's (1972) recent theory of justice has given rise to considerable attention and a whole literature has grown up around it. It is now generally agreed that it is virtually impossible to discuss philosophical issues of justice without taking account of Rawls's major contribution to the subject.

The idea of a hypothetical contract as it is conceived by Rawls assumes that free, equal, and "rational" persons who all aim to protect their own interests choose, in one joint act, the first principles of justice, determining thereby basic rights and duties and the division of social benefits. This hypothetical contract is negotiated behind what Rawls calls "the veil of ignorance," implying that nobody signing the contract knows what his position in society will be (e.g., his social status, intelligence and abilities). This ensures that the "original position" in which a certain conception of justice is chosen can be described as "fair" and "that no one is advantaged or disadvantaged in the choice of principles by the outcome of natural chance or the contingency of social circumstances" (Rawls, 1972, p. 12).

However, as various commentators have pointed out, there are difficulties in applying Rawls's theory of justice to the special problem of intergenerational justice, as Rawls himself seems to concede (see, e.g., Barry, 1977; Richards, 1983; Attfield, 1983). For, at one point, he says: "Now I believe that it is not possible, at present anyway, to define precise limits on what the rate of savings should be. How the burden of capital accumulation and of raising the standard of civilization and culture is to be shared between generations seems to admit of no definite answer" (Rawls, 1972, p. 286).

One of the particular problems involved in trying to apply the Rawlsian theory to the special issue of intergenerational justice is the question of who exactly participates in the original contract. At one point, Rawls explicitly states that "all generations are virtually represented in the original position" (1972, p. 288). If, following Rawls, we assume that justice requires that all generations are represented in the original position this implies that there might have to be an infinite number of parties to the original contract. The concept of a negotiation of a contract among an infinite number of parties is difficult to accept.

Another aspect of this problem is that there appears to be a logical inconsistency between the notion that virtually all generations are represented in the original position and the idea that, in this position, they will agree on the principles of justice, for the principles on which the participants would agree could affect how many generations will exist and hence how many will participate in the original contract. In other words, until the principles are agreed it will not be known how many generations are likely to come into existence, but until that is known the number of generations to be represented in the original position is not determined. And until the participants are determined it will not be possible to agree on the principles of justice. We have a typical "Catch 22" situation which highlights the manner in which the contingency feature of intergenerational justice distinguishes it from the more general theory of justice.

If we try to escape this dilemma by restricting participants to the present generation then we run into another difficulty. This is that the present generation will have to make possibly arbitrary decisions concerning how many future generations will, or ought to, come into existence and hence how many generations' interests need to be taken into account. This arbitrary decision would violate the basic Rawlsian principle of justice as fairness.

Logical problems concerning which generations are represented in the original position are, of course, not the only problems that arise in an attempt to extend Rawlsian theory to intergenerational justice. Another is that Rawls relies heavily on the positive proposition that people are concerned mainly with the welfare of their immediate offspring and that this provides the basis for a contract between each generation and the succeeding generation. But, as some commentators have pointed out, this constitutes a weak basis for a theory that may need to encompass concern with far more distant generations – a concern that would be relevant, for example, in the context of the proper sacrifice that present generations ought to make to avoid climate change a hundred years later (Richards, 1983, p. 137).

IV Discounting the Future and Equality of Treatment

Independently of the question of whether the original position in Rawlsian theory can fulfill its function of being a meeting-place of all generations at which they can agree on the terms of intergenerational justice (as well as of justice in general), the question of what the terms of this justice would be also arises. One interpretation would be that, from a moral point of view, all generations' needs count equally, but this then raises the next question of what is meant, in this context, by "counting equally"? As Kavka (1978) points out: "Location in space is not a morally relevant feature of a person determining his worthiness for consideration or aid. Why should location in time be any different?" Further, he argues that a rational person assigns the same importance to the satisfaction of present desires as to future ones, and "since rational prudence (which concerns the satisfaction of desires) sees no intrinsic importance in the temporal location of the desire, it would seem that rational morality (which concerns the well-being of people) should attach no intrinsic importance to the temporal location of people" (p. 188). David Richards goes as far as to say that "the failure to take seriously the moral fortuity of one's own generation is, I submit, a failure of moral imagination on a par with systematic forms of immorality like racism or sexism" (1983, p. 140).

These assertions seem to be claiming that it would be either irrational or immoral or both to give different moral status to different generations in the sense that the satisfaction of future needs should count less simply on grounds of their futurity. Does this claim amount to saying that discounting the future is either irrational or immoral? As Partridge points out: "The concept of discounting the future is a point of fundamental contention between economists and moral philosophers. To economists the concept is virtually axiomatic and thus beyond dispute. To many philosophers, the notion is, at best, arbitrary and unproved and, at worst, absurd" (Partridge, 1981, p. 8).

The controversy derives from the confusion as to what discounting of the future really means in economics. If it meant giving less consideration to future events *simply on account of their futurity* then it would really conflict with the claim that the location of something in time has no moral relevance. But, as far as I can judge, it would seem that, in economics, future events are discounted not on account of their futurity **per se** but on account of certain other characteristics that happen to be related to their futurity, such as the uncertainty or riskiness attached to future events.

For example, in his criticisms of the grounds for discounting the future, Derek Parfit dismisses the uncertainty argument for discounting on the grounds that "it is, therefore, a mistake to discount for time *rather than* probability." But the question is who really makes this mistake? The same applies to Parfit's rejection of discounting on the grounds that (i) future generations will have higher incomes than we do today, and (ii) we appeal to the law of diminishing marginal utility. Parfit argues that such considerations "do not justify a social discount rate. The grounds for discounting these future benefits is not that they lie further in the future, but that they will go to people who are better off. Here, as elsewhere, we should say what we mean" (1983, p. 31ff.). But perhaps economists do say what they mean – i.e., that they defend discounting the future explicitly on the grounds of uncertainty and the likely higher incomes in the future.

In other words, if every rational basis that may be advanced for discounting the future – e.g., uncertainty of future benefits, or higher future incomes – is to be dismissed on the grounds that this just happens to be a characteristic of the future, then, of course, one would be left in the position that the discounting practice would be irrational and indefensible. But the same would apply to rational grounds that may be advanced for most decisions that took the form "*X* is bad because *X* happens to have the characteristic Y." Parfit would, presumably, argue that this is an irrational condemnation of *X*, since it is not really *X* that is being criticized, it is *Y* that is to blame.

In the present context, for example, if it is agreed – as Parfit appears to agree – that it is rational to discount for uncertainty then, provided we also agree that the future is uncertain it would be rational to discount the future. This does not mean that we discount the future as such. It just happens that the future has this characteristic of being uncertain.

A useful clarification of the confusion concerning the discounting of the future can be found in Rawls, who says that

> the mere difference of location in time, of something's being earlier or later, is not itself a rational ground for having more or less regard for it. Of course, a present or near future advantage may be counted more heavily on account of its greater certainty or probability, and we should take into consideration how our situation and capacity for particular enjoyments will change. But none of these things justifies our preferring a lesser present to a greater future good simply because of its nearer temporal position." (1972, p. 293)

V Obligations Grounded in Affinity

The distinguished philosopher, John Passmore, in a particularly important contribution to this debate, expressed his doubts as to whether our present actions – however carefully planned and calculated – can shape the future in the manner intended.[1] As mentioned near the beginning of this paper, Passmore suggests that given our ignorance about the remote future, we might be justified in ignoring it totally and confining ourselves to dealing with present evils. "The supposition," he says, "indeed, that history lies entirely in man's hands, that men can deliberately create the world of their choice will not stand up to historical scrutiny" (1974, p. 82).[2]

However, Passmore argues that, despite all the doubts about the extent to which the fate of future generations will be the result of our deliberate actions, we do have a feeling of responsibility for posterity which is founded in our feeling of "love."[3] "Obligations deriving from loves," he says, "relate us to posterity just so far as we have some grounds for believing that the future will contain what we love" (1974, p. 91). Among the things we love are not only people, such as our children, but also places, institutions, and so on. But although our love has its temporal limits, as we seem to be unable to love things that are too remote in time, we still feel concerned for them thanks to the establishment of what Passmore called a "chain of love." For example, although we may not be able to love our grandchildrens' grandchildren, our concern for them derives from our expectation of our grandchildrens' love for their grandchildren.

---

[1] At one point he writes, "How confident can we be that, in attempting to cut down on growth in order to save the biosphere, we would not provoke social and political upheavals of the first order" (1974, pp. 84–85).

[2] This point is very much in line with one of the distinguishing features of the "Austrian school of economics," which – as far as I understand it – expressed some skepticism as to the possibility of predicting economic events. As one commentator has put it, "The beneficial effects of Austrian subjectivism is to curb exaggerated claims of accuracy and to temper expectations of ability to 'manage' economic phenomena, with some degree of scepticism" (Shand, 1990).

[3] The idea of deriving moral duty from a feeling of love may be very appealing to many people. It should be noted, however, that it differs from the idea of moral duty that is a central notion in Kant's ethics. For Kant our moral obligations to people have nothing to do with our feelings towards them. They are expressions of our observance of moral law which commands respect for other people on account of their rationality.

Although it is true, as is sometimes pointed out (Turner, 1988, p. 145), that Passmore's concept of obligation as a concept that is linked with his notion of "love" does not offer a sufficient basis for a policy towards the future, I see the main virtue of Passmore's approach to the question of intergenerational justice as being his emphasizing that we are in a situation of moral uncertainty from which we shall never escape. As I have tried to show briefly in my paper there is scope for different moral principles determining the extent of our obligations to posterity. Inevitably these principles may conflict with each other and with other moral obligations, so that in the face of such conflicts we are, as Kolakowski (1981) puts it, "driven by foggy intuition rather than precise calculation."

VI Conclusion

All this seems to lead to the conclusion that we cannot entirely avoid a situation of moral uncertainty. Obviously, such a situation may be a source of considerable intellectual or emotional discomfort from which we would like to escape. "No wonder," Kolakowski (1981) says, "that we are very satisfied when somebody succeeds in persuading us that there exists an absolute rule which is precise enough to make a decision for us. Although satisfaction is within our reach we enjoy it at the cost of moral self-mutilation."

Suppose then that there are no clear and precise rules that tell whether we have obligations to future generations or what these obligations are. It is still possible to say that our attitude to posterity is an attitude of concern. In my view it is an essential quality of our culture that we project our main undertakings and endeavors into the future. Social institutions, science, art, and other undertakings, are meaningful to us not only because they directly satisfy our present needs but also because they form and organize our vision of the future. Why the future should seem important to us in this manner is a question that I shall not pursue in this paper. I shall take it for granted that for one reason or another – our instincts, natural needs, cultural conditioning and traditions, and so on – it is important to us what the future of the human race is likely to be. We care about posterity partly, or mainly, because the conviction (conscious or otherwise) that the human race will endure gives some meaning to our lives. Hence, we are concerned about future generations not only (and perhaps not mainly) for their own sakes but for our own sakes. But whether actions undertaken out of apparent concern for posterity will prove to be successful in achieving the desired effects is a different matter, and here I have to admit that I share Passmore's reservations.

Bibliography

Attfield, R. 1983. *The Ethics of Environmental Concern.* Oxford: Blackwells.

Barry, B. 1977. "Justice between Generations." In: P.M.S. Hacker and J. Raz (eds.), *Law, Morality and Society*, Oxford: Clarendon Press.

Kavka, G. 1978. "The Futurity Problem." In: R.I. Sikora and B. Barry (eds.), *Obligations to Future Generations.* Philadelphia: Temple University Press.

Kolakowski, L. 1981. "Mala etyka" (Small Ethics). In: *Czy diabel moze byc zbawiony* (Whether the Devil Can Be Saved). London: Aneks.

Meadows, D. et al. 1972. *The Limits to Growth.* Report to the Club of Rome. NewYork: Universe Press.

Narveson, J. 1978. "Future People and Us." In: R.I. Sikora and B. Barry (eds.), *Obligations to Future Generations.* Philadelphia: Temple University Press.

Parfit, D. 1983. "Energy Policy and the Futher Future: The Identity Problem." In: D. MacLean and P.G. Brown (eds.), *Energy and the Future.* New Jersey.

Partridge, E. 1981. *Responsibility to Future Generations.* New York: Prometheus Books.

Passmore, J. 1974. *Man's Responsibility for Nature.* London: Duckworths.

Rawls, J. 1972. *A Theory of Justice.* Oxford: Clarendon Press.

Richards, D.A.J. 1983. "Contractarian Theory, Intergenerational Justice, and Energy Policy." In: D. MacLean and P.G. Brown (eds.), *Energy and the Future.* New Jersey.

Shand, A.H. 1990. *Free Market Morality: The Political Economy of the Austrian School.* London: Routledge.

Sterba, J.P. 1981. "The Welfare Rights of Distant Peoples and Future Generations: Moral Side-Constraints on Social Policy." *Social Theory and Practice* 7(1).

Sumner, L.W. 1978. "Classical Utilitarianism and the Population Optimum." In: R.I. Sikora and B. Barry (eds.), *Obligations to Future Generations.* Philadelphia: Temple University Press.

Turner, K. 1988. "Wetland Conservation: Economics and Ethics." In: D. Collard, D. Pearceand D. Ulph (eds.), *Economics Growth and Sustainable Development.* New York: St. Martins's Press.

Evolutionary Economics as an Approach to Environmental Problems

Georg Erdmann*

Introduction

According to the economic assessment of environmental problems, drawn from the predominant neoclassical theory, the most efficient strategy to improve the environment would be the application of so-called market approaches. Because the environment is economically a public good, this strategy requires the introduction of some environmental taxes (*Pigou tax*) or tradable pollution certificates. If the tax rate is fixed according to the marginal abatement costs, or if the number of pollution certificates corresponds to the socially optimal emission standard, these instruments allow the economy to be pushed to its stationary *Pareto-efficient* equilibrium, which is characterized by smaller markets for environmentally harmful goods and larger markets for environmentally favorable goods, as shown in Figure 1.

However, there are some doubts whether this strategy following a comparative static assessment of environmental problems is the most reliable approach towards the efficient management of the environment. As both the environment and the economy are by nature complex dynamic systems, it is rather questionable whether a policy designed to fit a *static* equilibrium approach is appropriate for the management of such systems. In a dynamic context, experience has shown that, in the course of economic development, a large number of economic and social problems have not been solved immediately through the correction of some

* My grateful thanks are due to Herbert Giersch, William D. Nordhaus and an anonymous referee who provided helpful ideas and comments.

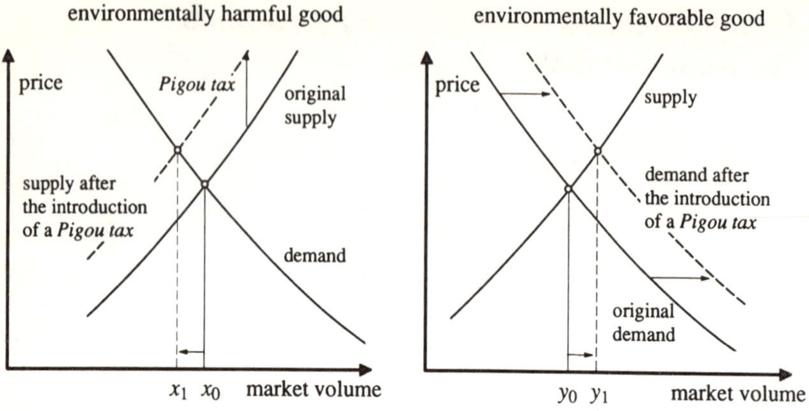

Fig. 1. Internalization of external costs via a Pigou tax.

market prices via political intervention, but rather by the accumulation and diffusion of knowledge and economic *innovations*, both in the areas of technology and of institutions. The history of energy markets presents strong evidence for this statement (see the examples given by von Weizsäcker, 1988), and actual trends in energy research and development (R&D) seem to strengthen this view further (see Martin, 1990). Thus, the contribution of innovations should be of special importance for solving environmental problems.

Of course, some contemporary ecological problems are the unintended result of economically successful innovations in the field of technology. Some people conclude that innovations cannot be a solution to problems that have their origin in earlier innovations. According to this opinion, it is basically impossible to control technological problems by means of technologies, because the complete set of implications resulting from new technologies can only be known ex post. Technological progress is assumed to become increasingly dangerous and uncontrollable due to its manifold and unpredictable interactions. The only sustainable way to solve environmental problems is supposed to consist in abandoning high standards of living.

As a reply, I would like to point to the fact that changing society in this direction requires the implementation of major innovations in the field of human behavior and social life. Thus the relevant question is not whether innovations are the solution to environmental problems or not, but rather what kind of innovations are appropriate, how those innovations can be stipulated, how the innovative process as a whole may be biased towards solving environmental problems, and what kind of policy is needed in order to overcome obstacles causing appropriate innovations to fail.

If the approach to environmental problems is to be designed by taking explicit recourse to dynamic economic theory of endogenous change, the process of knowledge accumulation and its implementation in the economy via innovations is of major importance. As expressed by the notion of "induced innovation," knowledge generation depends, among other things, on relative prices, but this statement covers only a partial aspect of economic change: the innovative process cannot be understood as a mere outcome of some mechanistic laws but rather should be regarded as the result of trial and error, rendering the innovative search open and unpredictable by nature. From a comparative static point of view, this openness overlays the impulses resulting from changing relative prices and leads to the conclusion that the immediate effects of changing relative prices on innovations are more or less random. If this idea is incorporated into a truly dynamic theory, some rules of endogenous economic change become obvious.

This paper proposes taking such a dynamic approach, known under the label *evolutionary economics*, as a background and point of reference for approaching environmental problems. This dynamic theory has not yet been established in form of a coherent school of thought comparable to neoclassical economics. There are a large number of rather different and only weakly compatible contributions to the rapidly growing literature on evolutionary economics (see Witt, 1991, for a current overview).

Among the conclusions that can be drawn from evolutionary economics is the statement that the unpredictable nature of the innovative process is the result of positive externalities linked with learning and knowledge accumulation. Thus, the solution of environmental problems via innovations not only has to deal with negative externalities, but also has to take the positive externalities – or, in terms of dynamic systems analysis, positive feedbacks – into account.

Based upon this approach the paper arrives at a new interpretation of the role of changing relative prices, environmental taxes and other instruments of environmental policy. It comes to the conclusion that environmental policy should try to irreversibly change the course of economic evolution by improving the conditions for appropriate innovations to succeed on the markets.

The organization of the paper is as follows: In the second part it presents some essentials of evolutionary economics, whereby this theoretical approach is not discussed in full detail but only as far as necessary to highlight the basic assumptions and implications of the theory. The paper then turns to the implications of and conclusions for an economic policy aimed at solving environmental problems. Among others, the evolutionary role of environmental taxes and the organization of the competition for environmentally favorable innovations is discussed.

I Sources and Essentials of Evolutionary Economics

Evolutionary thinking does not require a complete set of new methods for economic analysis but can rely on certain well-known concepts and insights of neoclassical economics as well as on ideas, which were developed by Schumpeter, von Mises, von Hayek and other economists outside the mainstream economic theory. One of the central paradigms of these economists is that economic change emerges spontaneously and in a *self-organized* manner, implying that it cannot be planned by any individual agent.[1]

The reason that these ideas have again become a focus of economic research is the recent scientific progress in physics, chemistry, biology and information science showing that certain dynamic phenomena in these rather different types of systems follow some common rules of self-organization that can be formally described by similar mathematical structures (see Nicholis and Prigogine, 1977; Haken 1978; 1988). This observation motivates a growing

[1] *Self-organization* is a modern term for the *invisible hand* described by Adam Smith more than 200 years ago.

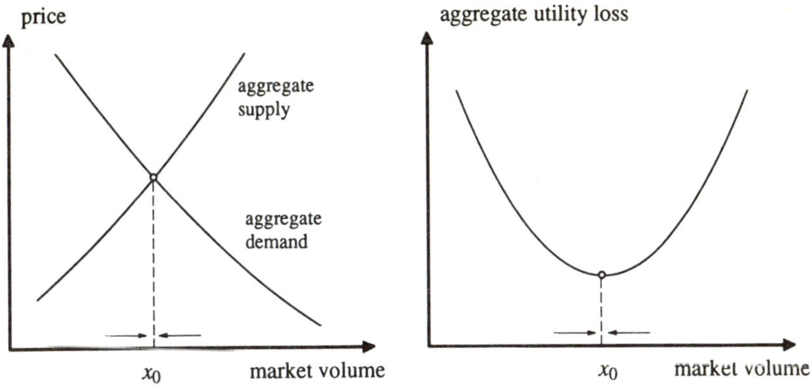

Fig. 2. Equivalence between the supply-demand equilibrium and the minimum of some potential function.

number of scientists to rethink the paradigm of self-organization in economics and social sciences, in the hope of advancing the theory of endogenous change by this line of research (see Nelson and Winter, 1982; Weidlich and Haag, 1983; Arthur, 1988; Erdmann, 1990, 1992). Accordingly, evolutionary economics can, in its current state, in part be understood as a formal reinterpretation of well-known arguments in the tradition of Schumpeter, Austrian economics, and subjectivist and institutional economics.

The following sections of this paper could proceed in formalizing the notion of self-organization by using the language of nonlinear stochastic differential equations in quantifying such a model and in simulating it in order to examine the patterns of economic evolution. But I will use another approach here by developing most of the arguments by using the graphical tool of *potential functions.*[2] Figure 2 presents on the right an example for such a potential function and it is used to explain how this graphical instrument is a straightforward extension of the traditional economic description of a market for some good, *x*. The traditional economic theory uses aggregate supply and a demand curves in a price-quantity diagram, indicating the Pareto optimal

[2] In physics, such potential functions represent the integral of some stochastic differential equation and describe the forces (for example, energy) acting on the system.

situation[3] by the intersection of both curves. The potential function shows the aggregate utility loss – based upon this supply and demand – as a function of the market volume x. The minimum of this function, x_0, corresponds to the allocation optimum in the price-quantity diagram.

The advantage of the utility potential function in explaining the rules governing the evolution of the market lies in the fact that it makes the dynamics of a market inside as well as outside its equilibrium x_0 explicit: the adaptive behavior (or arbitrage) of market participants trying to maximize profits and utility push the market to the minimum of its potential curve x_0. If the slope of the potential curve is steep for some market volume x, it indicates a strong stress on the market participants to adapt their behavior, because even small adjustments in behavior would lead to large aggregate utility gains. Therefore the corresponding market configurations will probably not hold for a long time, making it rather unlikely to find the market in those situations. But in situations where the slope is relatively small, there is no large utility improvement possible if the market behavior is modified a little. The adaptive dynamics will probably change the market rather sluggishly in the direction of the equilibrium x_0 and there is some likelihood of observing the market volume x in such configurations outside the equilibrium.

A Individually Heterogeneous Behavior

Besides these rather formal and abstract considerations there is another source of evolutionary economics. It is the view that the standard expected utility model, being the microeconomic foundation for the demand and the supply framework of neoclassical economics, is not a rather complete description of individual behavior – at least for economic situations where decisions concerning innovations are to be taken.

According to Schumpeter (1912), innovating means bringing about a new solution to a problem which is superior to former

---

[3] As far as the conditions of perfect competition hold.

solutions, which happens if some ingenuous and creative entrepreneurs venture to invest in unconventional search directions and business activities. Some of them are lucky and succeed in finding superior solutions, many others fail.

The superiority of a new solution may be measured ex post by a rent in favor of the entrepreneur, which sooner or later is transformed into some social benefit, depending, among other things, on the intensity of competition among the innovative entrepreneurs. But nobody is able to assess the superiority of an innovation ex ante. The key aspects and the major impacts of an innovation are not predictable in the course of its implementation. Formally speaking, there is no ex ante known function linking the amount of resources invested in certain innovative activities to the expected benefit to be drawn from this activity.[4] Dosi (1988a, p. 222) puts it as follows: "Almost by definition, what is searched for cannot be known with any precision before the activity itself of search and experimentation, so that the technical (and, even more so, commercial) outcomes of innovative efforts can hardly be known *ex ante*."

If there are no certainties as to the effect of additional efforts being invested in some search activity, there are hopes and subjective probabilities that fit into the microeconomic rational choice model. But the large number of factors determining subjective probabilities with respect to the expected success of certain search activities implies that a *deterministic* micro-model can hardly attempt to describe individual innovative behavior. A microeconomic model that is to describe the effects of external impulses on innovative activities obviously requires recourse to a stochastic approach.

A different attempt at describing individual innovative behavior is based upon insights from psychological decision theory (see Simon, 1984; Kahneman, Slovic and Tversky, 1985). According to this theory, individual decisions not only depend on preferences

[4] Case studies show that innovative success is often the unintended and unforeseen result of some venture activity. When major innovations, such as electricity or *EDP*, were first introduced into the market, they were designed and proposed for quite different purposes than those dominating today's applications.

and restrictions but also on psychological and social factors that may be called intuition, creativity, cleverness, strength, etc. The expected utility model is a special case describing behavior in situations where the problem is simple, its solution transparent, and psychological and social factors are of minor importance. In other, more complex situations – as is the case if decisions concerning innovative activities are to be taken – they matter.

But, again, a large number of variables and degrees of freedom interfering with the individual decision process come into consideration. This prevents the development of a *deterministic* psychological description of innovativeness. Instead, the psychological factors of individual behavior might be modeled by using random variables – an approach, which is always required if the rules governing the behavior of some subsystem are characterized by a large number of degrees of freedom. Nelson and Winter (1982, p. 175ff.) proposed an explicit model of innovation-led economic growth in formalizing intuition, creativity, cleverness, ingenuity, strength (and whatever else can be used to label individual behavior towards innovations) by means of random variables.

In a positive formulation, several companies deciding on the same type of innovative activity come to different results even if they are in identical economic situations, with equal assets, restrictions, and preferences. I will call this the paradigm of *heterogeneous individual behavior*.

The purpose of introducing heterogeneous behavior into economic modeling it is not to be able to predict whether a certain company will be engaged in a certain innovative activity, and whether it will be successful or not. Economics refers rather to the macroeconomic causes and impacts of some group of individuals behaving in a more or less heterogeneous manner, i.e., extending or reducing their search horizon in terms of Nelson and Winter (1982).

Heterogeneous behavior implies that the market allocation optimum corresponding to the intersection of the supply and the demand function, or the minimum of the potential curve, can be left by the global effects of individual search. In other words, the competition among innovative actors testing the markets with respect to configurations that may be superior to the current situation leads to continuous challenges of the given market equilibrium. The resulting disturbances are larger if the individual search horizon increases or if – in mathematical terms – the variance in individual behavior becomes larger.

The introduction of this idea into the model shown in Figure 2 leads to market trajectories that follow some more or less noisy path around the equilibrium x_0. Thus, the analysis presented so far seems to allow no basically different conclusions compared with the standard neoclassical model. However, if other effects concerning the competition for innovations are taken into consideration, the distinctive role of heterogeneous behavior becomes obvious.

B Nonconvexities and Positive Feedbacks

It is a well-known observation from neoclassical economics that in certain economic situations, nonconvexities and feedbacks are present, leading to positive externalities in the market – sometimes in addition to negative externalities. Among others, Hotelling (1929), Arrow (1962), Helpman and Krugman (1985), David (1987), Stiglitz (1987) and Lucas Jr. (1988) explained the theoretical reasons for such nonconvexities: indivisibilities of technologies, patents and norms, economies of scale, learning by doing, network externalities, spillovers between different innovative activities, sunk costs, adaptive expectations, etc.[5] The consequence of nonconvexities is that there may not be one single market equilibrium. Instead, multiple equilibria can exist.

For purposes of illustration, the example of *positive* R&D *externalities* may be used: Companies engaged in innovative activities are typically not able to keep the whole benefits of their search activities for themselves. Some of the R&D results will create external benefits in favor of competitors, imitators and customers. According to neoclassical economics, this effect leads to a

[5] In addition, the mutual benefit deriving from the relationship between science and technical progress is to be mentioned (see Fritsch, 1991). While science promotes technical progress, technical progress inversely improves the conditions for scientific work. Science is not only a source of innovations and technical progress, but also a consequence.

reduced propensity to invest resources in innovative efforts, which therefore may fall below the level that would be socially desirable (see Arrow, 1962). But if strategic interactions are taken into account, companies must be worried about their long-term competitiveness and market shares if they reduce innovative efforts while some competitors are still engaged in innovative activities. Instead of suboptimal overall investments being made in innovative activities, there is a likelihood for innovative efforts to occur in clusters: many companies devote much innovative effort to only a limited number of innovative activities, while other activities are neglected.

Dosi proposes the term *technological paradigm*, which defines "the needs that are meant to be fulfilled, the scientific principles utilized for the task, the material technology to be used" (Dosi, 1988b, p. 1127). It is likely that there exist a large number of technological paradigms, whereas R&D is actively executed along rather few of them while disregarding the others. Each combination of chosen and neglected technological paradigms represents a different pattern of the innovative process and leads to a different trajectory of the economy. Due to the costs (*sunk costs*) arising when entrepreneurs shift from one technological paradigm to another, these trajectories are (locally) stable in the mathematical sense. Thus it is reasonable to identify these different innovative patterns or trajectories as multiple equilibria.

The selective, self-reinforcing and thus partially irreversible structure of nonconvex markets can easily be introduced into the concept of *potential curves.* Figure 3 shows this for the most simple, nontrivial case of two stable equilibria in x_1 and x_2 and one unstable equilibrium in x_0. Each of the stable equilibria implies a different long-term market equilibrium.

If random forces reflecting heterogeneous behavior are introduced into this model, there exists a market constellation in which they play a decisive role in determining the future evolution of the market, namely the unstable equilibrium x_0. In the absence of random forces, the variable x would remain in this point forever. But a random influence acting in the economic situation described by the potential function – or a *fluctuation*, in the terminology of dynamic systems theory – will necessarily move the market to either x_1 or x_2. In other words, both equilibria x_1 and x_2 can be

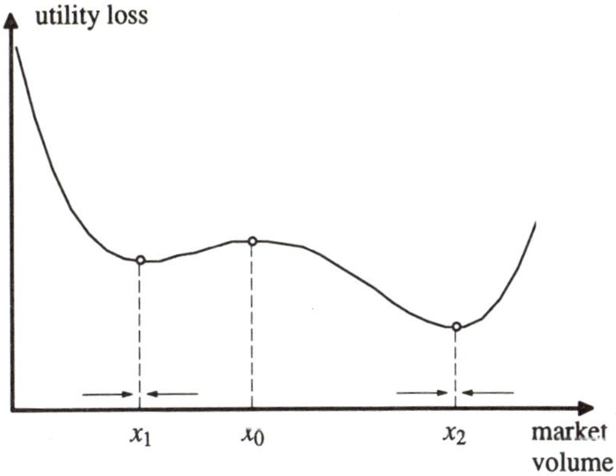

Fig. 3. Potential function showing two equilibria.

regarded as market niches that might be "discovered" by the manifold of individual search strategies. The solution of the market contingency happens when the individual search activities create an impulse strong enough to force the market irreversibly into the convergence basin of one of the stable equilibria. Afterwards the new equilibrium is approached by the adaptive market behavior. The resulting trajectory of the market volume x will look like a logistic curve and may be described formally by some diffusion law.

The superior equilibrium x_2 may turn out more likely than the inferior equilibrium x_1, but there is some chance for inverse evolution to happen (*lock-in* of an inferior equilibrium; see Arthur, 1988). David (1987) presents a number of examples where this effectively happened in the course of the introduction of new technologies.[6]

The role of random forces representing innovative behavior is also important for correcting the choice of an inferior trajectory. To show this, let us assume that the market is in the attraction

[6] An example related to environmental problems is that, according to estimates of the International Energy Agency (1989), up to 30% of electricity may be saved economically in the OECD countries. The fact that these economically feasible electricity savings are not realized can be explained by the existence of a potential barrier hindering the market from shifting to the overall economic optimum.

basin of the inferior equilibrium x_1. The only way to reach the superior equilibrium x_2 is if the presence of random forces are strong enough to move the market across the potential barrier in x_0. For example, the presence of some ingenious entrepreneurs who give up a given R&D direction in favor of another is required if a more favorable market niche is to be discovered. Such a market improvement is not necessarily the result of new problems emerging. It can happen in a *self-organized* manner as a spontaneous result of the individual search process.

In concluding this point, the discussion thus far shows that evolutionary phenomena are understood as the combined result of *chance* and *necessity*. Translated into economics, *necessity* is due to the laws of utility maximization, which are explained, among other things, by neoclassical economic models. *Chance* is the effect of individual intuition, creativity, cleverness, etc., and may be introduced into economic modeling by random variables.

C Phase Transitions, Contingencies and Nonpredictabilities

Random forces can irreversibly change the direction of the market evolution, but in Figure 3 this only occurs if the relevant economic variable is to be found far from the stable equilibria x_1 or x_2, but in the neighborhood of x_0. The reader may assume that this is rather unlikely to happen. In fact, far-from-equilibrium market configurations, where innovative impulses can chance to change the market evolution, are singular. Schumpeter already based his theory of economic change among others on that observation.

This idea is translated into the evolutionary model by the assumption that the shape of the potential curve describing the competition for innovations on a given market is not time-invariant. In particular, the number of stable equilibria may change. One source of such structural shifts of the potential curve is the success of a certain R&D project. At the same moment when this becomes obvious, the competing technological paradigms become useless, which may induce entrepreneurs to decide not to invest further innovative efforts into the related projects. If thereby a technological paradigm is definitively abandoned, the associated market structure loses its nature of being an equilibrium situation. On

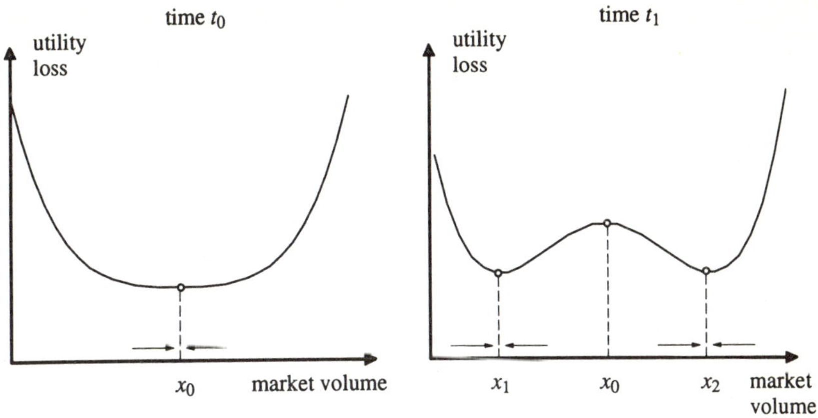

Fig. 4. Phase-transition of the potential function leading to a bifurcation.

the other hand, some originally nonequilibrium situations can become equilibrium configurations, if a new problem appears on the R&D agenda or a new scientific principle is taken into consideration for solving a given problem.

In dynamic systems theory, a structurally shifting shape of the potential curve is called a *phase transition* and it occurs if the parameters describing the relevant influences and forces acting upon the system under concern pass across some critical borders. A special case is shown in Figure 4, where the transition from the left to the right drawing is called a *bifurcation*. The market, which first is located in its stable equilibrium x_0, is later to be found far from any stable equilibrium. In this situation there are two directions open for the further market evolution, and without any detailed knowledge about the fluctuations resulting from individually heterogeneous behavior, the further direction of the market evolution cannot be predicted ex ante.

This is a weak form of the ignorance argument, which served as a starting point for the evolutionary theory of innovation. But there is also a strong version of this argument. In broadening the model presented thus far, a large number of interrelated markets and technological paradigms are evolving simultaneously. In regarding one particular market, the associated potential function is the result of feedbacks from innovative activities in the field of technology or from institutional arrangements and the associated evolution of other markets. Due to these ongoing influences, the shape of the potential function determining the environment of the innovative competition on that particular market in a given moment of time is continuously changing.

In addition, market participants cannot know more than only small segments of the potential function, and these they know not as the result of theoretical considerations taken from the office desk, but as the result of actively testing the market through explorative searches[7]. In a dynamic interpretation the changing shape of the potential function – or the changing market opportunities for innovations – must continuously be (re-)discovered by the search process, which is subject to trial and error.

II Implications for Approaching Environmental Problems

The concept of evolutionary economics presented so far gives some idea of the complex and unpredictable nature of the search and knowledge-generating process in the economy. The discussion further explained why a mathematical formalization should rely on the three elements (a) *utility potential* (or differential equations), representing utility-oriented behavior as depending on the market situation, (b) *random influences*, representing heterogeneous behavior concerning innovations, and (c) *phase transitions*, representing the openness of the economic evolution.

Not only the laws of economic evolution but also the environment may be described – in some relevant aspects – by these three elements of nonlinear systems theory. Formal isomorphs exist between both systems and may be a source of interdisciplinary exchange through the application of nonlinear stochastic models. But attempts to link both types of systems within one large model do not seem very promising to me. If such a model is to be a realistic representation of important aspects of the economy-environment interface and if it is to answer answer relevant ques-

[7] Competition is not only a way of coordinating decentralized decisions but also serves as a procedure for discovery. See von Hayek (1980), Schmidtchen (1990).

tions concerning the management of the environment, then it must be a large-scale model. Experiences have shown that such models are rather difficult to handle and ambiguous to analyze even if their mathematical structure is much easier.

I am also skeptical about any approaches that understand environmental economics as the mere task of translating the evolutionary terminology developed for natural sciences and mathematical systems analysis into economics. It is important not to confound the application of a new terminology – or certain mathematical isomorphs – with scientific progress in economics, which requires a sound analysis of the relevant aspects of the economic system under concern.

What else should then be the concept for applying evolutionary economics? I propose an instrumentalist view similar to the traditional economic proposals focusing on the internalization of external effects. The following discussion attempts to explain in what respect evolutionary theory broadens the economic view of efficiently approaching environmental problems. Its aim is to show that insights from dynamic systems analysis can improve the understanding of the requirements for a policy aiming at stimulating innovations in favor of the environment. However, as an implication of the concept of evolutionary economics discussed above, the answers and recommendations cannot take the form of a manual containing *deterministic* rules and procedures but must reflect the complex and stochastic nature of the innovative search process.

A Selecting Environmentally Favorable Innovative Strategies

It is straightforward to define the needs for an innovation-based environmental policy according to the evolutionary model presented above. Starting with the assumption that the competition for innovations is governed by multiple equilibria, it is reasonable to assume that there is one particular equilibrium market situation, which is best in terms of a certain environmental aspect. Assuming in addition (for the moment) prior knowledge about this, government policy should try to bias the explorative search process in a way that this environmentally best equilibrium becomes more likely to be selected through the competitive market process.

This selection problem is characterized by the presence of a double externality: Environmentally favorable technological paradigms might not be taken into consideration by the entrepreneurs as long as the costs of environmental damage remain external to the market. In addition to these negative externalities, positive externalities associated with R&D projects and innovations make the reorientation of appropriate innovative activities ambiguous and difficult even if the costs of environmental damages are internalized in the market prices. The two externalities imply that the market for innovations is distorted both in the comparative static sense and in the dynamic sense, i.e., with respect to the selection of the socially best equilibrium.

Figure 5 illustrates this point with two potential functions representing the market for an environmentally favorable good that offers an innovation opportunity. The reader may assume this figure to show the solar energy market. One potential function (drawn in a continuous line) describes the aggregate utility loss calculated by using market prices that exclude the external costs of environmental damages. It takes its overall optimum for the market volume x_1 and has another but inferior market equilibrium in x_2. The other potential function (drawn as a dotted line) reflects the aggregate utility loss calculated according to social

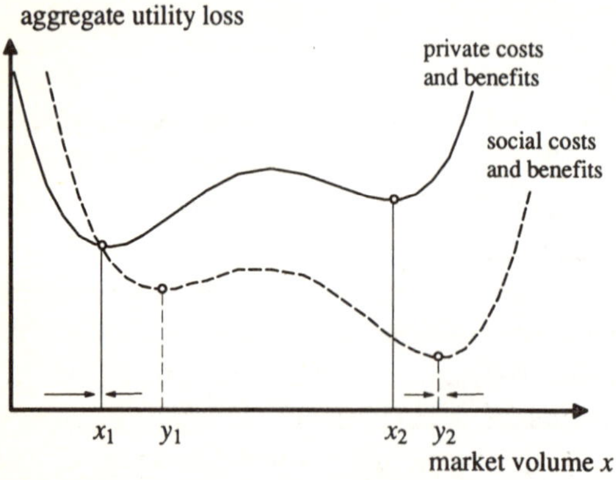

Fig 5. Potential functions for an environmentally favorable good reflecting private and social costs and benefits.

costs and benefits, including the external costs of environmental damages. It shows the overall optimum at y_2 and another market equilibrium in y_1.

Figure 5 suggests that the equilibrium x_1 will be selected more likely through self-organizing competition than the market niche at x_2 as long as the market participants base their decisions on prices that disregard the external costs of environmental damages. If innovative search efforts take the external costs and benefits into consideration, there is some chance that after some time the environmentally favorable market niche y_2 will be discovered and the market will expand to that equilibrium.

A formal model of this market evolution requires the use of stochastic differential equations describing the market forces (utility-oriented behavior) as well as the effects of individual search efforts. The later depend – according to one of the central ideas of evolutionary economics – on a large number of degrees of freedom. Therefore the success of innovative activities is a stochastic process overlaying utility-oriented behavior.[8]

Figure 6 gives an illustration of the pattern of market change for the case that individual behavior takes into account the external costs and benefits as reflected by the dotted potential function in Figure 5. It shows how the probability of observing the market volume y_2 grows in time, while the probability for the market equilibrium in y_1 declines. Anyhow it is still possible that the market remains at the inferior equilibrium y_1 or – in other words – that no innovative breakthrough occurs in favor of the environmentally favorable good.

B Role of Relative Prices

The double externalities governing the knowledge-generating process and the competition for environmentally favorable innovations require political measures in order to improve the likelihood

---

[8] The formal apparatus of such a model can be based on the master equation approach or the Fokker-Planck Equation. See Haken (1978), Weidlich and Haag (1983), Erdmann (1992).

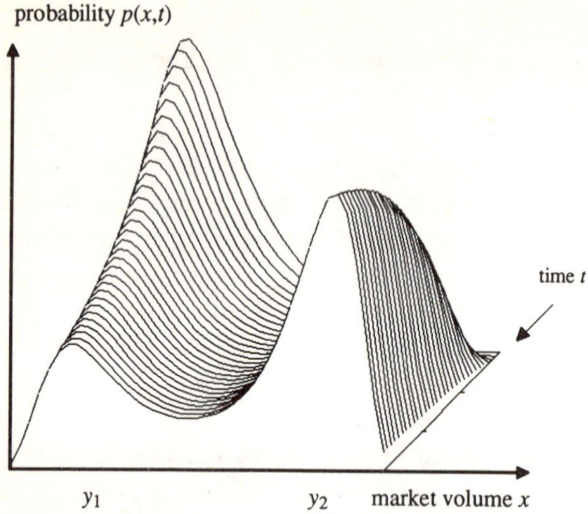

Fig. 6. Probability path for the evolution of the market volume for an environmentally favorable good.

that appropriate innovative efforts will succeed. Economists assume that the most efficient measure is the introduction of environmental taxes (*Pigou tax*) or tradable pollution certificates that correct the markets at least for negative externalities.

To analyze the evolutionary role of changing relative prices (or, more precisely, of changing price expectations) in more detail, one has to distinguish between the effect on substitution and that on innovations. To explain this distinction, the example of the two production factors *energy* and *capital* is used. While energy stands for an environmentally harmful good, capital is to be regarded as an overall environmentally favorable factor.

The introduction of an energy tax can be expected to stimulate the replacement of energy by capital through substitution. The empirical analysis of the elasticities of substitution between energy and capital shows a rather complex picture (see Berndt and Wood, 1975; Hunt, 1986), but the model presented in Figure 7 can serve as a starting point for the theoretical discussion. This figure expresses the technological choices given in a certain moment in time by an isoquant curve and shows how a tax-led rise in the relative price for energy implies a transition from x_1 to y_1, thereby reducing the energy intensity of the economy.

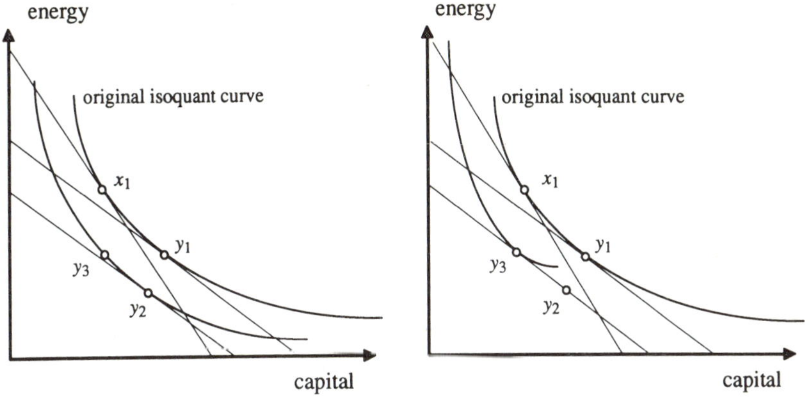

Fig. 7. Effects of changed relative prices on substitution and innovation.

In addition to this substitution effect along a given isoquant curve (or production function), successful innovative activities are assumed to occur and move the isoquant curve in the direction of the origin. According to the "Induced Bias Hypothesis" the situation shown in the left-hand side of Figure 7 should hold. With the higher relative price for energy, technical progress will be oriented towards saving more of this factor. Thereby the economically best technology becomes y_2, allowing a further reduction of the energy intensity – in addition to the substitution effect. In the case the of the right side of Figure 7 the contrary holds. Here the technology y_2 has not been discovered. The economically best technical choice is y_3 and allows no further reduction in energy use. In other words, in the left case an energy saving technical progress occurs, while in the right case there is no such bias in the direction of technical progress. The reader should recall that the same change in relative prices between energy and capital is assumed in both cases.

The "Induced Bias Hypothesis," according to which the introduction of an energy tax increases the likelihood of energy-saving technical progress, dates back to Hicks, who stated that a "change in the relative prices of the factors of production is itself a spur to invention, and to innovation of a particular kind – directed to economising the use of a factor which has become relatively expensive" (Hicks, 1932, p. 124f). The economic discussion following this hypothesis arrived at the conclusion that the success of

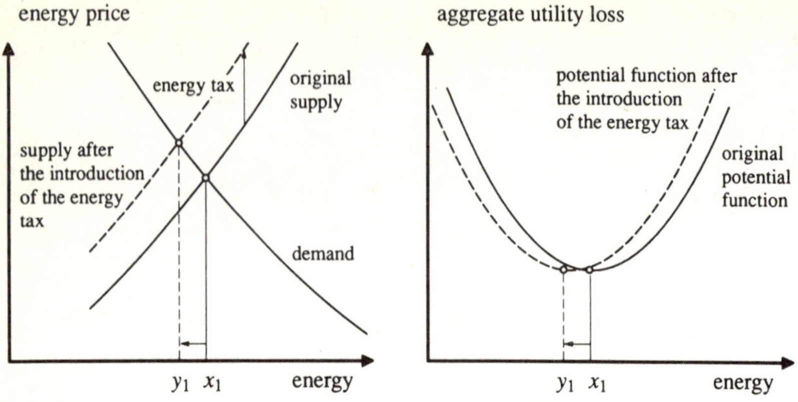

Fig 8. Energy tax and the energy market equilibrium.

innovative activities does not depend on relative prices alone but also on the existing innovation possibilities (see Kennedy, 1964; Stoneman, 1983, p. 52ff.), the costs associated with particular innovative efforts (see Binswanger, 1974) and the costs occurring if the innovation strategies and projects are changed (see Arthur, 1988).[9] Therefore it is not astonishing when empirical tests of the induced bias hypothesis "indicate that it is left unproven" (Stoneman 1983, p. 58)

The instrument of potential functions can be used to explain the doubts concerning the overall validity of an induced bias automatism on the direction of technical progress. Let me first discuss the role of *innovation possibilities.* An innovation possibility is the possibility that there is a market niche that might be discovered through innovative search efforts. In Figure 8 no such market niche is assumed to exist. The introduction of an energy tax should– similar to Figure 7 – create a substitution effect and thereby reduce the equilibrium energy market volume from x_1 to y_1.

[9] Theoretical considerations show that the factor-saving bias of technical change depends on the original factor shares. If the success of an innovative activity could be planned in advance, it would be biased towards saving more of a factor, the greater its cost share is. Thus, an energy tax creates a innovation bias in favor of a reduced use of energy if the elasticity of substitution between energy and other factors is less than unity. See Stoneman (1983, p. 54).

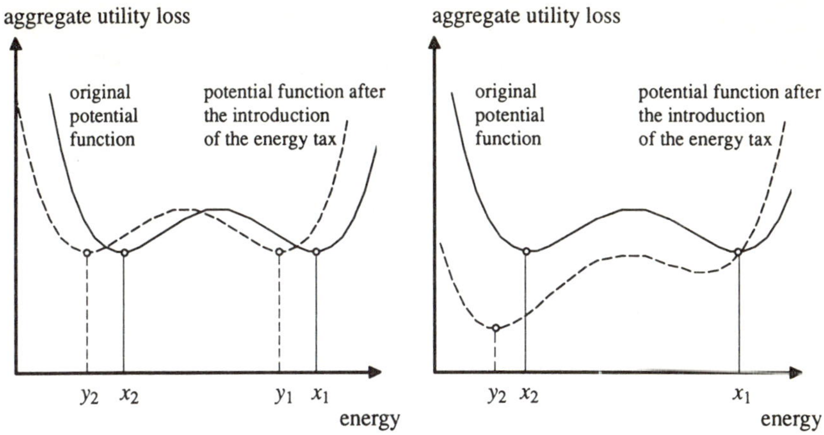

Fig. 9. Pigou tax on a market with innovation possibilities.

This is equivalent to a *horizontal shift* of the potential function and its local minima shown with dotted lines. Owing to the lack of an innovation possibility, no further reduction of the energy use is possible.

The existence of innovation possibilities may be affected by relative prices, but it also depends on other factors, such as the laws of physics and nature and the knowledge accumulated about them through basic research. In addition, the strength and market shares of the competitors on a market (Schumpeter hypothesis), institutional and legal aspects are important. There are numerous examples where government regulations explicitly determine the lack of market opportunities for innovative solutions in favor of reduced use of energy and environmental resources.[10] In these cases environmentally favorable innovative search activities cannot succeed as long as certain technical norms and regulations are not abandoned in order to enable a wider choice towards addressing environmental problems through innovations.

[10] An example is the nuclear energy industry. The introduction of a tax on CO_2 emissions would stimulate this industry and its technical progress (reactor safety, nuclear waste, proliferation, etc.), but as long as the nuclear moratorium continues to hold, this technical progress will hardly be stimulated by a CO_2 tax.

Let us now assume that there exists an innovation opportunity favoring a reduced energy intensity and discuss the question of what may hinder the market participants from discovering the appropriate market equilibrium in spite of the impulses they get from the energy tax. To illustrate this point, Figure 9 presents a market offering an innovation possibility. Let us assume that the market is in x_1 before the introduction of the energy tax and in y_1 thereafter. There is a market niche in y_2 (compare with the left case in Figure 7) which might be discovered through the innovative search. But whether the introduction of the energy tax (*Pigou tax*) improves the likelihood of this happening, depends on the effect this tax has on the shape of the potential function. In the left case of Figure 9 the changed relative prices are not particularly helpful in improving the conditions for successful innovations, while in the right case they are. Crucial is the effect of the tax on the potential barrier between the two market equilibria.[11]

There are several economic reasons for the existence of the potential barrier that may lock an environmentally inferior market equilibrium. At least three factors are to be mentioned.

(1) *Sunk costs.* If companies redirect their innovative efforts towards other problems some of their accumulated knowledge concerning R&D, management and markets is no longer used and has to be depreciated in the economic sense. The associated costs represent a threshold for changing an innovative strategy.

(2) *Network externalities.* If several companies are engaged in similar innovative activities, they benefit from each other through positive externalities. If, in this situation, a company decides to redirect its innovative activities towards other technological paradigms or problems, it hopes to increase its chances of acquiring a pioneering rent but it also loses some of the external benefits. This creates costs that challenge the shift to new strategies.

[11] Dosi suggests that political impulses "are going to succeed in radically changing the directions and procedures of technical progress only *if* and *when* they are able to foster the emergence of new (technological) paradigms" (1988, p. 1142).

(3) *Innovation risks.* Finally, the unpredictable nature of innovative success implies the reorientation of innovative activities such that they become a venture. The economic theory of risk taking explains the origin of the costs associated with such a decision which are especially important in all those cases where the capacity to take risks is exhausted.

To be a successful instrument favoring the success of environmentally favorable innovations, the introduction of an energy tax should not only change the attractiveness of appropriate market equilibria (see Figure 5) but also reduce the threshold resulting from the potential barrier. While this is obviously the case in the right-hand side of Figure 9, there is no such effect in the left-hand case.

Whether an environmental tax would be an appropriate instrument for changing economic evolution or not does not depend on the horizontal shift of the potential function that depends – according to neoclassical theory (compare Figure 8) – on the tax rate and the current elasticities of demand and supply. Rather, it matters how that measure influences the shape of the potential function. This effect is likely to be rather complex, because there is a large body of interrelated causes and effects with which to determine it.

In conclusion, it is not to be excluded that changing relative prices can have the desired effect on the directions of innovative efforts and technical progress. But it is likewise possible that the induced innovation effect is negligible. Certainly policymakers can influence relative prices, but they should recognize that an a priori assessment of this policy is rather ambiguous.

C Evolutionally Efficient Market Interventions

The reader might object that this statement opens no alternative to the market-oriented environmental policy based upon environmental taxes and tradable pollution certificates. The only conclusion is to be careful in assessing the effects of these instruments on the direction of innovations. But there is more that can be drawn from evolutionary economics.

The discussion above argued that the overall shape of the potential function is unknown to the market participants. It is also impossible to know in advance what shape would result if the potential function reflects social costs and benefits instead of private costs and benefits – in contrast to the assumption used for Figure 5. Thus it will hardly be possible to assess ex ante whether an energy tax really affects the direction of innovations and technical progress in the desired way.

But the evolutionary role of the tax can be checked ex post, without even knowing the shape of the potential function and the structural shifts resulting from the environmental tax. Its evolutionary role becomes obvious when the government withdraws the tax some time after its first introduction. If, in this case, the market returns to its original equilibrium x_1 (see Figure 9), there was no evolutionary impact at all. But if the market turns to x_2, the political instrument has *irreversibly* affected the economic evolution in the direction of a more favorable economic structure.

I propose calling the environmental tax in this second case *evolutionally efficient*. The relation between the evolutionary efficiency of an economic instrument and its efficiency in the comparative static sense is complex: an efficient environmental measure in the comparative static sense may not be evolutionally efficient and vice versa.[12] The evolutionary interpretation of changing relative prices thus leads to a different strategic orientation of environmental policy: while neoclassical economics focuses on the internalization of external effects, evolutionary economics assumes the irreversibility of the induced stimuli to be crucial.

Of course it is rather unlikely that the evolutionary efficiency of an environmental instrument can usually be determined ex ante, but it can be determined ex post by withdrawing the environ-

[12] Two examples for evolutionally efficient environmental measures might be cited. One is the oil price shock which occurred in 1979. In the meantime oil prices have returned to their pre-1979 values in real terms, but the world energy markets did not return to the previous structures. The other example is the introduction of unleaded fuel on the European gasoline markets through government regulation. Today no gasoline station could refrain from offering this fuel even if it were permitted to do so.

mental measure some time after its first implementation. If the market structure then returns to its original equilibrium, the instrument created reversible effects, otherwise it created irreversible effects.

Environmental policy should in fact examine the evolutionary efficiency of its instruments in this way by withdrawing them some years after the implementation. This strategy of deregulation is expected to keep the total number of environmental measures and interventions at its lowest possible level and thus improves the overall efficiency of environmental policy: environmental problems are basically solved by innovations, whereby the lowest possible number of political measures has to be applied.

D Role of the Search Horizon

The discussion so far has shown that environmental policy should try to employ its instruments in an evolutionally efficient way. But it has also shown that there is no guarantee at all that an instrument will succeed in allocating the market in its environmentally most favorable equilibrium. The potential barrier between different market equilibria is one of the factors preventing an automatic adjustment of an inferior market equilibrium once it has been selected, even if its inferiority has become obvious.

However, the strength of the potential barrier is not independent of the search horizon. A growing search horizon – or a growing variance of the stocastic variables describing individual behavior in favor of innovations – makes it easier for the market to jump across the potential barrier, thereby correcting former selection errors.[13]

Economic policy has some effect on the search horizon or the overall innovativeness in the economy. Numerous well-known conclusions and recommendations can be cited: the establishment

[13] There is an analogy to biological systems, where the survival of a species is improved if individuals have more adaptive and innovative skills. Similarly, an enlarged search horizon or an improved innovativeness helps market forces to correct innovation errors.

of the freedom to engage in innovative activities and market tests (the right to make errors included), the strengthening of autonomous decision making, free access to information, etc. In addition, other points of concern are measures determining the distribution of incentives (through the patent laws) and risks (through the bankruptcy laws) associated with innovative efforts, the treatment by the tax laws of investments into innovative projects, etc. Thus, governments have at their disposal a bundle of instruments for stimulating the overall innovativeness of the economy.

Many people argue that governments should, in addition, try to overcome both the potential barrier and the negative externalities hindering the self-organized selection of environmentally favorable market niches by subsidizing appropriate R&D efforts – perhaps with the financial help of the environmental tax revenues. Such a policy is expected to allocate more resources into the search for solving environmental problems than would occur without government intervention.

But the environmental effects of this policy are likely to be smaller than originally expected, because governments cannot know precisely which R&D projects are the most promising and should be subsidized. For the same reason a strategy to improve the efficiency of the innovative process by preventing hopeless, environmentally harmful, or duplicate R&D efforts from being subsidized is likely to be infeasible. Due to the unpredictable nature of innovative results, nobody has the appropriate information at his/her disposal that would generally allow the selection of an optimal R&D strategy towards solving a given environmental problem. Such information is lacking both in the private sector and in the government.

In terms of the potential function, its overall shape is usually not known to the market participants and nobody can predict the existence of an environmentally favorable market niche that might be discovered through a certain R&D project.

Certainly situations exist where this ignorance argument is of minor importance and the needs and requirements for innovations concerning a sustainable use of environmental resources can easily be defined. But the complex and unpredictable nature of the economy, the ecology and the interface between both implies that numerous environmental problems and technological paradigms exist where the decision about appropriate R&D projects and innovations is less transparent.[14] In these cases evolutionary economics proposes decentralized searches in a competitive environment, which probably will lead to the accumulation of more knowledge, to larger technical improvements and other forms of innovation through trial and error.

A step in this direction would be for public authorities to constrain their interference into private search activities by organizing a competition (in its original sense) for environmentally favorable solutions – for example, by publicly calling for the submission of innovative proposals concerning specific environmental problems. Technologically feasible and economically reasonable proposals would provide the basis for formulating a *Pigou tax* or an environmental norm in order to stimulate the diffusion of this proposal or technology, if necessary. These measures would be limited to a given period of time, depending on the period of product cycles, after which date they would expire automatically.

In repeating this procedure, a new round for submissions of new innovative proposals can be organized in the same rhythm of the product cycles if the emission level is still regarded as being unsatisfactory.

This approach has a strategic orientation similar to the patent law. It is known that the patent law stimulates and broadens the innovative search horizon.[15] The negative externalities associated with the existence of environmentally damages hinder the diffusion of environmentally favorable solutions. The entrepreneur holding the property rights to a patent will perhaps not be able to accumulate the royalty from a reliable solution to some given environmental problem if government does not interfere in the market. The required government intervention can take place by

[14] An example is the contemporary discussion concerning genetic engineering. There are some hopes that this technological paradigm may provide solutions to some of the environmental problems. But there are also fears that this technology may create new and worse environmental problems.

[15] It has also some limitations because it limits the capacity to allocate property rights correctly, but a deeper discussion of this issue lies beyond the scope of this paper.

using all types of environmental measures if they are applied during a *limited period of time.*[16]

The proposed approach for overcoming the external costs that distort the markets for innovations in favor of the solution to environmental problems has the advantage of increasing and biasing the search horizon in the right way even if the innovation possibilities, i.e., the shape of the potential function, are unknown ex ante. Public authorities are required to assess the results of private search activities as far as the environment is concerned – which would be done by the market if there were no environmental externalities. But public authorities execute no direct control of the directions and methods of innovative efforts. There are no government subsidies of private R&D projects (outside basic research) required. Rather, governments offer the promise of reacting upon proposals, thus stimulating the competitiveness for innovations and temporarily supporting the diffusion of the best available technology. This policy follows a trial and error approach aiming at stipulating irreversible improvements of the environment.

However, the central agency required to decide upon the competition for environmental innovations by fixing the environmental instrument (during the next product cycle) determines at the same time the market potential of the proposed technologies and the distribution of economic rents among the suppliers of environmental favorable technologies. According to "Public Choice Theory," serious doubts can be raised about the ability of the governments to efficiently follow environmental concerns (or any other public interests) in this way.

In the absence of any sound anticipatory evidence concerning the causes and effects of environmental policy this problem becomes even more important. If nobody can prove the correctness of the proposed measures or environmental norms, public agencies can easily follow *any private interests* by claiming that the

---

[16] Representatives of companies that could be potential pioneers in developing environmentally compatible technologies claim that a precondition for allocating more resources in related R&D projects is the expectation of some market potential for ecologically compatible products and processes. Such market expectations are created by the proposed approach.

proposed innovative solutions may generate some additional social welfare or not. There is much empirical evidence in Western market economies for this kind of environmental policy.

To overcome these problems, "Institutional Economics" has developed some statements that should be taken into consideration when implementing the competition for environmental solutions: The rules, according to which the government will react on innovative proposals, must be fixed in advance and the whole procedure must be transparent to the public. In addition, the rules should be based upon a broad consensus in business and society. This is to prevent entrepreneurs from allocating their resources to lobbying for environmental government intervention instead of R&D in favor of solving environmental problems.

III Conclusion and Outlook

What after all makes the difference for evolutionary economics concerning environmental policy with respect to theory, policy, and forecasting? While the neoclassical discussion of environmental policy focuses on the internalization of negative externalities, this paper proposes taking the existence of double externalities into consideration. Positive externalities are, among other things, a by-product of the knowledge-generating process and imply non-convexities and multiple market equilibria. Thus, the approach to environmental problems requires solving a selection problem that consists in finding the environmentally most favorable market equilibrium.

Real world competition solves the selection problem through a self-organized explorative search of heterogeneously behaving market participants acting in a weakly transparent economic environment. In general, the economic actors have rather limited knowledge about the market potential of certain innovative efforts. Thus they cannot know in advance whether they will find a new and attractive market niche that has to be understood as a new market equilibrium.

As to neoclassical economic theory, innovative searches usually disregard the external costs of environmental damages. Therefore, government intervention is required in order to correct this bias. But this intervention should not only be efficient in a comparative static sense (which, due to lack of knowledge about the external costs of certain economic activities, can at best be achieved approximately), but has also to be efficient in the evolutionary sense. This means that political measures should create irreversible effects on economic evolution in favor of the environment.

Of course this is hardly to be assessed either ex ante or ex post. Not only political instruments can create irreversible effects on the economy, but also (politically autonomous) changes in knowledge, technology, tastes, and institutional networks. Therefore it will be much more difficult to determine the evolutionary efficiency of an environmental instrument ex post than is assumed in the simple models shown in Figure 9.

There is another point to be noted. As discussed above, the complex and interdependent nature of economic evolution might be reflected by the concept of phase transitions and bifurcations. Such events are assumed to occur occasionally and to change the innovation possibilities as well as the possible effects of given environmental instruments. When the market is close to contingent situations, a much weaker impulse is required to irreversibly change the direction of the economic evolution than in situations where the market is close to an equilibrium configuration. Thus, an identical political instrument applied in favor of the environment can be evolutionally efficient in certain moments and inefficient in others.

In conclusion, there are a lot more aspects that determine whether a political measure in favor of the environment is evolutionally efficient or not than have been discussed in this paper. The work that is required to design concrete measures for approaching concrete environmental problems in an evolutionally efficient way is in its infancy. With respect to this task, interdisciplinary research on environmental issues is necessary, whereby – in addition to economics – the natural sciences, technical disciplines and business administration are of particular importance.

Bibliography

Arrow, K.J. 1962. "The Economic Implications of Learning by Doing." *Review of Economic Studies* 29:155–173.

Arthur, W.B. 1988. "Self-reinforcing Mechanisms in Economics." In: P.W.

Anderson, K.J. Arrow and D. Pines (eds.), *The Economy as an Evolving Complex System*, pp. 9–31. Redwood City: Addison-Wesley.

Berndt, E.R. and D.O. Wood. 1975. "Technology, Prices and the Derived Demand for Energy." *Review of Economics and Statistics* 57:259–268.

Binswanger, H.P. 1974. "A Microeconomic Approach to Induced Innovation." *Economic Journal* 84:940–958.

David, P.A. 1987. "Some New Standards for the Economics of Standardization in the Information Age." In: P. Dasgupta and P. Stoneman, (eds.), *Economic Policy and Technological Performance*, pp. 206–239. Cambridge: Cambridge University Press,

Dosi, G. 1988. "The Nature of the Innovative Process." In: G. Dosi et al. (eds.), *Technical Change and Economic Theory*, pp. 221–238. London, New York: Printer,

———. 1988. "Sources, Procedures, and Microeconomic Effects of Innovation." *Journal of Economic Literature* 26:1120–1171.

Erdmann, G. 1990. "Evolutionäre Ökonomik als Theorie ungleichgewichtiger Phasenübergänge." In: U. Witt (ed.) *Studien zur Evolutorischen Ökonomik I.*, 135–161 . Berlin: Duncker & Humblot.

———. 1992. *Innovation und Energie - eine evolutionsökonomische Analyse*. Tübingen: Mohr (forthcoming).

Fritsch, B. 1991. *Mensch, Umwelt, Wissen. Evolutionsgeschichtliche Aspekte des Umweltproblems*. 2. Auflage. Stuttgart, Zürich: Verlag der Fachvereine.

Haken, H. 1978. *Synergetics, An Introduction*. Berlin, Heidelberg, New York: Springer.

———. 1988. *Information and Self-organization. A Macroscopic Approach to Complex Systems. Berlin*. Heidelberg, New York: Springer.

Hayek, F.A. von. 1980. *Recht, Gesetzgebung und Freiheit. Band. I: Regeln und Ordnung*. München: Moderne Industrie.

Helpman, E. and P.R. Krugman. 1985. *Market Structure and Foreign Trade: Increasing Returns, Imperfect Competition and the International Economy*. Cambridge, Mass.: MIT Press.

Hicks, J.R. 1932. *The Theory of Wages*. London: Macmillan.

Hotelling, H. 1929. "Stability in Competition." *Economic Journal* 39:41–57.

Hunt, L.C. 1986. "Energy and Capital: Substitutes or Complements? A Note on the Importance of Testing for Non-Neutral Technical Progress." *Applied Economics* 18:729–735.

International Energy Agency (IEA), (ed.). 1989. *Electricity End Use Efficiency*. Paris: OECD.

Kahneman, D., P. Slovic and A. Tversky. 1985. *Judgment under Uncertainty*. Cambridge: Cambridge University Press.

Kennedy, C. 1964. "Induced Bias in Innovation and the Theory of Distribution." *Economic Journal* 74: 541–547 .

Lucas Jr., R.E. 1988. "On the Mechanics of Economic Development." *Journal of Monetary Economics* 22:3–42.

Martin, J.M. 1990. "Energy and Technological Change." *OECD Science and Technology Review* 7 (July):9–34.

Nelson, R. and S. Winter. 1982. *An Evolutionary Theory of Economic Change.* Cambridge, London: Harvard University Press

Nicolis, G. and I. Prigogine. 1977. *Self-Organization in Non-Equilibrium Systems.* New York: John Wiley & Sons

Schmidtchen, D. 1990. "Preise und spontane Ordnung." In: U. Witt (ed.), *Studien zur evolutorischen Ökonomik*, 75–113. Berlin, München: Duncker & Humblot.

Schumpeter, J. 1912. *Theorie der wirtschaftlichen Entwicklung. Eine Untersuchung über Unternehmergewinn, Kapital, Kredit, Zins und den Konjunkturzyklus.* 5. Auflage (1952) . Berlin, München: Duncker & Humblot.

Simon, H.A. 1984. *Models of Bounded Rationality.* 2 Vols. Cambridge: MIT Press.

Stiglitz, J.E. 1987. "Learning to Learn, Localized Learning and Technological Progress. In: P. Dasgupta and P. Stoneman, (eds.), *Economic Policy and Technological Performance*, pp. 125–153. Cambridge: Cambridge University Press.

Stoneman, P. 1983. *The Economic Analysis of Technological Change.* Oxford: Oxford University Press.

Weidlich, W. and G. Haag. 1983. *Concepts and Methods of a Quantitative Sociology.* Berlin, Heidelberg, New York: Springer.

Weizsäcker, C.C. von. 1988 . "Innovationen in der Energiewirtschaft." *Zeitschrift für Energiewirtschaft* 3(1988): 141–146:

Witt, U. 1991. "Überlegungen zum gegenwärtigen Stand der evolutorischen Ökonomik." In: B. Biervert and M. Held (eds.), *Evolutorische Ökonomik: Normen – Institutionen – Neuerungen.* Frankfurt: Campus.

Part II
Policy Instruments

Designing Markets for CO_2 Emissions and Other Pollutants

Johannes Heister and Peter Michaelis

Introduction

According to scientific evidence, the increasing concentration of carbon dioxide and other greenhouse gases in the earth's atmosphere will lead to a warmer climate and a change in life conditions on the planet in the decades to come. The primary cause for this global problem is the use of fossil fuels as a source of energy, such as coal, mineral oil and natural gas, which contain large proportions of solid carbon. The burning of these fuels leads to the emission of their carbon contents in the form of carbon dioxide, which contributes to global warming via the greenhouse effect.

Based on these findings, there is a growing consent among political leaders worldwide on the principal necessity to curb carbon dioxide emissions. But as yet, there is no clear conception of possible national and international policies by which such a goal can be reached. One problem is the design of appropriate emission control instruments that translate the political aim of reducing CO_2 emissions into corresponding behavior on the level of households and firms. Adequate individual incentives and, consequently, efficient pollution control cannot be ensured by command-and-control measures, which are widely applied in the case of other pollutants by many OECD countries (see, for instance, Opschoor and Vos, 1989). Particularly in the case of carbon dioxide, market-based instruments, such as emission charges and emission permits, have a much greater potential to minimize the overall costs of emission control and to induce an incentive for technical progress.

The objective of this paper is to show how to initiate a market for carbon dioxide and other greenhouse gases by introducing a feasible system of tradeable emission permits which can be applied as an efficient instrument of environmental policy in single countries and in the whole European Community after the EC internal market is in force.[1] This part of the paper summarizes the relevant framework conditions of the CO_2 problem and briefly reviews possible instruments for CO_2 control. Based on this, Part I develops an alternative to traditional permit systems. It describes the notion of tradeable emission coupons and applies this concept to CO_2 emissions. It deals with the intertemporal allocation of CO_2 emissions, opts for the initial distribution of CO_2 coupons by auction, stipulates the carbon content of fuel as the assessment base, selects importers and producers as the appropriate addressees of the coupon system for CO_2 and solves the (system's initial) problem with end-of-pipe technologies. Finally, it shows how to extend the coupon system to other greenhouse gases. Part II of the paper studies the performance of the system in the framework of the EC's future internal market. And finally, Part III deals with a possible application of the emission coupon system to pollutants other than greenhouse gases.

A The Background of Controlling CO_2 Emissions

Total man-made carbon dioxide emissions can mainly be attributed to two kinds of sources. In industrialized countries roughly half of the total quantity of CO_2 emissions is released by large combustion facilities (industry, energy conversion). The remaining half originates from smaller sources (skilled trades, households, traffic).[2] Under these conditions a reasonably sufficient exploitation of the reduction and substitution potential will only be achieved if possible policy instruments for CO_2 control do not focus only on major sources but include sources of minor CO_2 emissions as well. Unfortunately, measuring CO_2 quantities directly and continuously at their source – as would normally be necessary for the application of emission control instruments – incurs great expenses and would only be justifiable for large combustion facilities. However, the amount of CO_2 generated in combustion can be calculated on the basis of the specific carbon

Footnotes appear on pp. 131–132

content of the fuel. And, since there is no end-of-pipe technology available yet or even in sight, the total quantity of CO_2 generated in combustion is also released into the atmosphere. Hence, there is a linear relationship between the carbon content in fossil fuels and the related CO_2 emissions which allows emission coefficients to be established that are independent of the combustion technology and that indicate the quantity of CO_2 released per ton of fuel.[3] This makes it possible to do without directly measuring CO_2 emissions and instead calculate emission quantities indirectly on the basis of fuel input.

It is a great ecological advantage that carbon dioxide is a nontoxic and natural component of the atmosphere. Hence, the prevention of dangerous spatial concentrations (hot spots) is – in contrast to the cases of, for example, SO_2 or NO_x – of no importance here. As a consequence, a delineation of regions for CO_2 control is not required ecologically and the spatial allocation of total permissible CO_2 emissions can be left to the market. This, however, is not possible in the same manner when it comes to the long-term intertemporal allocation of CO_2 emissions. In this case, a clear and yet flexible steering mechanism must be invented (see Part 1).

With respect to environmental policy, carbon dioxide is an ideal case for the application of economic instruments. As CO_2 is a nontoxic and globally effective natural gas, the advantage of command and control measures which consists in their ability to tackle individual hazards selectively becomes irrelevant. Hence, there is room for the application of globally effective economic instruments of environmental policy. Moreover, direct regulations concerning CO_2 emissions have not yet been established in most countries. This should facilitate the adoption and implementation of economic instruments considerably, because, as experience has proved in the case of other pollutants, it is usually politically impossible to replace existing command-and-control regulations by economic instruments.[4] They can, at best, be complemented, and there remains little scope for economic instruments in cases that are already under command-and-control rule. This is particularly true when dynamic emission standards are applied, as, for instance, in the German air quality law. The requirement to adjust critical quantities and technical provisions to the state of the art as defined by the administration can in no way be reconciled with the application of economic instruments.

B Possible Instruments for CO_2 Control

There are basically four different instruments that may be applied for emission control, namely direct regulations, subsidies, charges and tradeable permits.[5] Their suitability for controlling CO_2 emissions can be judged on the basis of two major criteria.

(1) Instruments of emission control should be ecologically effective, i.e., they should reach the political target in terms of emission quantities as accurately as possible, and
(2) they should be economically efficient, i.e., emission abatement should be accomplished at minimal costs on the whole, including administration costs.

Additionally, the severe economic impact of CO_2 reductions suggests two further criteria.

(1) CO_2 policy instruments should feature a high degree of economic security, i.e., their macroeconomic impact should be predictable and they should provide a reliable planning basis for firms and individuals.
(2) And last, but not least, CO_2 instruments must be politically feasible, i.e., they must comply with a country's legal and institutional system, be adaptable to new situations, allow for a solution of related distributional problems, etc.[6]

Due to the linear relationship between fuel input and CO_2 emissions, most measures of direct regulation will have to be some kind of energy efficiency standards for production and, in the form of product norms, for commodities. Even if applied in the form of dynamic energy efficiency standards, which require the application of state-of-the-art technologies, it is obvious that the ecological effectiveness of direct regulations is very limited in the sense that a given overall CO_2 reduction target can hardly be achieved accurately. As is well known, also the economic efficiency of direct regulations is rather low, since marginal abatement costs for different sources will differ considerably and there is no incentive for innovation. Contrary to that, the economic security of direct regulations is relatively high, since the economic impact of command-and-control measures can be assessed relatively easily. And direct regulations are almost always politically feasible. However, considering the size of the task, these two advantages can hardly outweigh the lack of effectiveness and efficiency of direct regulations, and hence, direct regulations appear to be an inappropriate instrument for CO_2 control.

With respect to CO_2 reduction subsidies a similar judgment holds. To determine the correct dosage for achieving a given reduction target is very difficult, particularly since bandwagon effects must be taken into account and baselines for individual CO_2 sources would have to be established from which accomplished reductions can be measured. Furthermore, subsidies tend to be inefficient. When subsidies are given on a case-by-case basis, marginal abatement costs will differ. Furthermore, prices for carbon-intensive products remain too low, which implies that the consumers' potential to save energy is being wasted. Although the direct economic effects of CO_2 subsidies can be evaluated relatively easily, fiscal side effects of a subsidy scheme of sufficient size may be serious. This also reduces the political feasibility of a subsidy scheme as a general instrument for CO_2 abatement.

Hence, from an economist's point of view, a reasonable choice can only exist between some form of a CO_2 charge and a system of tradeable permits. Although both instruments levy a price on CO_2 emissions, there is an important difference with respect to the establishment of this price. In a charge system the price is fixed politically and total CO_2 emissions result endogenously mainly as a function of abatement costs. Hence, choosing the right charge rate for a given reduction target is rather difficult, if not impossible, since individual and future abatement costs are unknown to the policymaker. Consequently, a CO_2 charge is seriously defective with respect to ecological effectiveness: whether the ecological target will be reached remains uncertain. But the economic effects of a fixed charge rate can be appraised with relative certainty, and a fixed price provides a reliable planning base for firms and individuals, since they can calculate their future financial burden. Contrary to that, in a permit system total admissible CO_2 quantities are fixed directly in accordance with the political reduction target, and hence a permit system is ecologically safe. But this implies that the price for permits develops freely on the permit market depending on the relative scarcities and that it is not known ex ante. Hence, the macro- and microeconomic consequences of a permit system for CO_2 are much less certain.

The choice between a charge and a permit system must, in fact, face a trade-off situation between ecological and economic uncertainty, and the employment of permits instead of a charge system implies a partial relocation of uncertainty away from the ecological system into the economic system. It may, however, be argued that in the long run the economic system is less vulnerable to change than the ecological system, since experience shows that economies can, in the medium term, adapt to changes and deal with uncertainty relatively easily. Consequently, a permit system for CO_2 could be the more appropriate choice, on the condition that it is sufficiently flexible with respect to permissible CO_2 emission quantities in the short run. The coupon system described below is able to satisfy this condition.

Furthermore, in traditional analyses, charge and permit systems are usually judged to be equally efficient, since in both systems the price for emissions will render marginal abatement costs equal for all sources. However, for permit systems this effect will only result if perfect markets for permits exist on which an equilibrium market price is established. Studying the U.S. experience with emission trading programs, Hahn and Hester have shown that this condition is not automatically fulfilled and that cost savings through existing emission trading programs lag far behind their potential (see Hahn and Hester, 1989a,b). The reasons for these findings are manifold: in many cases permit rights are not a sufficiently guaranteed property, search and transaction costs are very high, permit markets are segmented and hence too small, there are problems with administration and enforcement, and there is a lack of experience and acceptance on the side of the market partners. In general, buying and selling tradeable permits implies a high risk. However, as will be seen below, the coupon system outlined in this paper is able to manage these problems efficiently.

To be politically feasible, charge and permit systems must both be in compliance with national and – for EC member states – with

EC legislation, and they must be harmonized with national energy policy. In contrast to a CO_2 charge, a permit system does not easily fit into the existing legal and institutional framework, and, moreover, permit systems are not easily adaptable or reversible, since the creation of guaranteed permit property rights depends on binding long-term political decisions. In the coupon system below, a change of policy is much less a problem.

It may be due to these considerations, together with a lack of experience with permits and a lack of information on their possible economic impact, that permit systems have so far only played a minor role in political decision making, at least in Europe. However, since the CO_2 problem appears to be an almost ideal case for the application of a permit system, economists should try to solve the problems identified above and demonstrate the feasibility and, if possible, practical and political superiority of a skillfully designed permit system for CO_2. It is the objective of the following sections of this paper to present a practical solution to this task, particularly with respect to market creation, administrability and economic security.

I The Coupon System

The attempt to solve the problems mentioned above, thereby making use of the favorable circumstances of the CO_2 case, leads to the development of a refined permit concept, called the coupon system, which corresponds in its basic structure to a flexible CO_2 charge. The coupon systems distinctive feature, compared with traditional charge systems, is seen in the fact that the charge rate is not fixed in a political process, but determined as a price for emission coupons by the market mechanism. The most important features of the system are presented and discussed in the following sections.

A The Design of CO_2 Coupons

A broad variety of permit systems have already been described in the literature (see, for instance, Tietenberg, 1980). These systems usually stipulate that the holder of an emission permit is entitled to discharge a certain quantity of the pollutant in question *per unit of time* during the period of validity of the permit. In contrast to this "traditional" approach, it is the distinctive feature of emission coupons that they have only one dimension: CO_2 coupons are solely defined in quantities of CO_2 and they are valid for an unlimited period of time. CO_2 coupons have two functions: First, they permit the emission of the stated quantity of carbon dioxide, but only once although at any point of time (function of entitlement). Second, after their use, they have to be submitted to the coupon authority, which withdraws and invalidates them (function of verification). Hence, CO_2 coupons can be interpreted as a specific CO_2 currency, which exclusively serves for the settling of CO_2 emissions with the coupon authority. This approach has a number of advantages over traditional permit concepts:

(a) Whereas traditional emission permits may differ from each other with respect to emission quantity per unit of time, temporal and spatial validity of the permit and possibly further criteria, emission coupons represent perfect substitutes, even with respect to time, and they are fully divisible. This guarantees that a homogeneous market and thus a market price for CO_2 emissions will develop, which ensures the optimum spatial allocation of the total permissible quantity of emissions. As perfect substitutes, emission coupons can easily be traded on a stock exchange. This reduces transaction costs and increases market transparency considerably.

(b) In the case of traditional emission permits, permanent supervision is inevitable. It is necessary to keep track of a permit whenever it changes hands in order to make sure that only its present holder uses the permit to justify his present emissions. Contrary to this, in the case of emission coupons, all supervision requirements are met if those economic agents who are charged with the coupon liability are obliged to submit a certain number of emission coupons to the coupon authority, which are then invalidated. The required number of coupons must correspond to the quantity of CO_2 emissions caused by the agent during the settlement period. The CO_2 emission quantity itself can be determined and supervised independently of the permits held by the owner of the source. Furthermore, it is not necessary to furnish proof of the possession of coupons for prolonged periods of time in the past, during which CO_2 was released. These features greatly reduce the administration costs of the system.

(c) When employing emission coupons, the control of CO_2 emissions over time can be effectuated by issuing a limited number of new coupons periodically in order to replace those coupons that have been used up (see below). There is no need to depreciate or limit the validity of emission permits as is necessary with traditional permit systems. The potentially unlimited validity of CO_2 coupons (until they are used) introduces a great deal of intertemporal flexibility into the coupon market. The limit to CO_2 emissions is not strict in each period of time, and this improves the adaptability of the economy.

(d) A system of CO_2 coupons has a high degree of reversibility and adaptability. This is important, since there is almost no experience with well-functioning permit markets yet. Reversibility could not be assured if traditional permits were introduced, which are property rights with an unlimited validity in the extreme case. Contrary to this, emission coupons in circulation will be permanently used up. Hence it is, if the occasion arises, possible to let the coupon system expire without having to expropriate those emission coupons that have already been granted. They could, for instance, be accepted as payments against CO_2 tax obligations if the coupon system were to be replaced by a CO_2 tax.

B Controlling CO_2 Emissions over Time

From a theoretical point of view, it would be conceivable to leave the intertemporal allocation of CO_2 emissions completely up to the market. On introducing the system, the total amount of CO_2 emissions that would be admissible in the long run – in the extreme case indefinitely – would be privatized and put on the market in the form of emission coupons. This stock would then be used up under the responsibility of the private sector just like the extraction of a non-renewable resource.

Such an approach, however, does not seem to be advisable and is not recommended here. For reasons of intertemporal externalities that would not be accounted for in the market price of emission coupons and on grounds of possible discrepancies between the individual and social decision parameters (e.g., time horizon, discount rate), it is not guaranteed that an ecologically justifiable and a socially desirable reduction path will result. Furthermore, given the present state of scientific knowledge, the total quantity of CO_2 emissions that would be admissible over time cannot be fixed definitively when initiating the system. Such a solution would, of course, also contradict the above-mentioned reversibility requirement.

Due to these reasons, the CO_2 reduction path has to be fixed at the political level. This means for the system in question that in each period of time only that number of (additional) emission coupons may enter the market which is equivalent to the (reduced) quantity of CO_2 emissions assigned to that very period. Hence, given the political will to reduce CO_2 emissions, the supply of emission coupons becomes ever tighter over time, which will naturally raise their market price and thereby induce further CO_2 abatement activities.

However, since the most economical reduction path is neither known to the political decision makers nor to the coupon authority, the emission path finally realized should be allowed to deviate to an ecologically and politically acceptable extent from that path which is predetermined by periodically issuing new emission coupons. The following two intertemporal flexibility mechanisms, which are inherent in the concept of emission coupons, enable market partners to react permanently to possible changes in technology and the economy in a most flexible way and thereby find the cheapest permissible path for the reduction of overall CO_2 emissions.

(1) First of all, it is possible to save emission coupons for later use, since their validity is not limited in time. Saving emission coupons is equivalent to transferring part of the CO_2 emissions assigned by the authorities for the current period to

future periods. Contrary to that, it is not possible to take advantage of future emission possibilities in the same manner, because the necessary emission coupons are not yet on the market. Thus the emission path is sealed off asymmetrically with respect to time.

(2) Second, to resolve this asymmetry the coupon authority may allow postponing the submission of a part of the emission coupons normally due as payment for CO_2 quantities emitted during the relevant settlement period. Delaying submission of coupons is equivalent to shifting CO_2 emissions originally assigned to future periods into the present. Hence, this expands actual present emission possibilities and lowers the coupon price, but at the expense of future periods. Since not paying for today's CO_2 emissions until the next settlement period has virtually the same effect as a bank credit, a fee must be charged. This fee must be at least as high as the interest on the implicitly given bank credit. It may be progressive and should become prohibitive at a certain level of accumulated debt.

Based on these intertemporal flexibility mechanisms, the coupon authority has instruments at its disposal with which it can – if necessary – influence the coupon market temporarily. With these instruments a fine-tuning can be effected which does not alter the number of emission coupons available in the long run.

- The coupon authority itself may keep a stock of emission coupons and may carry out an open-market policy by buying and selling coupons on the coupon stock exchange.
- It may pursue a "discount rate policy" by changing the fee that is charged for postponing payments with emission coupons.
- It may lengthen or shorten the settlement period, thus allowing for more or less automatic intraperiod flexibility.
- It may demand periodic anticipatory payments of coupons by those involved on the basis of their expected total payment, due at the end of the settlement period.[7]

If the policymaker considers these flexibility mechanisms to be still insufficient, the government may fix the overall emission target in the form of a target corridor. Within the bounds of this corridor and with a view to the current economic situation, the coupon authority itself would then determine the number of emission coupons that it will actually issue in each period. Obviously, this flexibility provision renders uncertain the number of carbon coupons that will be available in the long run. Hence, it should be applied with great care in order to avoid any unnecessary interference with the expectations of the market partners.

In addition to the flexibility mechanisms introduced above, it could be of advantage for the firms concerned if they were able to increase the certainty of their operational planning by securing emission coupons for future operations ahead of schedule. This can be made possible by prematurely issuing a number of those CO_2 coupons that have been assigned to future periods in the form of "dated emission coupons." Such coupons would become valid for the settlement of CO_2 emissions only *after* the imprinted date.[8]

C The Distribution of Emission Coupons

There are two basically different procedures for the initial distribution of tradeable emission permits: the allotment, free of charge, to the existing sources on the basis of their current real emissions (grandfathering) and the sale to the highest bidders in an auction.[9]

In the literature it is often suggested that the vested rights of existing polluters should be protected by supplying emission permits to them free of charge in equivalence to their current real emissions, at least for a transitional period. In the case of CO_2 this approach is to be rejected. The protection of acquired rights can also be ensured by announcing a permit system sufficiently in advance of its going into operation. This would render any grandfathering of emission coupons unnecessary, which, in the case of CO_2 emissions, would give rise to serious distributional problems: Since there are not yet any legal provisions for the limitation of CO_2 emissions, it is to be taken that to date *everybody* has a right to emit *any* quantity of carbon dioxide. If total CO_2 emissions were to be restricted now and allocated by tradeable emission permits, it would not be justifiable for scarcity-induced profits to accrue only to those who made use of their right to emit

CO_2 in the past, but not to those who held the same right but simply did not make use of it. Instead, the public at large, represented by the state, should be the beneficiary of any scarcity-induced profits arising from the privatization of a common right. Accordingly, under legal considerations tradeable emission permits should not be distributed free of charge. Rather, they should be sold by auction to the highest bidders.

There are other important reasons for the initial sale of emission rights: Auctioning emission coupons guarantees immediate access to the market for any new firm. The signaling effect of the true scarcity price can come into play as early as possible. And problems that relate to the establishment of a particular distribution formula can be avoided. A formula based on current real emissions would, for instance, provide an incentive to increase short-term emissions in order to obtain as many permits as possible. Any distribution formula would have to comply with some notion of distributional justice and would certainly be disputed by the pressure groups concerned. If revenues from coupon sales are treated as ordinary state income, possible distributional problems can be solved within the framework of the national budget, which is preferable for reasons of transparency and political control. Finally, it should be noted that a rise in the public share is not an unavoidable side effect, since it can be compensated by adequate fiscal measures, and therefore it should not be an argument for a particular design of a permit system.

D Assessment Base and Coupon Liability

Due to the constant ratio between the carbon contents of fossil fuels and the CO_2 emissions caused by burning these fuels, the coupon liability can either be based directly on the measured CO_2 emissions or indirectly on the weighted fuel input. Deciding between these two options implies a decision between conflicting goals. On the one hand, the innovation processes induced are most substantial if the financial burden is put directly on CO_2 emissions measured at their source. On the other hand, the existing substitution potential can only be fully exploited, if all sources of CO_2 emissions are included in the permit system. The latter, however, is not possible if directly measured CO_2 emissions are chosen as the coupon base, since a considerable share of the emissions is caused by minor sources for which an adequate and economically justifiable measuring technology does not yet exist. This means that at present only those systems can be realized that either do not include smaller sources or do not opt for directly measured CO_2 emissions as the coupon base.

Since neglecting minor sources seems to be economically unjustifiable and since the disadvantages of choosing fuel inputs as the coupon base can be compensated by an adequate supplementary mechanism (see below), the system developed here proposes determining the quantity of CO_2 emissions, for which emission coupons have to be submitted to the coupon authority, by weighting the fuel input with fuel-specific CO_2 factors. This is equivalent to chosing fossil carbon as the relevant assessment base. This approach warrants the inclusion of almost all man-made CO_2 emissions into the coupon system, as these emissions do not have to be directly measured at their individual source.

However, one modification is necessary, which is related to burning waste products in waste incineration plants. These products contain either nonfossil or fossil carbon. The emission of nonfossil carbon resulting from burning wood and other organic materials should not be included in a coupon system, since these quantities are a part of the natural carbon cycle and do not add to global warming. Contrary to that, CO_2 emissions resulting from burning products that contain fossil carbon (plastics and the like) should, in principle, be included in the coupon system. But since it is hardly possible to measure these CO_2 quantities separately in waste incineration facilities and since these quantities account for a relatively unimportant proportion of total CO_2 emissions, it seems reasonable to exclude them from the CO_2 coupon system. Moreover, the inclusion of CO_2 emissions from waste incineration could lead to an ecologically undesired substitution effect in favor of direct waste deposition (see below).

If fuel inputs are chosen as the assessment base, it is not necessary to place the coupon liability directly on the operator of a CO_2 source. This opens up an additional degree of freedom in choosing the licensee, a fact that can be used to reduce administration costs. These costs depend mainly on the number of licensees with which the coupon authority has to deal. Hence, leaving aside possible problems with competition, the coupon liability should be placed on that commercial level with the fewest participants. This is the level of importers and producers of fossil fuels. Placing the coupon liability on this group minimizes administration costs and reduces the possibilities for any unlawful circumvention of the permit liability.

In order to fulfill the coupon liability, fossil fuel importers and producers must procure emissions coupons. At the end of each settlement period they must transfer the required number of the coupons back to the coupon authority. In principle, the total CO_2 face value of the emission coupons to be handed in is directly equivalent to the quantity of fossil carbon supplied by a firm to the markets during the settlement period. The coupon costs will then be passed on to the consumers as a component of the price for the fuel. This results in a differentiated price increase, which is in direct proportion to the carbon contents and the CO_2 emissions of the respective fuel. This price increase is a signal to the consumer, which indicates the scarcity of permissible CO_2 emissions and induces the necessary energy saving and substitution effects.

Placing the coupon liability on the first commercial level may, however, impede the proper functioning of the coupon market. The number of licensees may not be sufficiently large to guarantee competition. This can be a problem for small economies and for countries in which monopolistic structures in the energy markets prevail. Fifty to one hundred licensees should be the minimum to constitute an active market for emission coupons. The number of potential market partners could, however, be much higher, since anyone may be permitted to buy and sell emission coupons. Opening the coupon market to market participants that wish to hold emission coupons as part of their portfolio will ensure that the coupon market operates under the condition of perfect competition whatever the number of licensees involved may be.

Then, any attempt by large companies or by cartels to dominate the permit market in order to push competitors on commodity and labor markets out of business would have no chance of success. Since emission coupons can be purchased, stocked and resold by anybody, the market for emission coupons is contestable. A cartel would therefore have to fight against an arbitrarily large number of potential market participants who have only small transaction costs. Furthermore, anyone who attempted to abuse the coupon market would undoubtedly have to reckon with open-market intervention by the coupon authority and by countermeasures on the part of the coupon exchange supervisory board.

E End-of-Pipe Technologies and Related Problems

Basing the determination of CO_2 emissions on the fossil fuel that is sold by fuel producers and importers gives rise to the following major problems for which a solution must be found if the coupon system is to retain its efficiency and be applied successfully.

(a) If the fossil carbon input is the relevant assessment base for the coupon liability then industry has no incentive to develop end-of-pipe technologies for holding back CO_2, since there would be no remuneration for reducing CO_2 emissions by installing such devices. Furthermore, if end-of-pipe devices were nevertheless applied, the coupon authority would in all extract more coupons from the economy than would be justified by total actual CO_2 emissions. The CO_2 target would then be undercut: it would de facto become tighter than was politically intended, and CO_2 emitting activities would have to be reduced by more than is required in order to reach the emission objective. Hence, CO_2 quantities held back by end-of-pipe devices must be exempted from the coupon liability.

(b) Similarly, fossil fuel quantities that are not used in combustion processes and therefore do not release CO_2 into the atmosphere would be unduly covered by the coupon system. This is a problem which mainly occurs in the chemical industry that uses oil to produce plastics and other carbon-containing durables. Nonenergetic use of fossil fuel causes a similar problem of equivalence between actual CO_2 emissions and emission coupons extracted from the economy. Therefore, these fuel quantities must also be exempted from the coupon liability.

(c) The same problem arises if fossil fuel products are (re)-exported, since any related CO_2 emissions will not occur in

> the home country, which is therefore not liable for them. Hence, these quantities should, in principle, not be subject to the domestic CO_2 restriction and they must therefore be exempted once they have crossed the border. This is easily achieved in the case of fuel exports by firms that bear the coupon liability themselves, since the calculation of their coupon payment due is based on their domestic sales. But a different solution must be found for fuel exports by retailers.

A solution to these problems cannot be found by exempting the fossil fuel quantities concerned from the coupon liability already at the first commercial level, since there a differentiation of fuel quantities with respect to their final use is impracticable, if not impossible. All three problems can, however, be solved at the level of fuel consumption. Any suitable mechanism would first of all have to compensate those who had to bear costs for CO_2 emissions that they have not caused, and second, it would have to neutralize the associated loss of CO_2 coupons to the economy. Such a mechanism must supplement the coupon system

It should be clear from the explanations above that emission coupons can be interpreted as a kind of money. Hence, they can be used for compensatory payments: those firms or individuals that have finally paid for CO_2 quantities that have not been released to the atmosphere are entitled to receive an equivalent amount of emission coupons. They are free to use these coupons as they wish. They may, for instance, use them to pay their fuel supplier or to exchange them for cash on the coupon market. Compensation payments with emission coupons remunerate those who have invested in end-of-pipe devices and, by reflecting the correct relative prices, compensation payments are an efficient incentive to do so. At the same time these newly issued compensatory emission coupons bring the total CO_2 emissions allowed and the number of coupons in circulation back into exact balance, thus solving the equivalence problem.

It is a precondition for the functioning of this compensation procedure that the quantity of CO_2 or of fossil carbon that has not been released to the atmosphere inside the country can be determined accurately. This is easily achieved in the case of fuel exports, since export data are either already available or are easy to collect at the border. The exporting firm will be granted emission coupons for free in equivalence to the quantity of fossil carbon that it has exported. In the case of nonenergetic usage of fossil fuel, the firms concerned must determine and declare the quantity of fossil carbon that has been bound in solid products and thus is sealed off from the atmosphere. After checking their declaration (if necessary, on the spot), the firms concerned receive the number of CO_2 coupons to which they are entitled.

The availability of end-of-pipe technologies will probably not become relevant for some time. But when it does, the measuring of the CO_2 quantity held back should be easy to achieve, since this CO_2 must exist in some storable and disposable, possibly solid, form. As an innovation incentive, all large CO_2 sources should be entitled to compensatory emission coupons as soon as the coupon system is implemented. In the case of small sources, private firms may act as an intermediary between source operators and the coupon authority and thus reduce transaction costs. They would measure (maybe also collect and dispose of) the CO_2 held back and deal with the coupon authority on behalf of their clients.[10]

F Extending the Coupon System to Other Greenhouse Gases

Besides CO_2 there exist several other human-made pollutants which contribute significantly to global warming. Hence, there is no reason at all to believe that a coupon system that aims exclusively at the reduction of CO_2 emissions represents the most efficient way to sustain the desired climatic conditions. Such a one-dimensional policy with respect to CO_2 can only be efficient if abatement costs for other greenhouse gases are prohibitively high. A condition that cannot be expected to be fulfilled in reality.

Moreover, a financial burden levied solely on CO_2 may lead to substitution effects that may be problematic from an ecological point of view. If, for example, waste incineration becomes more expensive due to a CO_2 coupon system, there will be a substitution effect in favor of direct waste deposition. However, landfills represent a major source of methane emissions, which contribute substantially to the greenhouse effect. This example shows that an encumbrance solely on CO_2 may lead to a substitution of pollutants that may – in the extreme case – even speed up global warming. Hence, including other greenhouse gases into the coupon system would be of advantage from both an ecological and an economic point of view. It would require a redefinition of the emission coupons in terms of greenhouse gas equivalents, i.e., emission coupons would permit the emission of a stated quantity of CO_2 *or* of a quantity of another trace gas that is equivalent in terms of its greenhouse effect. However, such a redefinition leads to a vast number of problems that can only be touched upon in this paper.

Besides carbon dioxide, the main greenhouse gases are methane (CH_4), nitrous oxide (N_2O) tropospheric ozone (O_3) and the chlorofluorocarbons CFC_{11} and CFC_{12}. However, not all of these gases are suitable to be included in a single coupon system. First of all, there is no straightforward way to include tropospheric ozone. This greenhouse gas is not directly emitted from anthropogenic sources, but is created by highly complex and nonlinear photochemical reactions in the atmosphere that involve nitrogen oxides and several other trace gases. Therefore, an unambiguous assignment of tropospheric ozone to individual polluters is not possible and hence nobody can be encumbered with the liability to provide coupons. The case of the CFCs has to be judged differently. Here it seems to be possible, at least in principle, to identify the responsible polluters, or at least the producers or suppliers of the CFCs. But according to international agreements, there will be a medium-term phasing out of CFC anyway, and their inclusion in a greenhouse coupon system could hardly speed up this process. Hence, it does not seem to be worthwhile to integrate the CFCs in a coupon system.

As a consequence, only methane (CH_4) and nitrous oxide (N_2O) are candidates for inclusion in the coupon system. At present, CH_4 and N_2O contribute approximately 20% to the greenhouse effect, and this share will increase considerably after the CFCs have been phased out. Main sources of CH_4 and N_2O are energy use, agricultural activities (use of fertilizers, cattle) and waste deposition. At least in principle it seems to be possible to identify those individuals and firms that are responsible for CH_4 and N_2O emissions and to encumber them with the coupon liability. However, whether measuring these emissions at the individual sources, as would probably be necessary, would technically be feasible at justifiable costs must remain an open question here.

In an extended greenhouse coupon system, the specific global warming potential of CH_4 and N_2O, defined as the warming effect of one ton of these gases relative to that of CO_2, would serve as a kind of "exchange rate" between the pollutants. According to estimates based on a time-horizon of 100 years[11] (IPPC, 1990), the greenhouse potential of one ton of CH_4 amounts to 21 tons of CO_2, whereas the figure for N_2O is 290 tons of CO_2. Therefore, it seems to be conceivable to define greenhouse emission coupons that permit the emission of one ton of CO_2 *or* 1/21 tons of CH_4 *or* 1/290 tons of N_2O. Admittedly, this is only a very rough approach, since it is not clear how, in the long run, the stock of greenhouse gases in the atmosphere would react to substitutions between the different greenhouse gases, how a moving time horizon can be integrated into the exchange rate and whether answering these questions would lead to an unfavorable differentiation of emission coupons with respect to time.

In a practical approach however, these difficulties may be less important, since the ecology of global warming should offer enough flexibility to deal with a short-run fluctuation in the greenhouse potential persistent in the atmosphere. Economically, the approach of a single greenhouse gas emissions coupon system would enable the market mechanism to identify the most efficient way of reducing the emissions of greenhouse gases.[12] However, many unsolved practical problems remain. They include, for example, the definition of the assessment base, the choice of the licensees and the general institutional setting.

II Emission Coupons for CO_2 and the EC's Single Market

The implementation of a system of emission permits (or similar measures) by one partner country in the European Community in a national go-it-alone approach is not advisable, neither for economic nor ecological reasons. Such an approach would significantly reduce the competitiveness of CO_2-intensive commodities in the EC and on world markets without being able to secure a real reduction in worldwide CO_2 emissions. In fact, this approach could even result in a global increase of CO_2 emissions. It is conceivable that the production of CO_2-intensive commodities would shift at least partially to countries in which the production of these goods would result in higher CO_2 emissions per unit because the CO_2 intensity of the production processes applied there may be higher. Hence, a cooperative international carbon dioxide policy that would stipulate comparable abatement efforts at least for the industrialized world is required.

In view of the theory of institutional competition (Giersch, 1990) and the principle of secondary liability (*Subsidiaritätsprinzip*), it would be of advantage if the decision on what kind of environmental policy instruments should be applied (command and control, charges, permits) could be made on the level of individual countries and thus would remain decentral. However, the decentralized application of policy instruments could cause serious problems in the coming EC internal market, since import restrictions will not exist any more and goods and services coming from all countries of the Community may be imported and sold in any other EC country without any restrictions. This means that the country-of-origin principle is generally in force, even with respect to product-related charges and directives as well as to other environmental regulations. For the case of the coupon system developed here, it will be shown below that under conditions of the Single Market a carbon dioxide policy with different instruments in the European Community is not viable.

Assume that one member state implements the coupon system as described above, whereas another EC country intends to fulfill her abatement obligations by employing adequate command-and-control regulations only (e.g., minimum effectiveness standards for power stations, etc.) and does not levy a financial burden on fossil fuel. In this situation, market prices for fossil energy (including coupon costs) would be higher in the "coupon country" than in the "command-and-control country." After the start of the EC's internal market, arbitrage would commence, i.e., retailers in the coupon country would buy their supplies in the command-and-control country, thus evading the coupon liability and related costs (except transportation costs). Such arbitrage would continue to reduce the domestic demand for emission coupons just until the coupon price were equal to the additional per unit transportation costs of purchasing fossil fuel in the command-and-control country. The coupon system would be undermined by the command-and-control system. The coupon policy would become ineffective and the emission target in the coupon country could not be met. Furthermore, EC-wide fossil fuel transportation costs would be excessive.

Basically the same market arbitrage would occur if one country decided for a CO_2 charge on individually measured real emissions or a tax on fossil fuels. In the case of an emission charge the above analysis holds, since the retail price for fossil fuel is not affected. In the latter case, the tax rate would most likely differ from the price for emission coupons initially. However, due to transfrontier arbitrage the price for emission coupons would adjust to the fixed tax rate by the process described above. The coupon system would thus degenerate to a tax system, where the coupon price would de facto be fixed by the "tax country's" tax rate (plus transportation costs). The final single price for CO_2 emissions in the two countries would, of course, be economically efficient as all polluters would be charged the same price for CO_2 emissions. However, the quantity target in the coupon country would be missed and transportation costs would be excessive.

Consequently, under conditions of the Single European Market the coupon policy would only make sense if the remaining EC partner countries also were to adopt a similar coupon strategy on the basis of fossil fuel sales. But if this were the case further problems would arise.

At first glance it does not appear to be necessary that national emission coupons be mutually tradeable in the whole Community in order to exploit the cross-country substitution potential which would minimize overall abatement costs. The prices for national emission coupons would adjust to each other throughout the Community through trade in fossil fuel, of course implying additional and unnecessary transaction and transportation costs. But additionally the problem arises that some EC partners themselves are large producers of oil, coal and gas and sell these to other EC countries. These quantities would, according to the country-of-origin principle, be subject to the coupon system of the extracting country, although they cause emission of CO_2 in the recipient country. Fixed national CO_2 emission limits on the basis of fossil carbon quantities imported from outside the Community or extracted by the country in question would thus impede the export opportunities of the fuel-producing countries concerned. And this would result in inefficient fossil energy markets in the European Community.[13]

This problem can be countered by extending the validity of the respective national CO_2 coupons to the entire Single Market so that national coupons can be traded Community-wide on a private basis and can be used to settle CO_2 accounts with all national coupon authorities. Under these conditions, the national prices for emission coupons would converge through cross-border private trade in coupons.

This situation, however, also implies that a member country cannot liberally choose its coupon policy any more without affecting all other national coupon markets.[14] This would, in turn, require a very close harmonization of national coupon policies, which would at least have to comprise binding rules for the supply of national markets with national emission coupons and for interventions in coupon markets by the national coupon authorities. But under these circumstances, a substantial difference with respect to a centrally organized Community coupon system, which would operate on the basis of a single CO_2 emission quantity for the entire Community, would de facto not exist.

Such a single Community coupon system, which could, of course, be opened up to include non-EC countries, would essentially be identical with the one described above for an individual country. Some differences would, however, occur with respect to the institutional setting, since a splitting-up of responsibilities between a Community coupon authority and corresponding national authorities seems to be advisable: in the Community system the CO_2 policy would be determined by the European Council of Environmental Ministers and implemented by the Community coupon authority. The latter would create the required quantity of Community CO_2 coupons and assign them to the respective national coupon authorities on the basis of a distribution key, which would have to be agreed upon in the preceding political negotiations.[15] The marketing of these coupons and the supervision and settlement of individual CO_2 accounts could then remain the responsibility of the national coupon authorities. This approach would ensure that the revenues raised by selling the coupons would fall under national control, whereas the coupon policy would be controlled by the Community coupon authority.

Finally, it should be noted that the problems which relate to the European Single Market are not specific for the case of CO_2 control by emission coupon. They arise whenever it is attempted to reduce CO_2 emissions by levying a financial burden on fossil fuel. Decentral decisions on how to curb CO_2 emissions would, under internal market conditions, only be possible if CO_2 emissions were measured directly at their source and levied accordingly. This, however, would imply that the tax or permit liability must be restricted to large CO_2 sources, and that a substantial proportion of the existing substitution potential cannot be exploited.

III Applying the Coupon System to Hot-Spot Pollutants

The positive features of the coupon system suggest considerations on whether this instrument can be made applicable to other pollutants. The application of emission coupons for the control of pollutants other than greenhouse gases is, however, not straightforward, since the coupon system for CO_2 described above relies strongly on some distinctive features of the CO_2 case. In particular, the fact that dangerous ambient concentrations of CO_2 cannot occur has been exploited to design the coupon system as a feasible and efficient policy instrument.

In contrast to CO_2, most other environmental pollutants (e.g., SO_2, NO_x, CO) can have strong local and regional effects and thus can produce dangerous "hot spot." This fact must be taken into account, when adapting the coupon systems to other pollutants. But if an adaptation is possible, the use of emission coupons can render the control of hot-spot pollutants much more efficient than present-day command-and-control systems.

A The Problem

Hot-spot pollutants can become dangerous if high enough concentrations prevail in the environment. Their global effect, however, is usually unimportant compared with their local or regional effect. Moreover, the damage done to the environment by one unit of such pollutants may differ considerably from region to region depending on the already existing ambient concentration of the substance and the prevailing regional conditions.

For this reason, the coupon concept developed above for CO_2 emissions cannot be applied to hot-spot pollutants without modifications. The fundamental features of emission coupons, namely that their validity is, at least in principle, neither restricted in space nor in time, makes them unsuitable for a treatment of hot-spot pollutants. Coupons may accumulate in industrial zones and allow the emission of such a quantity of the pollutant in question as may be harmful to the local environment and the resident population.

Traditional permit concepts propose to solve this problem by restricting the validity of the permits with respect to time and space. This leads to a system of differentiated emission (or ambient pollution) permits, which are traded on a number of different permit markets.[16] This approach is not compatible with the coupon concept, since the use of coupons for the control of emissions in separated regions would waive the favorable property of a homogeneous coupon market. A segmentation of coupon markets would be inevitable. Moreover, sufficient competition for coupons and a competitive coupon price could not be ensured, and transaction costs would be too high. And finally, emission coupons that are differentiated with respect to time cannot be regarded as a specific kind of money any more, since they are not a store-of-value asset. Hence, the favorable administration and market procedures of the CO_2 case could not be retained here. A system of differentiated coupons would become considerably more complicated and more expensive in terms of transaction and administration costs. Hence, such a system is not likely to be an efficient instrument.

A further problem arises due to the fact that in many countries direct regulations for hot-spot pollutants are in force and cannot be replaced easily by a permit system for political reasons. Such direct regulations may consist of emission standards, sometimes in the form of product norms, and ambient quality standards, which refer to pollutants in the ambient environment and on which the licensing of industrial facilities may be based. These standards may be tightened in the wake of time. Often "dynamic" emission standards are used that demand the application of state-of-the-art abatement technology and thus imply a continuous reduction of emissions from each source. It is obvious that in particular dynamic emission standards are in conflict with any permit system, since they stifle exactly that flexibility which makes a permit system workable and efficient.

B Two Objectives of Environmental Policy

The way to a genuine coupon system for hot-spot pollutants can be found by distinguishing two objectives of environmental policy. The first such objective is described by the principle of hazard prevention (*Gefahrenabwehrprinzip*). To protect the country's population against major hazards that threaten their lives, their health and property is one of the major responsibilities of any government. Hence, it must be the fundamental objective of environmental policy to fend off any situation in which pollutants in the environment may accumulate to such concentrations that are harmful to people. Therefore, policy instruments must be applied that prevent dangerous hot spots reliably and keep emissions and hence local concentrations at a level that is compatible with hazard prevention.

However, such a minimum level of protection is usually not enough. Even in small concentrations, ambient pollutants may become harmful to people and their property in the long run, sometimes in a way that is not yet completely understood and, therefore, not foreseeable. Pollutants may accumulate in the environment and eventually alter natural living conditions for plants and animals, irreversibly destabilize fragile ecological equilibriums, reduce biodiversity and even severely impede living conditions for the human society in the long run. Global warming is only one example for such a threat. These effects cannot be countered on the grounds of the principle of hazard prevention, since they are not definite enough: they do not (yet) pose a well-known and imminent threat to people or to property.

As a response to such considerations, the precautionary principle (*Vorsorgeprinzip*) has emerged from the (German) environmental policy debate. It has become a standing rule of environmental policy in Germany and can be considered a second distinguished objective. The German Federal Government described the Vorsorgeprinzip in 1976 in the following terms: "Environmental policy is not fully accomplished by warding off imminent hazards and the elimination of damage which has occurred. Precautionary environmental policy requires furthermore that natural resources are protected and that demands on them are made with care."[17] Hence, the precautionary principle surpasses the scope of hazard prevention, since it justifies and even demands government intervention already at a point in time when an immediate threat is not yet clearly discernible. The mere possibility of damage is enough. The precautionary principle aims at preventing environmental risks from becoming manifest in the first place. Hence, it intends to generally reduce environmental risks. This usually requires pushing total emissions well below the level that is derived from the principle of hazard prevention.

C Direct Regulations as a Backup for the Coupon System

Neither of these two objectives can be met in an acceptable way by only one policy instrument. Direct regulations are a reliable source-related and effective instrument, but economically they are inefficient. Charges are unreliable with respect to realizing a given emission target, since they depend on unrealistic information requirements, but they are spatially very well differentiable. Tradeable permits and emission coupons realize a given emission target accurately, but differentiating them in space and time reduces their efficiency potential. However, after modifying those instruments such that they are mutually compatible, each instrument can be assigned to a particular policy objective in such a way that its individual advantages can be exploited while its disadvantages are avoided.

Direct regulations are best suited, if not indispensable for legal and political reasons, to accomplish the objective of hazard prevention, particularly in hot-spot areas. But, as part of an instrument set, they must be clearly restricted to this objective. In particular, *dynamic* emission standards must not be used, since they usually require abatement activities that go far beyond the standard that is necessary to guarantee hazard prevention. Consequently, emission and ambient quality standards should be frozen and should only be tightened if new scientific knowledge requires so in order to prevent hazardous situations. Product norms and licensing of new industrial sites may be based on such minimum standards. But direct regulations must definitely not be employed in order to accomplish a higher environmental quality that may be pursued on the basis of the precautionary principle or simply because political preferences require so.

This, however, has usually been the case. On the instrument level, the precautionary principle has always been somewhat blurred, and, to a large extent, it has served rather political aims than clear-cut environmental objectives (Zimmermann, 1990). In German environmental policy the precautionary principle is usually simply associated with the application of state-of-the-art technology as required by direct regulations, which are adapted to the progress in abatement technology from time to time. A different approach is taken here. On the basis of a set of legal provisions that guarantee hazard prevention at any spot and any time, the precautionary principle can be interpreted as an objective that requires a more global improvement of environmental quality and is less interested in a particular local development. In this interpretation the precautionary principle can be made operational: it requires a certain level of *total* emissions, which is below the level consistent with hazard prevention.

In this form, the precautionary principle can and should, for efficiency reasons, be pursued by economic instruments. Compared with an emission tax, an overall emission coupon system seems to be particularly well suited for this purpose. It is able to realize directly and accurately any level of total emissions in the coupon market area that the policymaker deems consistent with the precautionary principle. For this, no knowledge on abatement cost functions is needed, as it would be necessary for finding the correct tax rate. With a minimum of direct regulations in force, a spatial and temporal differentiation of emission rights is unnecessary. Dangerous concentrations of pollutants cannot occur, since emission coupons only justify such an amount of emissions from an individual source as does not violate ruling emission or ambient quality standards. Also, with the use of emission coupons property right problems cannot occur in the presence of direct regulations, since coupons can always be saved for later use or sold at the market price. Consequently, the coupon system can display its advantages and ensure simultaneously a limitation or reduction of aggregate emissions and, within the bounds of hazard prevention, an efficient allocation of emission rights in space and time by means of a large and homogeneous coupon market.

Efficiency is reached in this setting for all those sources for which the coupon price is the binding constraint in the sense that these sources' marginal costs of compliance with the ruling direct regulations are lower than the coupon price. The coupon system induces these sources to abate emissions so much more than required by law that their marginal abatement costs are equal and equal to the single coupon price. And with an increase in the coupon price, for instance, due to a tighter coupon supply, the coupon system becomes the binding constraint for more and more emission sources, and this renders emission control more and more efficient in the course of time.

Of course, the opposite effect can occur if direct regulations are tightened and thus become binding for more and more emission sources whereas the supply of emission coupons remains constant. Then, emission control becomes less efficient. The total demand for emission coupons is reduced and the coupon price decreases. Moreover, the coupon market collapses if direct regulations are tightened to such an extent that the available emission coupons cannot be used up in the foreseeable future. Such an incident is a political mistake. It can occur whenever the emission reduction path that results from direct regulations becomes tighter in the course of time than the reduction path steered by the supply of emission coupons. Also, therefore, a freeze of direct regulations and their limitation to hazard prevention is inevitable for the functioning of the coupon system for hot-spot pollutants.

D Emission Charges for Regional Targets

Due to the market allocation of emission coupons, a certain regional differentiation of environmental quality may occur. In most cases, these quality differences, which occur within the bounds of the precautionary principle, may well be acceptable, since the average amount of emissions (or the average environmental quality) over the total emission space can be considered to be more adequate as a measure of precautions taken than the environmental impact in a rather small region.

However, the resulting environmental quality in a particular region may, nevertheless, be unacceptable for some (political) reason. For instance, emissions in an industrial area may remain on the highest permissible level, because the coupon price is too low to induce any reductions below the level of hazard prevention. In such cases a fine-tuning of emissions may become necessary in order to rectify regional ambient quality differences that are due to the market allocation of emissions coupon.

The use of direct regulations for this purpose would increase the already existing inefficiency of pollution abatement in this region. Instead, a regionally differentiated emission charge suggests itself as a supplementary instrument. In combination with a coupon system, an emission charge can easily be implemented and administered, since the charge can effectively be levied on the use of emission coupons. It would then be payable upon submission of the coupons to the coupon authority. Of course, the charge rate cannot accurately be targeted to realize the desired emission level. But this drawback is much less important here, since the emission charge should usually only be applied on a rather small scale as a supplement to the coupon system and is, therefore, probably less error-prone.

The additional emission charge increases the costs for emissions within the region concerned. If the charge rate is high enough this will bring regional emissions down to the desired level and improve the efficiency of pollution abatement in this region. But it will also reduce total demand for emission coupons and lower their price, which will result in an equal increase of emissions elsewhere. The price effect must be taken into account when setting the charge rate. The quantity effect will reduce the regional differences of environmental quality. Similarly to the tightening of direct regulations, an emission charge narrows the scope of the coupon market and may lead to its collapse, if applied excessively. Hence, the supplementary emission charge should remain an exception.

In total, the mutual interactions between those three instruments demand that both direct regulations and supplementary emission charges should be employed on a rather modest scale, so that their effect on the coupon market remains small. The coupon system should always carry the bulk of the incentive to abate the emissions dealt with and the coupon price should determine the abatement efforts of the large majority of sources.

Therefore, a thorough study into the relevant circumstances must be undertaken before this instrument set can be applied safely to a particular hot-spot pollutant. Such a case study would have to show that the scope of the planned coupon system would be large enough to generate an efficient coupon market. Furthermore, it would have to answer those questions that had to remain open here, namely who should assume the coupon liability on the ground of which assessment base and which administration and enforcement provisions would be necessary.[18] If favorable answers can be found to these questions, then the coupon system has the potential to render the control of hot-spot pollutants less expensive.

IV Conclusion

In the case of greenhouse gas emissions, in particular CO_2, a system of skillfully designed tradeable emission permits can have important merits as instrument of emission control. Making use of the favorable properties of the CO_2 case, the paper proposes a system of tradeable "emission coupons." Contrary to traditional permit concepts, emission (or CO_2) coupons are defined only in terms of a particular quantity of CO_2, and they are valid for an unlimited period of time. Hence, emission coupons allow the emission of the stated quantity of the pollutant in question only once – however, at any time.

CO_2 coupons are issued periodically by auction and in accordance with an initially fixed reduction path. By placing the coupon liability on companies that produce or import fossil fuel, the available reduction and substitution potential can be fully exploited with moderate transaction and administration costs. The liable companies must procure CO_2 coupons and transfer them back to the coupon authority according to the quantity of fossil carbon that they have supplied to the markets.

CO_2 coupons can be interpreted as a kind of specific CO_2 money, which serves as a means of payment and control of CO_2 emissions. This particularly favorable property allows repaying compensatory coupons to those firms and individuals who initially had to pay the coupon costs, but unduly, because they were able to avoid the related CO_2 emissions, e.g., by installing end-of-pipe equipment. Moreover, emission coupons for CO_2 can be redesigned to cover other greenhouse gases. In general, the coupon system for CO_2 emissions closely resembles a flexible charge system for CO_2, the charge rate of which is established on a market for emissions.

Under the conditions of the European Community's Single Market, a system of CO_2 coupons based on fossil fuel production and importation conflicts with alternative instruments that may be employed in other member countries. Hence, a decentral instrument choice is not possible, and a coupon system for CO_2 is only viable if applied to the entire European Community.

The emission coupon system can also have some merits when applied to hot-spot pollutants as part of an instrument set in which each instrument is assigned to a particular task. The instrument set comprises direct regulations that are employed to ensure hazard prevention and that are constrained to that effect, and an undifferentiated emission coupon system that pushes total actual emissions down to the protection level of the precautionary principle. Additionally, these two instruments may be supplemented by a regionally differentiated emission charge that may be applied to accomplish lower emission levels in an efficient way in areas in which the single coupon price is not high enough to achieve the desired ambient quality level. The skillful application of the instrument set can render the control of hot-spot pollutants considerably more efficient if the coupon price is the relevant constraint for most sources and direct regulations and emission charges are kept to a minimum. The application of the instrument set to a particular case requires a thorough study into the practical problems associated with this case.

Notes

[1] The paper is based in part on Heister and Michaelis et al. (1991), and Heister and Michaelis (1991).

[2] For example, in the Federal Republic of Germany (excluding the former GDR) about 740 million tons of CO_2 are emitted annually, roughly 60% by large combustion facilities and 40% by smaller sources.

[3] Determining CO_2 emissions by using emission coefficients can only be done correctly under the condition of complete combustion of the fuel, which is assumed here but may not always be fulfilled in reality.

[4] A well-known example is the German effluent charge, which serves only as an instrument to speed up the enforcement of the abatement requirements stated by the Water Management Law (*Wasserhaushaltsgesetz*).

[5] For a detailed comparison of these instruments with respect to their performance for CO_2 control, see Heister (1991).

[6] There is, of course, a multitude of further evaluation criteria in the literature which cannot be discussed here because of limited space. See Heister and Michaelis (1991).

[7] Note that neither the settlement period nor the date of payment need to be equal for all firms concerned.

[8] It can be expected that markets in futures and options for emission coupons will develop naturally. However, they would probably only cover shorter time periods. Therefore, futures and options created in the private sector are not in direct competition with dated emission coupons issued by the coupon authority, but supplement each other.

[9] The option of combining the allotment with a charge is only gradually different from a free-of-charge distribution of emission coupons, since additional criteria for discriminating between potential buyers have to be applied (unless the charge happens to equal the unknown market price).

[10] A model for this arrangement could be the measuring of individual heating consumption in private homes and flats by specialized firms in the Federal Republic of Germany.

[11] The global warming potentials are calculated such that they include the different lifetimes of CO_2, CHO_4 and N_2O in the atmosphere. Hence, the resulting figures are dependent on the time horizon applied in the calculation.

[12] Another way to ensure efficiency in the case of multiple greenhouse gases is the implementation of an efficient charge system. For a formal and empirical treatment, see Michaelis (forthcoming).

[13] It would, of course, be possible to channel fuel exports to member states through nonmember countries, thus making use of the compensation procedure described above. This would, however, imply excessive transportation and transaction costs.

[14] The situation is similar to that of a monetary system, in which national cur-

rencies are permanently linked to each other by fixed exchange rates, but national central banks may choose their monetary policy independently.

[15] Particularly a distribution key on the basis of population numbers could be considered. See, for instance, Grubb (1989).

[16] For formal treatments of this problem see, for instance, Montgomery (1972), Tietenberg (1974), Krupnick et al. (1983) and McGartland (1988). Compare also the literature on emissions trading rules; for example, Atkinson and Tietenberg (1987) and Hahn (1986).

[17] Umweltbericht (1976). "Umweltpolitik erschöpft sich nicht in der Abwehr drohender Gefahren und der Beseitigung eingetretener Schäden. Vorsorgende Umweltpolitik verlangt darüber hinaus, daß die Naturgrundlagen geschützt und schonend in Anspruch genommen werden" (Rdnr. 4). The translation is taken from Moltke, who offers a good introduction into the Vorsorgeprinzip in German environmental policy, which has no direct equivalence in the environmental policy of many other countries.

[18] For the case of NO_x emissions, such a study is presented in Heister and Michaelis et al. (1991).

Bibliography

Atkinson, S.E. and T.H. Tietenberg. 1987. "Economic Implications of Emissions Trading Rules for Local and Regional Pollutants." *Canadian Journal of Economics* 20(2):370–386.

Giersch, H. 1990. "Europa 1992 – Ordnungspolitische Chancen und Risiken." *Außenwirtschaft* 1:7–20.

Grub, H. 1989. *The Greenhouse Effect: Negotiation Targets.* London: The Royal Institute of International Affairs.

Hahn, R.W. 1986. "Trade-offs in Designing Markets with Multiple Objectives." *Journal of Environmental Economics and Management* 13:1–12.

Hahn, R.W. and G.L. Hester. 1989a. "Marketable Permits – Lessons for Theory and Practice." *Ecology Law Quarterly* 16:361–406.

———. 1989b. "Where Did All the Markets Go? An Analysis of EPA's Emissions Trading Program." *Yale Journal of Regulation* 6:109–153.

Heister, J. 1991. "An Analysis of Policy Instruments to Reduce CO_2-Emissions." Paper presented at the German-Norwegian Energy Conference, Bergen, June (forthcoming).

Heister, J., P. Michaelis. 1991. "Handelbare Emissionsrechte für Kohlendioxid." *Zeitschrift für angewandte Umweltforschung* 4(1):68–80.

Heister, J. and P. Michaelis et al. 1991. "Umweltpolitik mit handelbaren Emissionsrechten – Möglichkeiten zur Verringerung der Kohlendioxid- und Stickoxidemissionen." Kieler Studie No. 237. Tübingen: J.C.B. Mohr (Paul Siebeck).

Intergovernmental Panel on Climate Change (IPCC). 1990. *Policymakers Sum-*

mary of the Scientific Assessment of Climate Change. New York: WMO and UNEP.

Krupnick, A.J. et al. 1983. "On Marketable Air-Pollution Permits: The Case for a System of Pollution Offsets." *Journal of Environmental Economics and Management* 10:233–247.

McGartland, A. 1988. "A Comparison of Two Marketable Discharge Permits Systems." *Journal of Environmental Economics and Management* 5:35–44.

Michaelis, P. Forthcoming. "Global Warming: Efficient Policies in the Case of Multiple Pollutants." *Environmental & Resource Economics*.

Moltke, K. von. 1988. "The Vorsorgeprinzip in West German Environmental Policy." In: Royal Commission on Environmental Pollution, 12th Report, *Best Pratical Environmental Options*, pp. 57–70. London: HMSO.

Montgomery, W.D. 1972. "Markets in Licences and Efficient Pollution Control Programs." *Journal of Economic Theory* 5:395–418.

Opschoor, J.B. and H.B. Vos. 1989. *Economic Instruments for Environmental Protection*. Paris: OECD.

Tietenberg, T.H. 1974. "The Design of Property Rights for Air Pollution Control." *Public Policy* 22:275–292.

———. 1980. "Transferable Discharge Permits and the Control of Stationary Source Air Pollution: A Survey and Synthesis." *Land Economics* 56(4):391–416.

Umweltberichf. 1976. Fortschreibung des Umweltprogramms der Bundesregierung vom 14.07.1976 (BT-Drs.8/3713), Rdnr 4.

Zimmermann, K. 1990. "Zur Anatomie des Vorsorgeprinzips." In: *Politik und Zeitgeschichte*, Beilage zur Wochenzeitung *Das Parlament*, B6/90, 2. Februar, pp. 3–14. Bonn: Bundeszentrale für Politische Bildung.

Pollution Charges as a Source of Public Revenues

Wallace E. Oates*

Introduction

The economic theory of environmental regulation revolves around the concept of an externality – a form of social cost that is not borne by the agent who is its source. The theory carries with it a straightforward policy implication: to correct for the misallocation, in this case excessive emissions of pollutants, the regulatory agency can place a charge, a unit tax, on the offending activity that is equal to the marginal social damage. Such a Pigouvian tax serves to internalize the social cost associated with polluting emissions and can sustain an economically efficient level of environmental quality.

All this is well understood. What has received somewhat less notice is the fact that such taxes will generate revenues. This aspect of pollution charges has recently caught the attention of some policymakers. In the United States, for example, a bill was introduced in 1987 for a nationwide tax on sulfur and nitrogen oxide emissions. What was of particular interest about this bill was its source: it was not proposed by an environmental contingent of the U.S. Congress – it was rather introduced in the House Ways and Means Committee as a revenue-raising measure to help reduce the deficit in the federal budget! This brings to the fore an interesting

* I am grateful to Jean-Philippe Barde, Allen Kneese, Andrew Lyon, Paul Portney, and Friedrich Schneider for some very helpful comments on an earlier draft and to the National Science Foundation for its support of this research.

and important question: What role do pollution charges have to play as a source of public revenues?[1]

I will suggest in this paper that although there is a straightforward answer to this question in terms of the theory of optimal taxation, the issue is a more complicated one in a realistic policy setting. The basic problem is that we are likely to find ourselves trying to do two things with a single policy instrument: regulate environmental quality and raise public revenues. While the trade-off between these objectives can be resolved, in principle, by equating net benefits at the margin, this is not so easy in practice when different groups wrestle for control of the policy instrument for one or the other of these two objectives. For this reason, I will initially take up the optimal tax approach – which yields a clear conceptual solution to the problem. I will then proceed to a "public-choice" perspective that suggests some potentially quite troublesome matters – and also some guidelines for the proper use of environmental taxes.

Before turning to the optimal tax problem, I wish to return briefly to the theory of environmental regulation. The role of a Pigouvian tax as a corrective device is firmly imbedded in microeconomic theory. Although little is typically said about the precise disposition of the revenues from these taxes, there is one proposition that does flow out of the theory: the revenues should *not* be used to compensate victims of the pollution (Baumol and Oates, 1988, Chs. 3 and 4). The victims of environmental insults (or other forms of externalities) often have at their disposal "defensive activities" through which they can mitigate the effects of the pollution. Victims may, for example, be able to locate themselves away from the sources of the pollution or to employ cleansing devices. If, however, such victims are compensated for whatever damages they absorb, they will not have the proper inducement to engage

[1] A legitimate alternative to such taxes is a system of tradeable emissions permits where the total quantity of permits is set equal to the efficient level of emissions. Such a permit system can also be the source of public revenues if the permits are issued through a public auction. However, this need not be the case: the regulatory authority may choose to distribute the permits without charge to existing sources (or others). See, for example, Baumol and Oates (1988, Chs. 5 and 12).

in these defensive activities. Compensation, from this perspective, distorts the set of incentives required to induce the proper response to pollution: it results in excessive abatement by sources and too little in the way of defensive activities by victims. This is a point to which I shall return later in the paper.[2]

I An Optimal-Taxation Approach to Pollution Charges

From an optimal-taxation perspective, effluent fees become one of a set of potential revenue instruments. The objective is to design a system of taxation that produces the requisite level of revenues at the least cost to society. If we focus our attention on an efficient tax system, then the problem becomes one of choosing a set of tax rates for the various bases such that the excess burden (or deadweight loss) of an additional dollar of tax revenue is equated across all revenue sources.

More formally, our problem is to determine a set of tax rates $\mathbf{t} = (t_1, t_2, \ldots, t_n)$ applicable to the set of tax bases $\mathbf{b} = (b_1, b_2, \ldots, b_n)$ so as to:

$$\text{Min } D(\mathbf{t}) \quad \text{s.t. } \mathbf{tb} = R \qquad (1)$$

where R is the required level of revenues and D is the level of excess burden associated with the revenue system. The solution to this problem gives us the result:

$$D'(t_i)/b_i = D'(t_j)/b_j \quad \text{for all } i, j \qquad (2)$$

[2] This may seem a harsh dictum – one we may feel that, under certain circumstances, should be overturned on equity grounds. Particularly where individuals suffer damages from pollution over which they really had no control, we may wish to offer compensation in spite of its adverse effects on defensive measures. This is, however, a tricky issue. Where individuals choose to subject themselves to various forms of environmental damage (e.g., by locating near a smoky factory or a noisy airport) in return, perhaps, for lower rents on housing, the case for compensation is much less compelling. There is a further qualification of a different sort to the no-compensation argument. As Martin Bailey has shown, in instances where compensation becomes capitalized into local property values, it will not have any distorting effects on behavior by victims (on this point, see Baumol and Oates, 1988, pp. 230–4).

where D' denotes the partial derivative – or, in short, that the marginal excess burden from a dollar of revenues should be the same for all revenue sources.

The interesting and important aspect of introducing pollution charges as a revenue instrument is that, over some range at least, they have *negative* excess burden: they improve, rather than distort, resource allocation. This suggests that by substituting revenues from pollution charges for those from distorting taxes, we can improve the efficiency properties of the overall revenue system. An efficient tax system thus should, in principle, encompass taxes on activities that impose external costs on the environment.

David Terkla (1984) has actually developed some measures of the potential efficiency gains from pollution taxes. In a study of a hypothetical set of nationwide taxes on particulate and sulfur oxide emissions from stationary sources in the U.S., Terkla has estimated the gains that would result from using these revenues to replace partially those from either the federal income tax (on labor income) or the corporation income tax. He finds that the potential gains from a more efficient overall tax system range from $630 million to over $3 billion in 1982 dollars. These estimates, of course, rely on a set of specific assumptions concerning the scope and rates of pollution taxation. A broader set of pollution taxes could generate yet larger reductions in the excess burden of the tax system. There is, incidentally, an ongoing study at the U.S. Environmental Protection Agency of the revenue potential of taxes to contain carbon dioxide emissions. Such taxes could both provide a powerful incentive to reduce emissions of greenhouse gases and produce annual revenues running into the tens of billions of dollars.

The analysis thus suggests that from an optimal taxation perspective, we want to push the role for pollution taxes beyond that of solely an instrument for environmental regulation. From this broader perspective, the efficiency condition for effluent charges is no longer that marginal abatement cost (MAC) equal marginal social damage (MSD) – we now must set pollution taxes to account not only for environmental benefits and abatement costs, but also for the reduction in excess burden associated with reduced reliance on other taxes. As Dwight Lee and Walter Misiolek (1986) have shown, our new theorem says that, in an optimal taxation setting, MSD must diverge from MAC by an amount equal to the reduced excess burden from other taxes. Put more formally, we have that:

$$B'(E) - C'(E) = D'(R)R'(E) \tag{3}$$

where B is the benefits from reduced emissions, C is abatement costs, and E is the level of waste emissions. If the tax rates on pollutants are set so as to satisfy (3), then the net cost to society of another dollar of public revenues will be equated across all revenue sources.

This raises the interesting question of how pollution tax rates in an optimal-taxation setting compare with these rates under a purely environmental regime. One's first inclination is to assume that this will require that rates of pollution taxation be set higher than they would be for purposes solely of pollution control. However, as Lee and Misiolek show – and as a little reflection suggests – this is by no means necessarily the case. An optimal tax approach may well require that we set pollution tax rates *lower* than the level for which marginal social damage equals marginal abatement cost.

To take a polar case, suppose that MSD equals MAC just at the point of complete abatement. The environmental literature would thus have us set an effluent fee just sufficient to reduce waste emissions to zero. But such a tax would raise no revenues and would thus forgo the potential gains from substitution of these revenues for those from distorting taxes. The optimal-tax approach would, in this instance, have us reduce the pollution tax somewhat so as to generate some revenues from this source.

The basic point is that optimal-tax considerations require more revenues from taxes on pollution than under a purely environmental regime. But this may call for either an increase or a decrease in the tax rate depending on *tax elasticity*. If the elasticity at the environmental optimum (i.e., where MAC = MSD) is greater than unity, so that a reduction in tax rates on emissions leads to an increase in revenues, then the optimal tax rate on pollution will be lower than the rate for purely environmental reasons. In contrast, if tax elasticity is less than unity, then the optimal-tax rate on pollution is the higher of the two. Finally, in the special case of unitary tax elasticity, the rates under the two regimes are the same.

Lee and Misiolek draw on the existing empirical literature on pollution control to develop some estimates of the tax elasticity of pollution "demand." Interestingly, their elasticity estimates across a wide set of air and water pollutants exhibit considerable variation: some are well below unity, while the upper range for most reaches well above unity.[3] Their interval estimate, for example, of the tax elasticity for the emission of particulate matter from U.S. electric utilities is (0.99–1.34), suggesting that the rate on this source of emissions would, under an optimal-tax setting, likely be less than the "pure" environmental charge. It thus appears that there is no general prescription here: an optimal-tax approach is likely, in some instances, to require higher tax rates than a purely environmental regime – and, in other cases, lower tax rates.[4]

II A Public-Choice Perspective on Pollution Taxes

The optimal-taxation view of our problem produces a specific result, a first-order condition that must be satisfied for the optimal tax rate on *each* form of pollution. And this involves a basic trade-off between the efficiency gains from environmental cleanup and from reduced excess burden in the revenue system. Each pollution tax would have to be set such that the divergence of abatement costs from benefits at the margin from a cleaner environment (per dollar of revenues) equals the marginal excess burden from revenues from other taxes. While this result may be unimpeachable in

[3] These estimates of tax elasticity are based on a variety of different empirical studies of air and water pollutants. Some are based on elasticity estimates of pollution demand in the neighborhood of the conventional pollution target, while others represent the tax elasticity of pollution demand in the region where estimated marginal benefits equal estimated marginal abatement costs.

[4] The question arises here as to whether, as we move in the direction of greater stringency of environmental control and begin to climb the more steeply ascending portions of marginal abatement cost curves, it becomes more or less likely that optimal-tax considerations will point to higher rates for pollution taxes. I present a consideration of this issue in a brief appendix to the paper. There appears to be no general presumption on this matter.

principle, it is much less compelling in a realistic policy setting. To implement the optimal-tax result, we would need a very well informed public decision-maker whose interests transcend competing environmental and revenue pressures – a benevolent agent in a position to weigh environmental concerns against revenue needs.

This is a demanding institutional requirement. Pollution taxes are likely to be introduced in either of two forums: by an agency concerned with environmental management, or by those whose primary responsibility is budgetary management and who are seeking additional sources of revenues. In such cases, we are unlikely to get the kind of "weighing" of alternative costs between environmental and revenue objectives that is envisioned in the optimal-tax theorem.

This suggests that we turn to a public-choice perspective on the problem to see what insights this can provide. Suppose, for example, that the public revenue authority, the "Treasury" or "Legislative Tax Committee," were assigned the responsibility for determining the scope and level of pollution taxation. What might we expect? To take the extreme, Brennan and Buchanan (1980), in the public-choice literature, have argued that we can view the public sector as a revenue maximizer, a "Leviathan" that seeks to extract from the economy the most in public revenues that it can. For this polar case, we would expect to find a broad set of pollution taxes with rates set to maximize the inflow of revenues – rates determined so as to get us to the peak of the so called Laffer curve. In Figure 1, such an outcome is depicted by tax rate t_m, the revenue-maximizing rate.[5]

---

[5] In a somewhat similar vein, Adam Smith in *The Wealth of Nations* noted the potential peril in granting the revenue authority the control over tolls on the "turnpikes." Smith observes that

> if the tolls which are levied on the turnpikes should ever be considered as one of the resources for supplying the exigencies of the state, they would certainly be augmented as those exigencies were supposed to require ... The facility with which a great revenue could be drawn from them, would probably encourage administration to recur very frequently to this resource ... But the turnpike tolls being continually augmented in this manner, instead of facilitating the inland commerce of the country, as at present, would soon become a very great encumbrance upon it. (pp. 685–86)

How would such a single-minded pursuit of revenues influence the effectiveness of these taxes for environmental management? Some environmentalists have expressed the concern that in the quest for revenues, the tax authority would set tax rates that were too low from an environmental perspective – rates that would not provide an adequate incentive to polluters to reduce waste discharges. After all, if the rates were set at a high level, they would tend to kill off the tax base! Such an outcome would occur in Figure 1 if the optimal rate on environmental grounds were t_1: the revenue-maximizing tax authority would, in such a case, choose a tax rate below that for which the marginal benefits from pollution control (MSD) equal marginal abatement cost (MAC).

Once again, however, this outcome is not a general one. There are likely to be other cases where just the opposite occurs – where the revenue-maximizing rate is above the socially optimal rate such that the Leviathan outcome actually involves *increased* environmental protection. Such would be the case in Figure 1 if the optimal environmental rate were t_2.

The outcome again depends on the elasticity of the tax base. But this has to be interpreted with care. In a setting of revenue maximization, we might assume that other tax rates are already determined. *Given* an existing set of rates, the environmental authority might be expected to set pollution taxes such that MAC = MSD (although this is admittedly not, in general, an optimal deci-

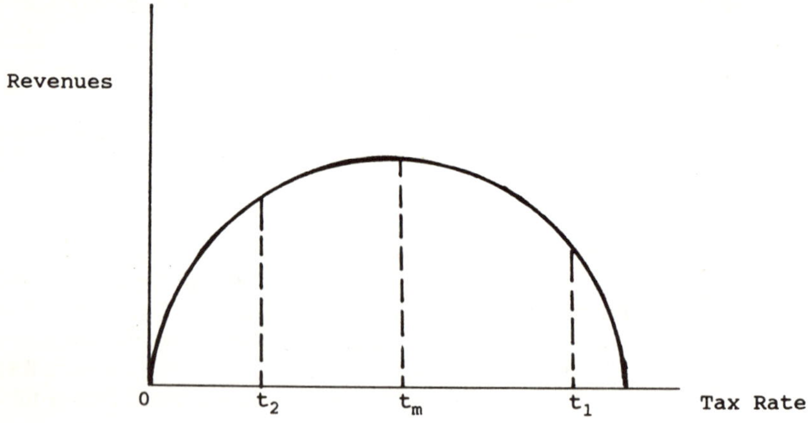

Fig. 1

sion in a distorted Leviathan setting). If the power to set pollution taxes were then transferred from the environmental authority to the Leviathan tax agent, we would find that Leviathan would either raise or lower pollution tax rates depending on whether or not the elasticity of the pollution-tax base was, respectively, less than or greater than unity.[6] There really is no general presumption here, other than that it is unlikely that revenue-maximizing rates on polluting waste emissions would coincide with the rate that provides the level of environmental protection for which MSD = MAC. Leviathan, in short, could prove to be either a friend or foe of the environment![7]

Note also that, for our polar case of revenue maximization, pollution taxes generate no added benefits in the form of reduced reliance on other distorting forms of taxation. Leviathan simply uses the new source of revenues to augment the flow of funds into the public treasury. The benefits, in this case, come solely from whatever net gains there may be in terms of enhanced environmental protection.

The Leviathan view with its assumption of pure revenue maximization is, of course, a cynical and quite controversial view of the public sector. More realistically, we might expect even a revenue authority to give some weight to environmental issues (in part in response to lobbying efforts from concerned groups) in determining the rates of pollution taxes. It is interesting in this regard that the recent adoption of "eco-taxation" in Sweden took place in an explicitly revenue neutral setting: existing taxes were, in fact, reduced with the introduction of pollution charges (Barde, 1991,

[6] Note that the elasticity of the pollution tax base must, in this instance, be understood to be the elasticity in the context of a set of distorted Leviathan taxes on other tax bases. This means that we cannot easily compare outcomes (e.g., levels of pollution tax rates) between Leviathan and optimal-tax regimes because the rates of taxation on other tax bases are likely to be quite different – and the elasticity of the pollution tax base is likely to depend to some extent on the rates of other taxes.

[7] In a related context, Oates and Schwab (1988) have shown that revenue-maximizing behavior can be unambiguously anti-environmental. In a setting of intergovernmental competition for new economic activity, "local" officials, to maximize local taxes, will tend to set excessively lax environmental standards in order to attract new capital and expand the local tax base.

p. 7). Likewise, attempts (albeit unsuccessful) to introduce environmental taxes in Austria involved a packaging of the proposed levies with cuts in other taxes. In the United States, there is the potential for such coordination in Congress where "interested" committees have joint jurisdiction over certain regulatory programs. While such instances are encouraging, my suspicion is that they are likely to be the exception rather than the rule: tax authorities are likely to view such taxes primarily as a vehicle for revenues and adjust rates to meet revenue needs rather than environmental circumstances.[8]

In contrast, if the authority for levying and adjusting pollution taxes is vested in an agency responsible for environmental management, then pollution control is likely to be the predominating objective. Whatever revenues are generated by the taxes (with a qualification to be introduced in the next section) will tend to be regarded as a "side effect." The revenues can indeed provide some benefits through reduced reliance on other distorting taxes, but the benefits will be serendipitous – not the result of the calculated tradeoff embodied in equation (3).

In a realistic policy setting, we may well be faced with the choice of placing the determination and administration of pollution taxes with either a tax or an environmental authority. The analysis does not provide any sort of rigorous basis for a preference for one over the other: it would appear very difficult to establish a general proposition that says that the tax rate for which MAC = MSD will result in a higher (or lower) level of social welfare than the revenue-maximizing tax rate.

However, I wish to argue that from a policy perspective there are reasons for preferring one locus of authority for pollution taxes to the other. There is, I think, a strong case for placing such taxes under the aegis of an environmental regulator. Pollution taxes are a potentially powerful tool for environmental management – one

[8] Friedrich Schneider has called my attention to another potential difficulty in the management of pollution taxes. He notes that such levies are likely to produce substantially more revenues in the short run, following their introduction, than over the longer term when sources have introduced new abatement technology in response to the taxes. The tax authority should thus be prepared for an "erosion" of the tax base over time.

of the most effective policy instruments available for controlling polluting activities. There is a large theoretical and empirical literature in environmental economics that makes a compelling case for a heavy reliance on economic incentives for pollution control.[9] To take pollution taxes out of the sphere of the environmental authority is effectively to place one of the primary determinants of levels of waste emissions under the management of another public body. This is likely to constrain quite severely the options for environmental management – and to force environmental regulators to turn to less effective, command-and-control instruments for pollution control.

Tax authorities, in contrast, have a substantial range of tax bases from which to choose. Revenues from pollution taxes can ultimately finance only a modest portion of the budget. This suggests, it seems to me, that it would make sense for the tax authority to take tax rates on pollution basically as given by environmental regulators. The tax authority would view these funds as largely an exogenous (but welcome) revenue source – and would then determine rates on other tax bases so as to produce the requisite overall level of revenues. The outcome would admittedly diverge from the optimal-tax result described in equation (3), but it is, I suspect, about as good as we can hope to do in the policy arena. I would stress in this regard that pollution taxes, effectively administered for purposes of environmental management, are the potential source of sizeable revenues – and the "side benefits" in terms of a less distorting tax system are likely to be quite substantial. This conclusion, however, is subject to an important qualification to be taken up next.

III Some Reflections on Environmental Trust Funds

As we have discussed, in the economics literature, pollution taxes have traditionally been addressed as instruments for pollution control, not as sources of public revenues. The basic theorems in environmental economics call for unit taxes on polluting waste

[9] See Cropper and Oates (forthcoming) for a recent survey of this literature.

emissions to be set equal to marginal social damages or, in a second-best setting, at a level designed to achieve certain predetermined targets for environmental quality (Baumol and Oates, 1971).

Theory and practice have, however, diverged in important ways. Environmental authorities around the world have not made extensive use of pollution taxes for environmental management. But there are some noteworthy uses, especially in Europe. France, Germany, and the Netherlands, for example, have employed effluent taxes for water-quality management. But, interestingly, in all these cases, the revenue aspects of the taxes have been quite important. As Robert Hahn (1989) and others have pointed out, environmental authorities have typically set rates in such a way as to generate the revenues needed for various pollution-control projects and other related costs. They have looked on these taxes as a source of revenues to fund programs for water-quality management, not primarily as instruments for the regulation of waste flows.[10]

This is an important issue in the "political economy" of pollution taxes. I mentioned earlier the legislation proposed in the U.S. in 1987 for a nationwide tax on sulfur and nitrogen oxide emissions. There was in that bill a provision to direct the revenues collected by the taxes into a special "Sulfur and Nitrogen Emissions Trust Fund" which would be used to assist polluters in meeting their control costs. More generally, there seems to be a strong force that leads to the earmarking of such revenues for environmental purposes.

This is a force to be resisted! If the revenues from pollution taxes are siphoned off into increased spending for environmental projects, then they will obviously make no contribution to the improvement of the overall tax system by reducing the reliance on distorting taxes. The case for pollution taxes as a revenue source rests on their use to replace other taxes. If, as some public-choice writers fear (Brennan and Buchanan, 1980), the new source of

---

[10] There are a few instances in which incentive effects have figured importantly in environmental taxes: fees on discharges into Dutch river basins and some of the new "eco taxes" in Sweden on carbon and other airborne emissions. But these appear to be the exception – not the rule.

revenues serves as a means for expanding the public budget, then its role as a revenue source may have perverse results.

Moreover, certain trust-fund uses may themselves have troublesome implications for efficient resource use. In the proposed U.S. bill, a primary use of the revenues would have been to assist polluters in covering their control costs. From the perspective of economic efficiency, this is misplaced assistance. The tax is itself to serve as a signal to polluters to guide decisions on levels of control activities – and rebates on control costs would distort this signal. Over the longer haul, it is important that sources bear the full cost of their abatement activities *and* pollution taxes so that profits (net of these costs) will provide the right incentive for entry and exit decisions into the industry (Baumol and Oates, 1988, pp. 52–54).

An alternative use of such funds is the compensation of victims for any damages they suffer from pollution. But, as we discussed earlier, such compensation also can create undesirable incentives: it discourages victims from engaging in efficient levels of defensive activities.

All this is certainly not to say that important environmental projects should not be undertaken. But they should have to meet the same budgetary and economic tests as other public-sector projects – and should not be undertaken simply by virtue of the availability of some earmarked funds. In short, the revenues generated by pollution taxes should be treated in the same way as other tax receipts: they should make up part of the general fund and other tax rates should be determined in light of the contribution from this source.

This is admittedly a tough stance – since earmarking of revenues has played a central role in many of these programs. There are, for instance, cases where funding is needed for public projects (e.g., waste-water treatment plants) related directly to the emissions of the taxed sources. The "Polluter Pays Principle" can be used to justify earmarking of revenues for the finance of such publicly provided environmental services. In addition, Jean-Philippe Barde has suggested to me that such trust funds can been seen as a kind of second-best measure where the heavy costs of taxes would make their introduction politically infeasible without some earmarking assistance, or as a transitory solution in a setting where charges are raised gradually over time to the desired level.

While such cases can be made, I think that, in general, we do best to discourage earmarking of funds from pollution taxes – and to regard them as a valuable source of general revenues that can be used to improve the structure of the overall tax system.

IV Some Concluding Remarks

Environmental economics has viewed pollution taxes, quite properly, as a potentially effective instrument for environmental management. But such taxes will produce revenues. And, from an optimal-taxation perspective, the design of these taxes should, in principle, consider both their contribution to pollution control and to an improved tax system. While it is straightforward to characterize the nature of this tradeoff and the conditions to be satisfied by an "optimal" tax on pollution, it is more difficult to envision an institutional setting in which the potentially conflicting goals of environmental and revenue management will be effectively coordinated.

This suggests that for purposes of institutional design, we should probably consider two alternatives: placing the responsibility for levying and administering these taxes under either the environmental, or the tax, authority. The analysis indicates that it is impossible to say, in general, which regime is likely to adopt the higher rate structure. But broader concerns of effective environmental management suggest, I think, a strong case for placing the authority for pollution taxes with an environmental regulator. The revenues from these taxes would then flow into the general fund and provide a special "side benefit" in terms of reduced reliance on taxes that distort the functioning of the economy.

The magnitude of these "side benefits" depends on the excess burden *at the margin* from existing distorting taxes. There is now a substantial empirical literature in the economics of taxation that attempts to estimate the magnitude of marginal excess burden. While there is far from a consensus on any precise figures, many of these studies produce quite sizable estimates. Charles Ballard, John Shoven and John Whalley (1985), for example, making use of a multisector, computational general-equilibrium model, find that the marginal excess burden of taxes in the United States is large.

They estimate that the welfare loss from a one-percent increase in all distortionary tax rates is within the range of 17 to 56 cents per dollar of extra revenue.[11] Such estimates suggest that the "side benefits" from pollution taxes could be quite sizable indeed!

Appendix

As Lee and Misiolek have shown, there is no general presumption concerning the relationship between the optimal tax rate on pollution and the rate under a purely environmental regime. What we know is that the optimal tax solution will call for more *revenues* from pollution taxation (relative to the environmental regime), but this may entail a higher or lower tax rate (and more or less pollution), depending on the tax elasticity at the environmental optimum.

A further question arises here. There now exists a large body of empirical work on the costs of abatement for a wide range of pollutants. Nearly all these studies find that *marginal* abatement costs (MAC) behave in textbook fashion. After a range of relatively low and slowly rising marginal costs, abatement efforts encounter rapidly rising costs at the margin. Figure A.1 depicts such a prototypical MAC curve.

In this context, we can ask whether or not as we move, say, from a point like *G* to a point like *H*, reflecting an increasing stringency of environmental control, tax elasticity tends to rise or fall. The issue here is how optimal tax considerations are likely to affect the *levels* of the tax rate and emissions as the stringency of environmental regulation rises. Or, put slightly differently, is tax elasticity higher at *G* or *H*?

One's initial surmise may be that elasticity is higher at *G*, since the steepness of the MAC curve at *H* indicates that a unit reduction in taxes will not have much influence on the level of emissions. But the matter is more complicated. It is also true at *H* that the *level* of emissions is lower, so that the relative size of the *percentage* change in emissions at *G* and *H* is unclear.

---

[11] See Don Fullerton (1991) for a helpful attempt to reconcile some of these diverse estimates.

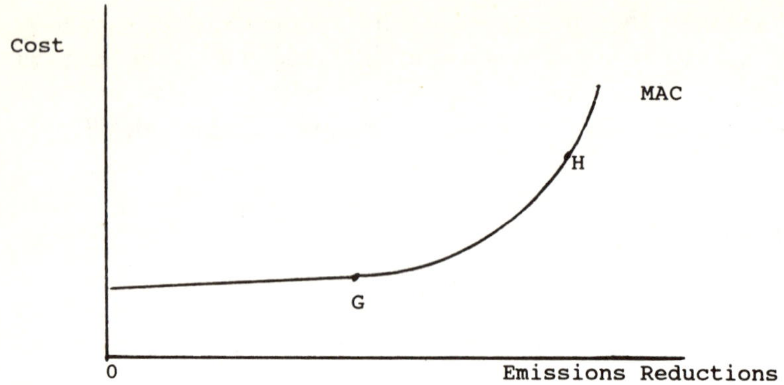

Fig. A.1

I will show here that no general presumption emerges from the consideration of a simple case. In carrying out the analysis, note that all that is at issue here is the shape and position of the MAC curve. Cost-minimizing polluters respond to taxes on effluents by setting MAC equal to the tax rate . It is this response to variations in the tax rate that determines whether revenues rise or fall as tax rates are increased.

For purposes of the analysis, I take as a simple representative case a marginal abatement cost function of the form:

$$C = f + gA^2 \tag{A.1}$$

where C is marginal abatement cost, A is the level of abatement (i.e., reduction in emissions from the uncontrolled level), and f and g are parameters.

The level of revenues (R) from the tax is simply the product of the level of emissions (E) and the tax rate (t):

$$R = tE. \tag{A.2}$$

Note next that emissions are related to abatement by:

$$E = E_0 - A \tag{A.3}$$

where E_0 is the uncontrolled level of emissions.

Cost-minimizing behavior by polluters implies that marginal abatement cost will equal the tax rate:

$$C = f + gA^2 = t. \tag{A.4}$$

Substituting (A.3) and (A.4) into (A.2) gives us:

$$\begin{aligned} R &= E(f + gA^2) \qquad \text{(A.5)} \\ &= E[f + g(E_0 - E)^2] \\ &= (f + gE_0^2)E - 2gE_0E^2 + gE^3. \end{aligned}$$

Taking the derivative of revenues (R) with respect to the level of emissions (E) yields:[12]

$$dR/dE = (f + gE_0^2) - 4gE_0E + 3gE^2. \tag{A.6}$$

Examining the right side of (A.6), we see that the first and third terms are positive and the second term is negative, suggesting that the sign of the entire expression is likely to be ambiguous. Taking the second derivative:

$$d^2R/dE^2 = -4gE_0 + 6gE.$$

We thus find that "marginal revenue" is decreasing over the range 0 to $(2/3)E_0$ and increasing from $(2/3)E_0$ to E_0. But this does not permit us to determine, in general, how the sign of the derivative, dR/dE, varies with E. Hence, in terms of Figure A.1, it not possible, in general, to determine whether tax elasticity at a point like G is greater or less than tax elasticity at a point like H.

In short, as environmental measures become more stringent and we move up the MAC curve, it is unclear whether optimal tax considerations are more or less likely to require further increases in the tax rate.

Bibliography

Ballard, C.L., J.B. Shoven and J. Whalley. 1985. "General Equilibrium Computations of the Marginal Welfare Costs of Taxes in the United States." *American Economic Review* 75(March): 128–138.

[12] It is easier to work with the relationship between R and E than between R and t. Since E and t are monotonically nonpositively related, we can infer the relationship between R and t from that between R and E.

Barde, J.-P. 1991. "The Use of Economic Instruments for Environmental Protection in OECD Countries." Unpublished paper.

Baumol, W.J. and W.E. Oates. 1971. "The Use of Standards and Prices for Protection of the Environment." *Swedish Journal of Economics* 73(March): 42–54.

———. 1988. *The Theory of Environmental Policy*. Second Edition. Cambridge: Cambridge University Press.

Brennan, G. and J. Buchanan. 1980. *The Power to Tax: Analytical Foundations of a Fiscal Constitution*. Cambridge: Cambridge University Press.

Cropper, M.L. and W.E. Oates. 1992. "Environmental Economics: A Survey." *Journal of Economic Literature* 30(June): 675–740.

Fullerton, D. 1991. "Reconciling Recent Estimates of the Marginal Welfare Cost of Taxation." *American Economic Review* 81(March): 302–308.

Hahn, R.W. 1989. "Economic Prescriptions for Environmental Problems: How the Patient Followed the Doctor's Orders." *Journal of Economic Perspectives* 3(Spring): 95–114.

Lee, D.R. and W.S. Misiolek. 1986. "Substituting Pollution Taxation for General Taxation: Some Implications for Efficiency in Pollution Taxation." *Journal of Environmental Economics and Management* 13(Dec.): 338–347.

Oates. W.E. and R.M. Schwab. "Economic Competition among Jurisdictions: Efficiency Enhancing or Distortion Inducing?" *Journal of Public Economics* 35(April): 333–354.

Smith, A. 1937. *The Wealth of Nations*. New York: Random House, The Modern Library.

Terkla, D. 1984. "The Efficiency Value of Effluent Tax Revenues." *Journal of Environmental Economics and Management* 11(June): 107–123.

The Role of Economic Incentives for Natural Resource Management in Developing Countries

Edward B. Barbier*

Introduction

The costs that environmental degradation imposes on developing economies are considered significant. However, these costs are difficult to assess. The impacts of environmental degradation often occur *externally* to any market system and involve complex processes of ecological-economic interaction. Both the economic *causes* and *effects* of environmental degradation are difficult to discern and analyze in developing countries.

Much excessive degradation of the environment and natural resources in developing countries is thought to result from individuals in the marketplace and by governments not fully recognizing and integrating environmental values into decision-making processes. If markets fail to reflect adequately environmental values, *market failure* is said to exist. Where government decisions or policies do not fully reflect these values, there is policy or *government failure.* Throughout the developing world, the existence of poorly formulated input and output pricing policies, insecure land titling and registration, tax thresholds and rebates, cheap and restricted credit facilities, overvalued exchange rates and other policy distortions has exacerbated problems of natural resource management. By failing to make markets and private decision makers accountable for forgone environmental values, these policies may contribute to market failure. At worst, the direct private

* I am grateful to Bruce Aylward, Joshua Bishop, Joanne Burgess, Johann Holmberg and Anil Markandya for their constructive comments. All errors and omissions are of course mine alone.

costs of resource-using activities are subsidized and/or distorted, thus encouraging unnecessary environmental degradation.[1]

The following paper argues that designing public policies to encourage proper economic incentives for sustainable and efficient management of natural resources is crucial to developing economies. These economies, especially the lower-income countries, are highly dependent on primary production as the foundation of long-term, sustainable economic development. Successful exploitation of primary production – agriculture, fishing, forestry and minerals – in turn depends on efficient and sustainable management of the resource base supporting primary productive activities. Moreover, as developing countries industrialize and as their populations concentrate in urban settlements, the role of the environment in assimilating waste products and providing life-support amenities will become increasingly important. Protection and conservation of key natural systems and important ecological functions will also be essential, not only in terms of their potential value for recreation and tourism but also because these systems and functions may provide valuable support and protection for economic activity and human welfare. This paper will concentrate mainly on the role of economic incentives for efficient and sustainable management of the resource base supporting primary production and key ecological functions in developing economies.

I Economic Instruments and Incentives

Traditional discussions of appropriate policy instruments for providing the necessary *economic incentives* for natural resource management usually focus on the relative merits of regulatory as opposed to economic instruments.

Regulatory, or *direct control*, instruments involve the direct limitation or reduction of activities that degrade the environment, in accordance with some legislated or agreed standard. Examples include quotas or bans on renewable resource harvesting, re-

[1] For a recent review of the economics of environmental degradation in developing countries, see Barbier (1991).

strictions on air pollution emissions, controls on hazardous waste transport and dumping, zoning laws and ambient water quality standards. Such controls are usually mandatory and enforceable through litigation, fines/penalties, revocation of licenses or other judicial or administrative sanctions. Regulatory controls on environmental degradation have an important role to play in developing economies, but their effectiveness is often limited by poorly functioning judicial, administrative and monitoring/enforcement procedures.

In contrast, *economic*, or *market-based*, instruments do not directly control or restrict activities that degrade the environment. Rather, they create the economic incentives for individuals to choose freely to modify or reduce their activities, thus indirectly producing an environmental improvement. The aim of economic instruments is to alter private costs and benefits so that any unaccounted social costs (and benefits) of environmental degradation can be "internalized" to ensure the desired environmental improvement. Examples include effluent charges (taxes), stumpage fees or other "additional" prices to be paid for the social costs arising from environmental damages; subsidies to assist individuals in altering activities or conforming to environmental standards; tradeable (marketable) pollution permits or harvesting quotas; deposit/refund for recycling or fee/rebate systems such as reforestation rebates on timber stumpage fees; and finally, compensatory financing such as debt-for-nature swaps.

However, the effectiveness of such market-based instruments in adjusting private costs to reflect the social costs of environmental degradation may depend on how well market systems reflect private costs in the first instance. The pervasiveness of market and policy failures underlying many of the environmental degradation problems in developing economies suggests many instances where public policies and incomplete markets frequently reduce the direct costs to individuals of utilizing the environment. Thus many authors stress as a priority for developing countries the role of *policy reforms* as an "economic instrument," i.e., the removal of subsidies and other public policy interventions that distort the *private* costs of resource use and pollution discharge (Panayotou, 1990; Pearce, 1990). Similarly, *institutional reforms* such as the improvement or establishment of property and resource right regimes, legal titling, environmental sanctions, contract enforcement and so forth are equally important policy instruments for improved natural resource management in developing countries in that they assist or even establish markets for environmental goods and services.[2]

Although regulatory and market-based instruments for environmental improvement are important to developing economies, this paper will focus on the key role of policy and institutional reforms for improving natural resource management in these economies.

II Poverty, Environment and Degradation

A common assumption is that the effectiveness of public policies and economic incentives in controlling environmental degradation in developing economies is limited by the existence of a poverty-environment "trap." Given the presence of both high levels of poverty and environmental degradation in developing countries, it is tempting to conclude that poverty causes environmental degradation. However, recent evidence suggests that poverty-environmental linkages cannot be reduced to simple unidimensional cause-effect relationships (Jagannathan, 1989; Barbier, 1989; Conway and Barbier, 1990; Pearce and Warford, 1991). There are numerous complex factors that influence poor peoples' perceptions of the environment and their behavior towards natural resource management. These range from the economic distortions arising from policy and market failures, to underlying labor and capital endowments and constraints, to access to alternative employment and income-earning opportunities, to institutional and legal factors such as tenure or access security, property rights and delivery systems. Often what is perceived to be a *direct* link between poverty and environmental degradation proves to be an *indirect* link under careful analysis. Public policies and other factors often af-

[2] Given the economic importance of such institutional reforms, Panayotou (1990) includes them in the category of "economic" instruments; however, the conventional view is to consider institutional reforms to be "noneconomic" policy instruments.

fect the incentive structures and redirect capital and labor flows between sectors and regions, with adverse consequences for the poor and their ability or willingness to manage resources sustainably (Jagannathan, 1989).

As poor people have little or no access to capital and must rely on family or low-skilled labor for earning income, it would seem economically perverse that they would degrade any "natural capital" at their disposal. Many studies have revealed that poor people and communities are often acutely aware of the essential role of natural resources in sustaining their livelihoods, and equally, of the costs and impacts of environmental degradation.[3] This would suggest that, ceteris paribus, there exist tremendous *incentives* for the poor to manage and sustain the stock of natural capital at their disposal in order to maintain or enhance both their immediate and future livelihood options. Where they choose to degrade their environment – and there may be rational grounds for doing so under certain circumstances – it is because changing economic and social conditions have altered the incentive structures of the poor, including perhaps their control over or access to essential resources. Often increased "immiserization" is an outcome, or part of the "cumulative causation" process, that is symptomatic of the subsequently observed poverty-environment "trap."

Thus from an economic perspective, simply observing that poor people are "driven" to degrade the environment – even when this appears to be the case – is not helpful. Designing appropriate policy responses to alleviate problems of poverty and environmental degradation therefore requires careful analysis of the *determinants* of individual behavior. Such an analysis would clarify the factors leading them to degrade their environment, their responses to environmental degradation and the incentives required to induce conservation.

Where further analysis reveals that poverty is not the direct "cause" of environmental degradation, designing appropriate policy responses will nevertheless be affected by poverty's indirect role. The response of poor people and communities to incentives

[3] On indigenous knowledge and views of the role of natural resources in the livelihood security of the poor, see Chambers (1988), Richards (1985) and Wilson (1988).

encouraging sustainable resource management may be affected by special factors influencing their behavior, such as high rates of time preference induced by greater risk and uncertainty over livelihood security, labor and capital constraints, insecure tenure over and access to resources, imperfect information and access to marketed inputs and a variety of other conditions and constraints (Barbier, 1989b, 1990b).

Moreover, the poor are not a homogenous group. The work of Lipton (1983, 1988) highlights how the "ultra" or "core" poor, other poor and the nonpoor in developing countries all differ in terms of demographic, nutritional, labor-market and asset-holding characteristics.[4] A recent study in Malawi highlights how the poor and the "core" poor face different incentives and constraints in combatting declining soil fertility and erosion, which is a serious problem afflicting smallholder agriculture (Barbier and Burgess, 1990). Some of the results of the study are indicated in Table 1.

In Malawi, female-headed households make up a large percentage (42%) of the "core-poor" households. They typically cultivate very small plots of land (<0.5 ha) and are often marginalized onto the less fertile soils and steeper slopes (>12%). They are often unable to finance agricultural inputs such as fertilizer, to rotate annual crops, to use "green manure" crops or to undertake soil conservation. As a result, poorer female-headed households generally face declining soil fertility and lower crop yields, further exacerbating their poverty and increasing their dependence upon the land. The special constraints and needs of poor female-headed households must be carefully considered when designing economic policies to alleviate poverty and control land degradation. Otherwise, an important subset of the rural population will not respond fully to policy measures and incentives to improve environ-

[4] The exact numbers and composition of poor and ultra-poor will obviously vary by country and region; however, as an approximate indication Lipton (1988) suggests that the ultra-poor can be defined as those at significant risk of income-induced caloric undernutrition and the poor as those with sufficiently low income to be at risk of hunger but not undernutrition, with the former usually falling in the bottom 10–20% income category (e.g., the "poorest quintile").

Table 1. Women, Poverty and Land Degradation, Malawi

A. Smallholder Poverty Profile, Malawi

	Core Poor	Other Poor	Nonpoor
Sex of Head of Household (% female)	42	34	16
Number of Labor Days/Year – per household	532	606	762
Average Land Holding (ha) – per household	0.39	0.73	1.76
Agricultural Services			
– % using fertilizer	9	16	35
– % maize yield (1000 tn/ha)	1.2	1.3	1.4

B. Fertilizer Use by Household Type, Blantyre Agricultural Development Division, Malawi

Total Households	883			
Gender of Household Head	Male		Female	
	No.	%	No.	%
	556	63.0	327	37.0
Fertilizer Farmers	208	37.4	90	27.5
Nonfertilizer Farmers	348	62.6	237	72.5

C. Credit Disbursement and Input Use to Smallholders, Malawi

	83/84	84/85	85/86	86/87	87/88	88/89	89/90
Seasonal Loans ('000 Malawi Kwacha)	11460	15555	19065	18283	26871	42211	57075
No. of Beneficiaries ('000)	180	212	208	206	243	301	315
Women as % of Beneficiaries	15.0	16.2	19.4	25.4	29.8	24.8	29.9

Table 1 (continued)

D. Adoption of Soil Conservation, Ntcheu Rural Development Project, Malawi

Activity	Target (1)	Achievement (2)	(1/2) (%)
Farms Plans	M: 8	M: 3	37.5
	W: 2	W: 0	0.0
Contour Marker Ridges	M: 600	M: 232	38.7
	W: 300	W: 42	14.0
Composting	M: 1500	M: 1051	70.1
	W: 1000	W: 156	15.6
Manuring	M: 4500	M: 3347	74.4
	W: 2500	W: 1002	40.1
Alley Cropping	M: 170	M: 30	17.6
	W: 80	W: 14	17.5
Buffer Strips	M: 8	M: 3	37.5
	W: 2	W: 0	0.0
Raised Boundaries/Paths	M: 200	M: 321	160.5
	W: 100	W: 199	199.0
Gully Reclamation	M: 80	M: 104	130.0
	W: 20	W: 20	100.0
Farmer Training	M: 500	M: 157	31.4
	W: 220	W: 245	111.4

Notes: M: Men W: Women.
Source: Table A from World Bank (1990).

mental management, and the problem of land degradation may continue unmitigated.

In confronting poverty-environmental degradation problems, policymakers are therefore faced with difficult challenges. On the one hand, existing policy and market failures may distort the incentives faced by all individuals for managing environmental assets efficiently and sustainably, suggesting that public policies are a legitimate means of ensuring that these distortions are corrected. This is reinforced by the important role that resources often play in the livelihoods of the poor. In other words, efficient and sustainable resource management may be an important *prerequisite* for ensuring livelihood security and avoiding any poverty-environment trap rather than a *by-product* of efforts to improve incomes. On the other hand, designing appropriate policies to alleviate poverty and reduce environmental degradation is not an easy task.

In many instances, our knowledge and analysis of the linkages between policy changes at the sectoral or macro level and their effects on the incentives facing diverse groups of poor people in a variety of differing ecological, economic and social circumstances is simply not adequate. This reinforces the urgent need for more research and policy analysis of this kind.

A worrying trend in developing economies is the concentration of the poorest groups in "ecologically fragile" zones – areas where environmental degradation or severe environmental hazards constrain and even threaten economic welfare. As indicated by Leonard (1989), around 470 million, or 60 percent of the developing world's poorest people, live in rural or urban areas that can be classified as "ecologically fragile."[5] Around 370 million of the developing world's poorest people live in "marginal" agricultural areas. These less favorable agricultural lands, with lower productivity potential, poorer soils and physical characteristics, and more variable and often inadequate rainfall, are easily prone to land degradation due to overcropping, poor farming practices and inadequate conservation measures.

The result is that **the economic livelihoods and welfare of the poorest income groups in low potential areas are at greater risk from increasing environmental degradation**. It is this risk combined with the impact of public policies, institutions and investments on the economic incentives that the poorest face that may have the most profound – and often perverse – effects on the willingness and ability of the poorest groups to counteract degradation.

Another major "poverty reserve" in developing countries is peripheral urban areas, or "squatter" settlements. Recent evidence from West Java and Nigeria confirms that the informal employment sector and settlements around urban and semi-urban settle-

---

[5] The "poorest people" are defined by Leonard (1989) as the poorest 20 percent of the population in developing countries. In commenting on the data presented by Leonard, Kates (1990) argues that it is too simplistic to equate all land of low agricultural potential and squatter settlements with "areas of high ecologically vulnerability." Thus "while there is good reason to expect an increasing geographic segregation of the poor onto the threatened environments, both the purported distribution of the hungry and the actual state of environmental degradation needs to be examined much more carefully."

ments are often the preferred "open access resource" for the poor (Jagannathan, 1989). Although precise estimates of how many of the 1.3 billion urban dwellers in developing countries live in "squatter" settlements are scarce, it is common for between 30–60 percent of the population in large cities to live either in illegal settlements or in tenements and cheap boarding houses. In smaller urban centers of less than 100,000 inhabitants – which contain about three quarters of the developing world's urban population – the proportion of people living in illegal settlements may be smaller than in the large cities. However, the proportion living in areas with inadequate infrastructure or services may be as high or even higher in small compared to larger urban centers (Cairncross, Hardoy and Satterthwaite, 1990).

The result is that **the economic welfare of a substantial, and growing, number of the poorest urban dwellers is threatened by the environmental hazards and health risks posed by pollution, inadequate housing and poor sanitation, water and other basic infrastructure services.**[6]

The concentration of the poorest groups in developing countries in "ecologically fragile" areas suggests that it is the welfare of the poorest in developing economies that is at the greatest risk from continued environmental degradation. As argued by Kates (1990), throughout the developing world the poor often suffer from three major processes of *environmental entitlement* loss:

- the poor are *displaced* from their traditional entitlement to common resources by development activities or by the appropriation of their resources by richer claimants;
- the remaining entitlements are *divided* and reduced by their need to share their resources with their children or to sell off bits and pieces of their resources to cope with extreme losses (crop failure, illness, death), social obligations (marriages, celebrations) or subsistence; and
- the resources of the poor are *degraded* through excessive use and by failure to restore or to improve their productivity and

[6] Further examples of the impact of urban environmental problems and substandard living conditions on the welfare of the urban poor can be found in Hardoy and Satterthwaite (1989) and Hardoy, Cairncross and Satterthwaite (1990).

regeneration – a process made worse by the concentration of the poor into environments unable to sustain requisite levels of resource use.

As a result of these processes, the economic livelihoods of the poor become even more vulnerable to the risks posed by environmental degradation, and their ability and willingness to manage resources sustainably may become even more constrained.

Moreover, statistics indicate that the poorest groups in the relatively more affluent developing regions of Latin America and Asia are even more concentrated in ecologically fragile areas than the poorest groups in Africa (Leonard, 1989). This would suggest that the problem does not easily disappear with economic growth and rising national income.

In short, whether poverty is directly, or only indirectly, the "cause" of environmental degradation seems less relevant a concern when compared to the implications of pervasive environmental degradation for the livelihoods of the poor. This is the real "poverty-environment" link that should be the focus of development efforts. If poverty alleviation is an ultimate aim of economic development, then efficient and sustainable environmental management is a necessary means for achieving this goal.

Thus the continuing dependence of most of the world's poorest economies on their resource base should give environmental management a high priority as a development concern. This is particularly the case given that past economic policies and investments have led to rapid changes – frequently with adverse economic consequences – in resource stocks and patterns of use. Demographic trends have often worsened the relationship between population and resource-carrying capacity in many regions. Continuing agricultural extensification into marginal lands has increased the susceptibility of economic systems and livelihoods to environmental degradation.

As pointed out elsewhere, a reappraisal of demographic and agricultural policies to take into account the new realities of resource-carrying capacity constraints and the need to improve the potential of marginal lands while sustaining the productivity of high potential lands is required (Conway and Barbier, 1990; Barbier, 1989b; FAO, 199O; Leonard et al., 1989; Pearce, 1991;

Repetto, 1987; Repetto and Holmes, 1983). With regard to population-environment linkages, one useful approach is to view the role of population growth in terms of increasing the "scale" of human demands on limited natural systems (Foy and Daly, 1989). As will be discussed in the following sections, rethinking public policies for developing countries is also a necessity.

III Public Policies and Natural Resource Management

As discussed above, the result of market and policy failures is a distortion in economic incentives. That is, the private costs of actions leading to environmental degradation do not reflect the full social costs of degradation, in terms of the environmental values forgone. There are several reasons for this outcome:

First, the market mechanisms determining the "prices" for natural resources and products derived from conversion of natural resource systems *do not automatically take into account wider environmental costs*, such as disruptions to ecological functions, assimilative capacity, amenity values and other environmental impacts or forgone option and *existence values* – i.e., the value of preserving certain natural environments, species and resources today as an "option" for future use or simply because their "existence" is valued. Nor do market mechanisms account for any *user cost* – the cost of forgoing future direct or indirect use benefits from resource depletion or degradation today.

In addition, even the direct costs of harvesting resources or converting natural resource systems *are often subsidized and/or distorted by public policies*. As a result, individuals do not face even the full *private costs* of their own actions that degrade the environment. Unnecessary and excessive degradation ensues.

For example, in the Brazilian Amazon subsidies and other policy distortions are estimated to have accounted for at least 35% of all forest area altered by 1980 through tax incentives for capital investment (e.g., industrial wood production and livestock ranching); rural credits for agricultural production (mechanized agriculture, cattle ranching and silviculture); subsidized small farmer settlement; and export subsidies (Browder, 1985). In addition, government-financed investment programs – for road-building, colonial settlement and large-scale agricultural and mining activities – may *indirectly* be contributing to deforestation by "opening up" frontier areas that were previously inaccessible to smallholders and migrants.

Similarly, in Malaysia and Indonesia, government policies to encourage the switching from the export of raw logs to processed timber products have led to substantial economic losses, the establishment of inefficient processing operations and accelerated deforestation (Repetto and Gillis, 1988). Throughout Southeast Asia the allocation of timber concession rights and leasing agreements on a short time scale, coupled with the lack of incentives for reforestation, have contributed to excessive and rapid depletion of timber forests. In the Philippines, the social gains from logging old-growth forest was found to be negative (around US$130 to US$1,175 per hectare), once the social costs of timber stand replanting, the costs of depletion and off-site damages were included (Paris and Ruzicka, 1991).

There is also evidence of *noneconomic* policy distortions contributing to excessive deforestation (Binswanger, 1989; Browder, 1985; Pearce, Barbier and Markandya, 1990; Southgate, Sierra and Brown, 1989). Formal property law and titling regulations often ensure that clearing of land is a prerequisite for guaranteeing claims to frontier forest landholdings. Given the insecurity of many frontier tenure regimes, private individuals and firms often clear excessive amounts of forest lands in order to safeguard their tenuous claims to holdings and to "capture" agricultural rents. As the capacity of many governments to "manage" vast tracts of publicly owned tropical forests is often minimal, encroachment into forest reserves and protected lands is not controlled. At the same time, proper consideration of customary land tenure arrangements and access claims by indigenous forest dwellers and users is often lacking in government decisions to allocate forest land or determine titling.

Finally, many large-scale public investment projects and programs, such as hydroelectric dams, irrigation schemes, commercial agricultural development schemes, road-building, and so on, have significant environmental impacts. Some of these impacts may impose additional costs on society. Given such costs, to appraise the net benefits of the investment project or program in terms of its *direct costs* and benefits alone would be a misrepresentation of its economic net worth to society. The *forgone net benefits* associated with any environmental impacts must also be included as part of the opportunity costs of the development investment.

In recent years, many advances have been made in applying economic valuation techniques to analyzing the environmental impacts of investment projects and programs in developing countries (Anderson, 1987; Dixon et al., 1988; Bojo, Maler and Unemo, 1988; Gregersen et al., 1987). Frequently, appraisal of the environmental impacts of major public investments has shown that the investments should be modified, and in some cases should not

Table 2. Comparison of Present Value Net Economic Benefits Kano River Project Phase I and Hadejia-Jama'are Floodplain, Nigeria (N7.5 = US$1, 1989/90)

Per Hectare[a]	(8%, 50 yrs)	(8%, 30 yrs)	(12%, 50 yrs)	(12%, 30 yrs)
HJF (N/ha)	1276	1176	872	846
KRP (N/ha)	233	214	158	153
Per Water Use[b]				
HJF (N/10^3m^3)	366	337	250	242
KRP (N/10^3m^3)	0.3	0.3	0.2	0.2

[a] Based on a total production area of 730,000 ha for Hadejia-Jama'are floodplain (HJF) and a total crop cultivated area of 19,107 ha in 1985/86 for the Kano River Project Phase I (KRP).

[b] Assumes an the annual average river flow into Hadejia-Jama'are floodplain (HJF) of 2,549 Mm^3 and an annual water use of 15,000 m^3 per ha for the Kano River Project Phase I (KRP).

Source: E. Barbier, W. Adams and K., Kimmage (1991). The economic importance of the wetlands suggests that the benefits it provides cannot be excluded as an opportunity cost of any scheme that diverts water away from the floodplain system. When compared to the net economic benefits of the Kano River Project, the economic returns to the floodplain appear much more favorable. This is particularly the case when the relative returns to the Project in terms of water input use is compared to that of the floodplain system. The result should cause some concern, given that the existing and planned water developments along the Hadejia-Jama'are river system, such as the Kano River Project, will continue diverting water from the floodplain.

proceed at all. Table 2 summarizes an analysis of the net benefits of the Hadejia-Jama'are floodplain in Northern Nigeria, which is under threat from upstream irrigation development investments, such as the Kano River Project. The analysis shows that the economics benefits of the floodplain system are considerable, particularly in comparison with the irrigation project, which would suggest that the opportunity cost of diverting water to upstream developments could be high.

IV The Challenge for Public Policies: "Optimal Ignorance"

If public policies are to be redirected to achieve efficient and sustainable management of natural resources in developing countries, then clearly major changes are required. Economic valuation of the environmental impacts arising from market and policy failures is essential for determining the appropriate policy responses. Often, however, insufficient data and information exist to allow precise estimation of the economic costs arising from market and policy failures. In most cases, cost estimates as orders of magnitude and indicators of the direction of change are sufficient for policy analysis. (See, for example, the case studies in Pearce, Barbier and Markandya, 1990, and the discussion of tax and regulation policies in developing countries in Anderson, 1990.)

However, with many natural resource problems in developing countries we are not even at this state of "optimal ignorance" to begin designing appropriate policy responses. In the face of such uncertainty we should be humble in our public policy prescriptions. Even the standard economic tool of "improved pricing policy" should be invoked with caution. In most developing countries there is little empirical understanding of the linkages from price changes to short- and long-term supply and demand responses to natural resource impacts. The situation is complicated by the presence of underemployment, informal and incomplete markets, labor and capital constraints, and above all, the problem of widespread poverty. Thus we are often ignorant of the impact of public policies on the economic incentives faced by individual producers and households for managing natural resources, particularly in the case of the poorest groups who are on the "margin" of the formal economic and social systems.

This problem occurs frequently in the economic analysis of *dryland degradation.* The term "drylands" is usually applied to all arid and semiarid zones, plus areas in the tropical subhumid zone subject to the same degradation processes that occur on arid lands. Accounting for about one third of global land and supporting a population of 850 million, the world's drylands are rapidly being degraded through population growth, overgrazing, cropping on marginal lands, inappropriate irrigation and devegetation. Yet these areas are being asked to support increasing numbers of the world's poorest people. The process of dryland degradation is often referred to as "desertification," where the productive potential of the land is reduced to such an extent that it can neither be readily reversed by removing the cause nor easily reclaimed without substantial investment.

However, there are few economic studies of the costs of dryland degradation.[7] Even further behind – and more controversial – is the analysis of the effects of economic and resource management policies on dryland degradation in developing countries. This is often attributed to the superficial identification of the causes of desertification and to the frequently poor identification of the reasons behind the failures of dryland projects (Nelson, 1988). Although the majority of "causes" are attributable to population growth and natural events, dryland degradation is also symptomatic of an agricultural development bias that distorts agricultural pricing, investment flows, R&D, and infrastructure towards more "favored" agricultural land and systems (Barbier, 1989b). Where drylands "development" is encouraged, it is usually through the introduction of large-scale commercial agricultural schemes that can conflict with more traditional farming and pastoral systems.

The complexity of social, economic and environmental relationships is formidable. Not enough is often known about dryland farming and pastoral systems; open access use and common property resource rights; land tenure regimes and security; the distri-

---

[7] For recent examples of such studies, see Bishop and Allen (1989), Bishop (1990) and Lallement (1990).

bution of wealth and income; and coping strategies under the presence of variable climatic conditions, frequent drought, market instability, political conflicts and other factors influencing risk and uncertainty. A common misperception is that the extension of private property rights, commercial agriculture and markets will "automatically" solve dryland management problems in the long run. At the same time, not all dryland farmers and pastoralists, even in the most distant and resource-poor regions, are totally isolated from agricultural markets. Virtually all subsistence households require some regular market income for cash purchases of some agricultural inputs and basic necessities; many farmers and pastoralists provide important cash and export crops. As a result, alterations in market conditions – whether from changes in policies, climatic conditions, R&D innovations, or other factors – do have a significant impact on the livelihoods of rural groups in dryland areas. Understanding their responses to these changing market conditions is a crucial aspect of the dryland management problem.

For example, a study of gum arabic production in Sudan indicates that fluctuations in the real price of gum and its price relative to those of other agricultural crops have had important impacts on farmers' cropping patterns, diversification strategies and decisions to replant gum – with important consequences for Sudan's gum belt (IIED/IES, 1990; Barbier, 1990). Even though it is economically profitable *and* environmentally beneficial to grow gum, it is only when these economic incentives are properly dealt with by the government will rehabilitation of the important gum belt of Sudan take place.

Soil erosion and land degradation are not confined just to drylands and other marginal lands; the problem is pervasive throughout all agricultural systems, degraded forest lands, public and privately owned lands, and large and small holdings in the Third World. Designing appropriate policy responses to control soil erosion and land degradation for all types of cropland in developing countries is again hampered by the data limitations and the lack of microeconomic analyses of farmers' responses to erosion and incentives to adopt conservation measures.

The limited evidence that does exist suggests that relationships – such as the effects of agricultural input and output pricing on farm-level erosion – are complex and difficult to substantiate.

Nevertheless, there are some indications that subsidies for non-labor inputs, notably inorganic fertilizers, can artificially reduce the costs to farmers of soil erosion and, on more resource-poor lands, substitute for manure, mulches and nitrogen-fixing crops that might be more appropriate. On the other hand, the *inaccessibility* of inorganic fertilizers – e.g., shortages caused by rationing cheap fertilizer imports – can actually lead to suboptimal application and encourage farming practices that actually increase land degradation. Similarly, the relationship between erodibility and profitability of different cropping systems needs to be carefully analyzed, particularly in relation to changing *relative prices* of different crops and changes in *real producer prices and incomes* over time. More complex incentive effects arise from the relationships between erosion and the availability of labor, off-farm employment, population pressure, tenure and access to frontier land, the development of post-harvesting capacity and other complementary infrastructure and the availability of credit at affordable interest rates (Barbier, 1988; Barbier, 1989a, Ch. 7; Barbier and Burgess, 1990; Mortimore, 1989; Southgate, 1988).

A tentative conclusion is that there are often strong economic incentives determining farmers' decisions to invest in soil conservation. Farmers will generally not modify their land management practices and farming systems unless it is in their direct economic interest to do so. Such modifications are expensive and may involve risk. Unless soil erosion is perceived to be a threat to farm profitability, or alternatively unless changes in land management lead to at least some immediate economic gains, farmers will be less willing to bear these substantial costs. In addition, the more productive or profitable the land use, the more farmers will be willing to maintain and invest in better land management and erosion control practices. Higher productivity and returns will also mean that farmers can afford to maintain terraces and other conservation structures and to continue with labor-intensive erosion control measures. On the other hand, poorer farmers dependent on low-return cropping systems, such as maize or cassava, may be aware that soil erosion is reducing productivity but may not be able to afford to adopt conservation measures. At the other extreme, farmers with very profitable crops that are extremely erosive, such as temperate vegetables on steep upper volcanic slopes with deep topsoils, may not consider soil conservation measures if their returns do not appear to be affected by soil erosion losses. Unfortunately, in most developing regions, we still do not understand sufficiently the economic and social factors determining these incentives for soil conservation.

Nor do we appreciate fully the special role of women and female-headed households in economic-environment linkages. Women's relationship with the environment is not just confined to the poverty link. Even in those households that are not classified as poor the women are active participants in agricultural and household production. Thus, *women's use, perception, knowledge and management of the land* can be contrasted to that of men across all households. For example, a detailed study of the effects of agricultural commercialization among smallholders in the Zomba district of the southern region of Malawi emphasizes how the type of crops cultivated differ between men and women (Peters, Herrera and Randolph, 1989). Female-headed households on average cultivate maize on 90% of their land and rarely grow any cash crops, whereas men grow maize on 81% of their land with the remainder mostly under the cash crop tobacco.

Women confront a multitude of *constraints* that are nonexistent or less binding for men which hinder economic opportunities and improved land management (Becker, 1990). For example, both men and women may be constrained in adopting new maize varieties as they require relatively intensive fertilizer inputs as compared to traditional maize. However, female-headed households often have extremely low incomes and are unlikely to be able to raise sufficient financing from their own sources or to obtain credit to purchase hybrid maize and fertilizer (see Table 1). Large labor, demands on women within the household – such as child bearing and rearing, fuel and water collection, cooking, land preparation, planting and weeding – further limits their ability to undertake sound land management – constructing ridging along contours, building bunds, maintaining buffer strips, planting trees and so on. Off-farm employment opportunities for women to supplement farm income may also be constrained by gender discriminations in the labor market; for example, male labor is usually preferred to female labor for wage employment on tobacco estates.

Smallholders in Malawi appear aware of the problems posed by persistent soil erosion – especially farmers cultivating steep slopes who frequently cite problems of run-off and declining yields. Extension advice on how to deal with the problems posed by soil erosion mainly reaches more prosperous, male farmers who are credit club members. Extension messages tend to be very general and are not customized to the needs and requirements of women, particularly the labor and other economic constraints they face. This is indicated in the relatively poor adoption of soil conservation measures by female as opposed to male farmers (see Table 1).

An equally important challenge for economic analysis in the future is to examine the causes of large-scale land use changes and resource degradation. Thus clearing forest land for agriculture is thought to be the major cause of tropical deforestation. A number of economic studies have been launched, particularly in Latin America, to analyze the main factors inducing people to settle in and to clear "frontier" forest lands for agriculture.

For example, Binswanger (1989) and Mahar (1989) make the case for the role of subsidies and tax breaks, particularly for cattle ranching, in encouraging land clearing in the Brazilian Amazon. However, more recent analyses by Schneider et al. (1990) and Reis and Margulis (1990) emphasize the role of agricultural rents, population pressures and road-building in encouraging small-scale frontier settlement. In Northern Brazilian Amazon, the total road network (paved and unpaved) increased from 6,357 to 28,431 km over 1975–88. A simple correlation between road density and the rate of deforestation shows that as road density increases, the rate of deforestation increases in larger proportions (Reis and Margulis, 1990). Schneider et al. argue that these factors encouraging frontier agriculture – "nutrient mining" – far outweigh the more publicized impacts of fiscal incentives for cattle ranching. A statistical analysis by Southgate, Sierra and Brown (1989) of the causes of tropical deforestation in Ecuador indicates that colonists' clear forest land not only in response to demographic pressure but also to "capture" agricultural rents and to safeguard their tenuous legal hold on the land.

Although there are an increasing number of case studies examining the factors behind tropical deforestation and agricultural frontier expansion, there have been few attempts to explore these linkages through statistical analysis. One such analysis by Palo, Mery and Salmi (1987) for 72 tropical forest countries identified a strong link between tropical deforestation and population density, population growth and increased food production. A study by Capistrano (1990) and Capistrano and Kiker (1990) examined the influence of international and domestic macroeconomic factors on tropical deforestation.[8] The econometric analysis indicates the role of high agricultural export prices in inducing agricultural expansion and forest clearing, as well as the influence of domestic structural adjustment policies, such as exchange rate devaluation and increased debt servicing ratios. Comparative analysis of 24 Latin American countries also highlights the strong but indirect relationship between population pressure and frontier expansion – increasing numbers of urban consumers raise the demand for domestic production and hence for agricultural land – and the countervailing role of increased agricultural productivity and yield growth in slowing agricultural expansion (Southgate, 1991). A statistical analysis by Burgess (1991), covering all tropical forest countries, confirms the relative importance of frontier agricultural expansion (represented by an index of food crop and meat production) and debt-servicing on tropical deforestation. Increases in domestic roundwood (representing both industrial use and fuelwood) and GNP per capita also had significant but much smaller positive impacts. Surprisingly, population had a slightly negative effect on deforestation.[9]

Clearly, both microeconomic analysis of individuals' behavior influencing and responses to environmental degradation and

[8] Capistrano (1990) and Capistrano and Kiker (1990) use changes in timber production forest area as a proxy for total deforestation. Although the authors argue that there is a close correlation between average area of closed broadleaved forest and timber production forest area, there are many tropical forest countries where industrial logging is not a significant source of overall deforestation. Thus their analytical results are more relevant to the deforestation of tropical timber production forests than to overall tropical deforestation.

[9] The results of Burgess (1991) indicating that annual increments in population are *negatively* correlated with deforestation conflict with the earlier findings by Palo, Mery and Salmi (1987). Clearly, further work needs to be undertaken to examine the explicit relationship between population growth, population density and deforestation.

macroeconomic analysis of the broader economic-environmental linkages affecting degradation will be required if coherent and effective public policies for natural resource management in developing countries are to be designed and implemented.

IV Conclusion

This paper has argued that efficient and sustainable natural resource management has a vital role to play in economic development and poverty alleviation. Improved economic analysis of both the impacts and the causes underlying environmental degradation will become crucial in the years ahead. Substantial policy distortions and market failures affecting natural resource management in developing countries do exist, and it is necessary to reorient public policies to correct for these distortions as best as possible. However, we should also be cautious in advocating "sweeping" policy changes. For many environmental problems in developing countries, we are not even at the state of "optimal ignorance" to begin advocating new policy directions. More difficult is the problem of "political will"; even when the economic evidence is clear and the policy direction self-evident, short-term political and economic interests in developing countries may predominate – especially when powerful special interest groups have a vested interest in maintaining the *status quo*.

Bibliography

Anderson, D. 1987. *The Economics of Afforestation.* Baltimore: Johns Hopkins University Press.

———. 1990. "Environmental Policy and the Public Revenue in Developing Countries." Environment Working Paper No. 36. Washington D.C.: The World Bank.

Barbier, E.B. 1989a. *Economics, Natural-Resource Scarcity and Development: Conventional and Alternative Views.* London: Earthscan.

———. 1989b. "Sustainable Agriculture on Marginal Land: A Policy Framework." *Environment* 31(9): 12–17 and 36–40.

———. 1990a. "The Economics of Controlling Degradation: Rehabilitating Gum Arabic Systems in Sudan." LEEC Discussion Paper 90-03. London: London Environmental Economics Centre.

———. 1990b. "The Farm-Level Economics of Soil Erosion: The Uplands of Java." *Land Economics* 66(9): 199–211.

———. 1991. "Environmental Degradation in the Third World." In: D.W. Pearce et al., *Blueprint 2: Greening the World Economy*. London: Earthscan.

Barbier, E.B., W.M. Adams and K. Kimmage. 1991. "Economic Valuation of Wetland Benefits: The Hadejia-Jama'are Floodplain, Nigeria." LEEC Discussion Paper 91-02. London: London Environmental Economics Centre.

Barbier, E.B. and J.C. Burgess. 1990. *Malawi-Land Degradation in Agriculture*. Report to the World Bank Economic Mission of Environmental Policy, Malawi Country Operations Division, The World Bank, Washington D.C.

Becker, H. 1990. "Labour Input Decisions of Subsistence Farm Households in Southern Malawi." *Journal of Agricultural Economics* 41(2): 162–171.

Binswanger, H. 1989. "Brazilian Policies that Encourage Deforestation in the Amazon." Environment Department Working Paper No. 16. Washington D.C.: The World Bank.

Bishop, J. 1990. *The Costs of Soil Erosion in Malawi*. Washington D.C.: Malawi Country Operations Division, The World Bank.

Bishop, J. and J. Allen. 1989. "The On-Site Costs of Soil Erosion in Mali." Environment Department Working Paper No. 21. Washington D.C.: The World Bank.

Bojo, J., K.-G. Maler and L. Unemo. 1990. *Environment and Development: An Economic Approach*. Dordrecht: Kluwer Academic.

Browder, J.O. 1985. *Subsidies, Deforestation, and the Forest Sector in the Brazilian Amazon*. Washington D.C.: World Resources Institute.

Burgess, J.C. 1991. "Economic Analysis of Frontier Agricultural Expansion and Tropical Deforestation." M.Sc. Thesis, Economics Dept., University College London, London.

Cairncross, S., J.E. Hardoy and D. Satterthwaite. 1990. "The Urban Context." In: Hardoy, J.E., Cairncross, J.E. and Satterthwaite, D., *The Poor Die Young: Housing and Health in Third World Cities*. London: Earthscan.

Capistrano, A.D. 1990. "Macroeconomic Influences on Tropical Forest Depletion: A Cross-Country Analysis." Ph.D. Dissertation, Food and Resource Economics Dept., University of Florida, Miami.

Capistrano, A.D. and C.F. Kiker. 1990. "Global Economic Influences on Tropical Closed Broadleaved Forest Depletion, 1967–85." Mimeo, Food and Resource Economics Dept., University of Florida, Miami.

Chambers, R. 1987. "Sustainable Livelihoods, Environment and Development: Putting Poor Rural People First." Discussion Paper 240. Institute of Development Studies, University of Sussex, Brighton.

Conway, G.R. and E.B. Barbier. 1990. *After the Green Revolution: Sustainable Agriculture for Development*. London: Earthscan.

Dixon, J.A., R.A. Carpenter, L.A. Fallon, P.B. Sherman and S. Manipomoke. 1988. *Economic Analysis of the Environmental Impacts of Development Projects*. London: Earthscan.

Dixon, J., D. James and P. Sherman. 1989. *The Economics of Dryland Management*. London: Earthscan.

FAO. 1990. "Sustainable Development and Natural Resource Management." Part Three in *The State of Food and Agriculture, 1989*. Rome: FAO.

Foy, G. and H. Daly. 1989. "Allocation, Distribution and Scale as Determinants of Environmental Degradation: Case Studies of Haiti, E1 Salvador and Costa Rica." Environment Department Working Paper No. 19. Washington D.C.: The World Bank.

Gregersen, H.M., K.N. Brooks, J.A. Dixon and L.S. Hamilton. 1987. *Guidelines for Economic Appraisal of Watershed Management Projects*. Rome: FAO.

Hardoy, J.E., S. Cairncross and D. Satterthwaite, (eds.). 1990. *The Poor Die Young: Housing and Health in Third World Cities*. London: Earthscan.

Hardoy, J.E. and D. Satterthwaite. 1989. *Squatter Citizen: Life in the Urban Third World*. London: Earthscan.

IIED/IES. 1990. *Gum Arabic Rehabilitation Project in the Republic of Sudan: Stage I Report*. London: IIED.

Jagannathan, N.V. 1989. "Poverty, Public Policies and the Environment." Environment Working Paper No. 24. Washington D.C.: The World Bank.

Kates, R.W. 1990. "Hunger, Poverty and the Environment." Paper presented at the Distinguished Speaker Series, Center for Advanced Study of International Development, Michigan State University, Lansing, May 6.

Lallement, D. 1990. *Burkina Faso: Economic Issues in Renewable Natural Resource Management*. Washington D.C.: Agricultural Operations, Sahelian Department, Africa Region, The World Bank.

Leonard, H.J., with M. Yudelman, J.D. Stryker, J.O. Browder, A.J. De Boer, T. Campbell and A. Jolly. 1989. *Environment and the Poor: Development Strategies for a Common Agenda*. New Brunswick: Transaction Books.

Lipton, M. 1983. "Labour and Poverty." World Bank Staff Working Papers No. 616. Washington D.C.: The World Bank.

———. 1988. "The Poor and the Poorest: Some Interim Findings." World Bank Discussion Papers No. 25. Washington D.C.: The World Bank.

Magrath, W.B. and P. Arens. 1987. *The Costs of Soil Erosion on Java – A Natural Resource Accounting Approach*. Washington D.C.: World Resources Institute.

Mahar, D. 1989. *Government Policies and Deforestation in Brazil's Amazon Region*. Washington D.C.: The World Bank.

Mortimore, M. 1989. "The Causes, Nature and Rate of Soil Degradation in the Northernmost States of Nigeria and an Assessment of the Role of Fertilizer in Counteracting the Processes of Degradation. "Environment Department Working Paper No. 17. Washington D.C.: The World Bank.

Nelson, R. 1988. "Dryland Management: The 'Desertification' Problem. "Environment Department Working Paper No. 8. Washington D.C.: World Bank.

Palo, M., G. Mery and J. Salmi. 1987. "Deforestation in the Tropics: Pilot Scenarios Based on Quantitative Analysis." In: M. Palo and J. Salmi (eds.), *Deforestation or Development in the Third World*. Helsinki: Division of Social Economics of Forestry, Finnish Forestry Research.

Panayotou, T. 1990. "Policies, Incentives and Regulations: The Use of Fiscal Incentives." Conference on Environmental Management in Developing Countries, OECD Development Centre, Paris, October 3–5.

Paris, R. and I. Ruzicka. 1991. "Barking Up the Wrong Tree: The Role of Recent Appropriation in Tropical Forest Management." Environment Office Discussion Paper, Asian Development Bank, Manila.

Pearce, D.W. 1990. "Policies, Incentives and Regulations: Recent Thinking in OECD Countries." Conference on Environmental Management in Developing Countries, OECD Development Centre, Paris, October 3–5.

———. 1991. "Population Growth." In: D.W. Pearce et al. (eds.), *Blueprint 2: The Greening of the World Economy*. London: Earthscan.

Pearce, D.W., E.B. Barbier and A. Markandya. 1990. *Sustainable Development: Economics and Environment in the Third World*. London: Edward Elgar.

Pearce, D.W., E.B. Barbier, A. Markandya, S. Barrett, R.K. Turner and T. Swanson. 1991. *Blueprint 2: The Greening of the World Economy*. London: Earthscan.

Pearce, D.W. and J.J. Warford. 1991. *Environment and Economic Development: The Sustainable Management of Natural Resources in the Developing World*. Washington D.C.: World Bank (forthcoming).

Peters, P.E., M.G. Herrera and T.F. Randolph. 1989. *Cash Cropping, Food Security and Nutrition: The Effects of Agricultural Commercialization Among Smallholders in Malawi*. Report to the U.S. Agency for International Development, Harvard Institute for International Development, Cambridge, Mass.

Reis, E. and S. Margulis. 1990. "Options for Slowing Amazon Jungle-Clearing." Paper presented at the Conference on *Economic Policy Responses to Global Warming*, Rome, 5–7 September.

Repetto, R. 1987. "Population, Resources, Environment: An Uncertain Future." *Population Bulletin* 42(2).

———. 1988. "Economic Policy Reform for Natural Resource Conservation. "Environment Department Working Paper No. 4. Washington D.C.: World Bank

Repetto, R. and M. Gillis, (eds). 1988. *Public Policies and the Misuse of Forest Resources*. Cambridge: Cambridge University Press.

Repetto, R. and Holmes. 1983. "The Role of Population in Resource Depletion in Developing Countries." *Population and Development Review* 9(4):609–632.

Richards, P. 1985. *Indigenous Agricultural Revolution*. London: Hutchinson.

Southgate, D. 1988. "The Economics of Land Degradation in the Third World." Environment Department Working Paper No. 2. Washington D.C.: The World Bank.

———. 1991. "Tropical Deforestation and Agriculture Development in Latin America." LEEC Discussion Paper 91-01. London: London Environmental Economics Centre.

Southgate, D., R. Sierra and L. Brown. 1989. "The Causes of Tropical Deforestation in Ecuador: A Statistical Analysis." LEEC Discussion Paper 89-09. London: London Environmental Economics Centre.

Wilson, K.B. 1988. "Indigenous Conservation in Zimbabwe: Soil Erosion, Land-use Planning and Rural Life." Paper submitted to the Panel Session *Conser-*

vation and Rural People, African Studies Association of UK Conference, 14 September.

World Bank. 1989. "Malawi–Country Economic Memorandum: Growth through Poverty Reduction." Washington, D.C.

Part III
Trade Issues

The Impact of Domestic Environmental Policy on International Trade

James A. Tobey*

Introduction

The trade impact of policy measures to protect the environment has been the subject of some concern and discussion ever since the late 1960s when most industrialized countries first began introducing serious pollution control programs. Some of these concerns were voiced at the 1972 United Nations Stockholm Conference on Development and Environment. At that time it was stated that (United Nations, 1972):

> Environmental issues are going to exercise a growing influence on international economic relations. They are not only a formidable competitor for developed countries' resources but they are also a factor which is, to an ever increasing degree, going to influence the pattern of world trade, the international locations of industry, the competitive position of different groups of countries, and their comparative costs of production. Environmental actions by developed countries are going to have a profound and manifold impact on the growth and external economic relations of developing countries.

Trade effects of environmental policies have been explored in some detail using standard models of international trade (Asako, 1979; McGuire, 1982; Pethig, 1976; Siebert, 1974). It has been shown that environmental control costs encourage reduced specialization in the production of polluting outputs in countries with

---

* This paper, though new, draws heavily on my previous paper, "The Effects of Domestic Environmental Policies on Patterns of World Trade: An Empirical Test," *Kyklos*, Vol. 43, No. 2, 1990. The views expressed in this paper are those of the author alone and should not be attributed to the U.S. Council on Environmental Quality.

stringent environmental regulations. In contrast, countries that fail to undertake an environmental protection program should increase their comparative advantage in the production of items that damage the environment. These potential trade effects have a strong element of a priori plausibility and proposed environmental regulations are, in fact, often opposed vigorously on the grounds that they will impair the international competitiveness of domestic industries.

The magnitude of any impact of domestic environmental policies on international competitiveness is an empirical issue. Some studies have made use of existing input-output (I-O) and multisector macroeconometric models to assess the likely magnitude of the trade effects of environmental controls (D'Arge, 1974; Robison, 1986; OECD, 1985). These studies use estimates of the costs of pollution control programs on an industry basis to get some sense of the likely effects of these programs on trade and payment flows. Generally, they find small, but measurable, effects. One report (OECD, 1985) finds that pollution control measures in France, the Netherlands, and the United States may have reduced the level of total exports by approximately one-half to one percentage point; no change, or only very slight effects were found for Austria, Finland, and Norway.

Other studies, relying on ex post assessments of the historical evidence have not been able to confirm the predicted trade effects of environmental policy. One methodology for addressing this issue involves the study of trade and foreign-investment flows for several key industries and countries. These "location of industry" studies (Leonard, 1988; Pearson, 1987, 1985; Walter, 1985) have found little evidence that pollution-control measures have exerted a systematic effect on international trade and investment. Leonard (1988) observes that the differentials in the costs of complying with environmental regulations in industrialized and industrializing countries have not been sufficiently large to offset larger political and economic forces in shaping international comparative advantage. These forces include, for example, access to markets, raw material supplies, political stability, availability of supporting infrastructure, and transport costs.

In this paper, an ex post assessment of the impact of environmental regulation on patterns of international trade is conducted using the Heckscher-Ohlin-Vanek (HOV) model of international trade. A growing number of applied trade efforts have employed this framework to conduct empirical tests of the sources of international comparative advantage (Leamer, 1984; Bowen, 1983; Murrell, 1990).

The paper first identifies the commodities to be studied and the HOV equations that form the framework for the empirical tests. Then, several empirical tests are conducted. Finally, the empirical results are interpreted, and, the question of potential future impacts is addressed.

I Identification of Pollution-Intensive Commodities

Commodities whose production draws heavily on environmental resources – termed "pollution-intensive" commodities – can be identified by the pollution-abatement costs incurred in their production. Direct pollution abatement costs are reported by the U.S. Department of Commerce (1975) and the Environmental Protection Agency (1984). In addition to the direct pollution abatement costs, we also need to consider the abatement costs embodied in intermediate goods purchases, or the indirect pollution abatement costs. By multiplying direct pollution abatement costs by the total expenditures I-O table, others have generated an estimate of total (direct and indirect) pollution abatement costs per dollar of industrial output (Kalt, 1985; Robison, 1986).

Commodities termed pollution intensive are defined as the products of those industries whose abatement costs in the U.S. are equal to or greater than 1.85 percent of total costs. The cut-off of 1.85 percent is chosen because it results in a set of industries that are generally considered the most polluting (metals, chemicals, and paper industries) throughout the world.[1] Moreover, there is a considerable difference between the pollution-abatement costs in these industries and in those of the remaining group of industries.

[1] This cut-off does not include the petroleum industry. Petroleum is excluded because it is believed that the dynamics of this industry during this time (early to mid-1970's) were heavily influenced by extraordinary circumstances affecting the availability and processing of crude oil.

Table 1

I-O Industry	SITC	Description	Direct and Indirect Pollution Abatement Costs as Percentage of Total Costs[1]
	Mining		
5	281	Iron ore, concentrates	2.03
6	283	Ores of nonferrous base metals	1.92
	Primary Nonferrous Metals		
38	681	Silver, platinum	2.05
38	682	Copper	2.05
38	683	Nickel	2.05
38	685	Lead	2.05
38	686	Zinc	2.05
38	687	Tin	2.05
38	689	Nonferrous base metals, n.e.s.	2.05
	Paper and Pulp		
24	251	Pulp and waste paper	2.40
24	641	Paper and paperboard	2.40
24	642	Articles of paper	2.40
	Primary Iron and Steel		
37	671	Pig iron	2.38
37	672	Ingots	2.38
37	673	Iron and steel bars	2.38
37	674	Universals, plates	2.38
37	675	Hoops and strips	2.38
37	676	Railway material	2.38
37	677	Iron and steel wire	2.38
37	678	Tubes and fittings	2.38
37	679	Iron, steel castings	2.38
	Chemicals		
27	513	Inorganic elements	2.89
27	514	Other inorganic chemicals	2.89
28	581	Plastic materials	2.36

[1] Kalt (1985)

In Table 1, the input-output industries defined as pollution-intensive are matched to 3-digit SITC commodities and aggregated into five commodity groups, including paper and pulp products (paper), mining of ores (mining), primary iron and steel (steel), primary nonferrous metals (nfmetals), and chemicals (chems).

II The Heckscher-Ohlin-Vanek Equations

The HOV equations are a multifactor, multicommodity extension of the Heckscher-Ohlin model of international trade. They have been used in several different ways. The factor content studies and cross-commodity regressions use measures of factor intensities and trade to infer factor endowments. The third methodology and the approach taken in this study, regresses trade in a specific commodity across countries on country characteristics, or, resource endowments. In that resource endowments are the explanatory variables, such regressions reveal the direct influence of resources on trade in a specific commodity. Since this study seeks to reveal information on the most pollution-intensive commodities across countries, the cross-country analysis is chosen as the most appropriate approach.

To derive the HOV equations we specify world production, consumption, income, and trade relationships, and solve for net exports. It is assumed that each country produces I commodities and that the quantity of each commodity produced is a function of the quantity of primary factors used in a sector. The relative endowments of factors varies from country to country. Given these assumptions, production is represented by:

$$Q_{it} = \sum_{k=1}^{K} a_{ki} V_{kt}$$

where Q_{it} is the production of commodity i in country t, a_{ki} is the amount of resource k used to produce one unit of commodity i, and V_{kt} is country t's endowment of factor k.

Consumption is represented by $C_{it} = c_i G_t$, where C_{it} is the consumption of commodity i by country t, c_i is the proportion of national income spent on good i, and G_t is the national income of country t.

Income is represented by:

$$G_t = \sum_{i=1}^{N} p_i Q_{it}$$

where p_i is the price of good i.

Finally, trade is represented by $N_{it} = Q_{it} - C_{it}$, where N_{it} are net exports of commodity i by country t.

Substituting equations for production, consumption, and income into the trade equation it is possible to obtain the following HOV equation:

$$N_{it} = \sum_{k=1}^{K} \left(a_{ik} - c_i \sum_{i=1}^{N} p_i a_{ik} \right)^* V_{kt} = b_{ik} V_{kt}$$

where $b_{ik} = a_{ik} - c_i \sum_{i=1}^{N} p_i a_{ik}$.

A set of eleven resource endowments for the year 1975 is used to explain net exports of the most polluting industries under the HOV model. These endowments are provided by Leamer (1984) and include:

1. CAPITAL (CAP) Accumulated and discounted gross domestic investment flows since 1948, assuming an average life of 15 years.
2. LABOR 1 (LAB1) Number of workers classified as professional or technical.
3. LABOR 2 (LAB2) Number of literate nonprofessional workers.
4. LABOR 3 (LAB3) Number of illiterate workers.
5. LAND 1 (LND1) Land area in tropical rainy climate zone.
6. LAND 2 (LND2) Land area in dry climate zone.
7. LAND 3 (LND3) Land are in humid mesothermal climate zone.
8. LAND 4 (LND4) Land area in humid microthermal climate.
9. COAL (COAL) Value of production of primary solid fuels (coal, lignite, and brown coal).
10. MINERALS (MINLS) Value of production of minerals: bauxite, copper, flourspar, iron ore, lead, manganese, nickel, potash, pyrite, salt, tin, and zinc.
11. OIL (OIL) Value of oil and gas production.

With the endowments from Leamer, the HOV model can be summarized as follows:

$$N_{it} = \mathrm{CST}_{i0} + b_{i1}V_{1t} + b_{i2}V_{2t} + \cdots + b_{i11}V_{11t} + \mu_{it} \tag{1}$$

where b_{ik} are the coefficients which indicate the total effect (production and consumption) of an increase in a resource on net trade of a specific commodity, μ_{it} is the disturbance term, and CST_{i0} is the equation's constant term.

If the environmental endowment, measured by the stringency of environmental regulation, has an effect on trade patterns then the set of eleven endowments in equation (1) is incomplete.[2] In this case, estimation of the HOV trade equations implies a specification error involving an omitted variable. Several approaches are taken to test the effect of the environmental endowment on trade patterns under the HOV model when cross-country quantitative data on the environmental endowment are not available. In the first, a qualitative variable is included in equation (1) to represent the omitted variable; in the second, an omitted variable test is conducted, and, in the third, a fixed-effects test is undertaken.

III Introducing "Environmental Endowments" in the HOV Model

To test the pollution haven hypothesis under the first approach, the following equation is estimated using ordinary least squares (OLS):

$$N_{it} = \mathrm{CST}_{i0} + b_{i1}V_{1t} + b_{i2}V_{2t} + \cdots + b_{i11}V_{11t} + b_{iE}D_{Et} + \mu_{it} \tag{2}$$

---

[2] Although pollution emissions are a joint product of the production process, they can also be interpreted as an input, or endowment, in the production function because they can be viewed as one of the various uses of the environment (Baumol and Oates, 1988). Since use of the environment is typically a public good, the environmental endowment has no price attached to it and will be used freely by industries until pollution control measures are introduced. Thus, a country's environmental endowment can be measured by its stringency of pollution control measures.

Table 2. Index of the Degree of Stringency of Environmental Policy
(7 = strict, 1 = tolerant)

Industrialized Countries		Index	Less Developed Countries		Index
1	Austria	4	1	Chile	4
2	Australia	5	2	Columbia	5
3	Belux	3	3	Cyprus	1
4	Denmark	5	4	Israel	4
5	Finland	6	5	Liberia	1
6	Germany	5	6	Malta	1
7	Japan	7	7	Nigeria	2
8	New Zealand	5	8	Panama	4
9	Netherlands	5	9	Singapore	6
10	Norway	6	10	Spain	4
11	Sweden	7			
12	UK	4			
13	USA	7			

Source: Walter and Ugelow (1979).

where D_{Et} is a qualitative variable measuring the stringency of pollution control measures in country t based on an UNCTAD survey described in Walter and Ugelow (1979).

The degree of environmental stringency is measured on a scale from one (tolerant) to seven (strict); the mean score for developed countries is 6.1, while for developing countries it is 3.1. There are observations for 23 countries; 13 industrialized and 10 developing countries (Table 2).

The OLS regression results are presented in Table 3 (absolute value of the t ratio shown in parentheses beside the estimated regression coefficient). In no instance is the t ratio found to be statistically significant on the measure for the stringency of environmental policy in the five regressions of net exports of polluting industries.

Aside from the Walter and Ugelow index, no cross-country data or synthetic measures of the stringency of environmental policies are available. However, to extend the analysis to a larger group of countries, equation (2) was estimated using a dummy variable (equal to one for industrialized countries with enforced environmental regulations, and zero for developing countries with-

Table 3. Equations (D.F. = 10)

Variable Name	Mining ($R^2 = 0.99$)	Paper ($R^2 = 0.96$)	Chems ($R^2 = 0.93$)	Steel ($R^2 = 0.89$)	NFMetals ($R^2 = 0.92$)
CAP	−192(2.4)	177(1.6)	583(5.6)	1537(2.6)	−89(1.0)
LAB1	735(1.9)	−267(0.5)	981(1.9)	−1434(0.5)	−550(1.2)
LAB2	−111(3.2)	−25(0.5)	−154(3.5)	54(0.2)	44(1.1)
LAB3	−15(0.6)	50(1.5)	−49(1.6)	84(0.5)	69(2.5)
LND1	385(1:5)	278(0.8)	521(1.6)	237(0.1)	−254(0.9)
LND2	−104(0.7)	−192(1.0)	−31(0.2)	503(0.5)	−247(1.5)
LND3	1295(2.8)	100(0.2)	−268(0.5)	−2898(0.9)	−414(0.8)
LND4	435(0.9)	6089(9.2)	−2003(3.2)	−1374(0.4)	−589(1.1)
COAL	−78(0.6)	−110(0.6)	−283(1.6)	−83(0.1)	88(0.6)
MINLS	338(1.6)	330(1.4)	88(0.4)	26(0.1)	715(3.7)
OIL	−30(1.6)	−110(4.3)	−20(0.8)	−142(1.0)	17(0.8)
D	−10314(0.3)	2454(0.1)	−1531(0.1)	98844(0.4)	48658(1.3)
CST	−5669(0.1)	−168370(1.0)	−107110(0.7)	−697020(0.8)	−122980(0.9)

out enforced environmental regulations) for a group of 58 countries – 17 industrialized and 41 developing. The dummy variable was not statistically significant in any of the five HOV equations.

IV Omitted Variable Test

A second approach to testing the effect of pollution control measures on trade patterns investigates the bias in the regression residuals when the variable representing counties' environmental endowments are not included in the HOV equations.

Consider first a simple HOV equation with one known and one unknown independent variable. Let x_{t2} represent a factor endowment for country t. Under the null hypothesis that the environmental factor (x_{t3}) has no effect on the pattern of trade, the equation specifying net exports (N_t) may be written as:

$$N_t = \beta_1 + \beta_2 x_{t2} + \tilde{\mu}_t. \qquad (3)$$

The alternative to the null hypothesis is represented by the following equation:

$$N_t = \beta_1 + \beta_2 x_{t2} + \beta_3 x_{t3} + \mu_t. \qquad (4)$$

If equation (3) is correct, the least squares estimators of β_1 and β_2 using equation (3) will be unbiased and efficient for all sample sizes. If equation (4) is correct, the estimation of equation (3) will still generate an unbiased estimator or β_2 given the following assumption:

A1: The omitted variable is not correlated with any of the included independent variables.

Given assumption A1, estimation of equation (3) when the omitted variable (x_{t3}) does not equal zero will not affect β_2. Its presence will, however, be embodied in the constant and disturbance term. Solving for $\tilde{\mu}_t$, the following equation can be derived:

$$\tilde{\mu}_t = \beta_3(x_{t3} - \overline{X}_3) + \mu_t. \tag{5}$$

Under the null hypothesis that x_{t3} has no effect on the pattern of trade, so that $\beta_3 = 0$, $\tilde{\mu}_t$ is a consistent estimator of μ_t. Under the alternative case where pollution control measures have an effect on the pattern of trade, so that $\beta_3 \neq 0$, then (given assumption A1) $\tilde{\mu}_t$ provides a consistent estimate of equation (5).

A methodology to test the effect of pollution control measures on the pattern of trade may now be presented. Under the alternative hypothesis that equation (4) is correctly specified and assuming it also has all the properties of the classical regression model, then the sign of μ_t is expected to be random. Therefore, the expected sign of $\tilde{\mu}_t$ in equation (5) is the same as that of $\beta_3(x_{t3} - \overline{X}_3)$. β_3 is expected to be negative if pollution control measures reduce net exports of pollution-intensive commodities. To determine the sign of $x_{t3} - \overline{X}_3$, consider the distribution of the stringency of environmental regulations, x_{t3}, over the world. Industrialized, high-income countries have environmental endowments greater than the population mean, $\overline{X}_3$, and less-developed countries have environmental endowments less than the population mean. Thus, the pattern of sign of $\tilde{\mu}_t$ under the alternative hypothesis depends on the distribution of x_{t3} over countries. Given the distribution suggested above, the proportion of error terms that are positive for developing countries is expected to be significantly greater than the proportion of error terms that are positive for industrialized countries.

Let T_n represent the true proportion of errors for countries in group n (where $n = 1$ corresponds to industrialized countries and

$n = 2$ corresponds to developing countries). The null hypothesis (H_0) states that the proportion of errors that are positive is the same for both industrialized and developing countries. The alternative hypothesis (H_1) states that the proportion of such errors is greater for developing countries than for industrialized countries.

$$H_0: T_2 = T_1$$

$$H_1: T_2 > T_1.$$

A nonparametric statistical procedure was chosen to conduct the statistical test because it requires few assumptions regarding the distribution of the error terms. Under the null hypothesis, the test statistic may be given as:[3]

$$A = \frac{R_2 - R_1}{[T \times (1 - T)[(1/I \times J_2) + (1/I \times J_1)]]^{1/2}}$$

where $R_n = S_n/(I \times J_n)$ represents the proportion of estimated errors that are positive; I equals the total number of commodity groups ($= 5$), J_n equals the total number of countries in country group n; and, S_n equals the number of estimated error terms for countries in group n that are positive.

T is an estimate of the true proportion under the null hypothesis. The best estimate of the true population proportion is constructed by combining the observations for both industrialized and developing countries as follows:

$$T = (S_1 + S_2)/(I \times (J_1 + J_2)).$$

To perform the omitted variable test, a set of 58 countries is arranged in three groups (Table 4). Group one consisted of industrialized, high-income countries. Environmental regulatory costs in this group are predicted to generate a comparative disadvantage in the production of polluting commodities. Group two is composed of upper-income developing countries and semi-industrialized nations without a stringent environmental program in 1975. Group three is composed of middle to low-income developing countries, also without stringent environmental programs.

---

[3] See Yamane (1967).

Table 4. Country Observations

Country	GDP per capita[1]	Country	GDP per capita[1]	Country	GDP per capita[1]
		(1975 constant US$)			
Group One		Group Two		Group Three	
Australia	5,919	Argentina	3,159	Afghanistan	380
Austria	4,994	Brazil	1,978	Burma	312
Belux	5,569	Chile	1,834	Colombia	1,596
Canada	6,788	Costa Rica	1,835	Dom Rep	1,443
Denmark	5,969	Cyprus	1,811	Ecuador	1,300
Finland	5,192	Greece	3,360	Egypt	929
France	5,864	Hong Kong	2,559	El Salvador	1,005
Germany	5,758	Ireland	3,067	Ghana	952
Iceland	5,201	Israel	4,154	Honduras	871
Japan	4,904	Italy	3,870	India	472
Netherlands	5,321	Malta	2,154	Indonesia	536
New Zealand	4,769	Mexico	2,276	Jamaica	1,763
Norway	5,419	Panama	2,026	Korea	1,530
Sweden	6,749	Peru	1,860	Liberia	830
Switzerland	6,082	Portugal	2,397	Lybia	6,680[2]
UK	4,601	Singapore	2,875	Malaysia	1,532
USA	7,132	Spain	4,032	Mauritius	1,260
AVERAGE	5,661	Turkey	1,738	Nigeria	1,179
		Yugoslavia	1,960[2]	Paraguay	1,186
		AVERAGE	2,567	Philippines	912
				Sri Lanka	661
				Thailand	930
				AVERAGE	1,002[3]

[1] Heston and Summers (1984).

[2] 1977 GNP per capita, from World Bank, 1979 *World Development Report.*

[3] Excluding Libya.

A summary of the results when equation (1) is estimated using this set of 58 countries is shown in Table 5. It is not possible to reject the null hypothesis that $T_2 = T_1$ in the comparison of industrialized countries with any combination of the developing country groups. These results reinforce the earlier finding that used a qualitative variable to represent the environmental endowment and which also found no effect of pollution control measures on HOV trade patterns.

Table 5. Positive Residuals

Country Group	Paper	Steel	Chems	NFMetals	Mining	S_n[1]	J_n[2]	R_n[3]	A[4]
One	7	9	5	8	11	40	17	0.47	—
Two	5	10	9	5	6	35	19	0.37	−1.32
Three	10	18	15	5	11	59	22	0.54	0.96
2 + 3	15	28	24	10	17	94	41	0.45	−0.15

[1] S_n is the number of errors for group n that are positive.
[2] J_n is the number of countries in group n.
[3] $R_n = S_n/(I \times J_n)$.
[4] A is the test statistic comparing group one countries against groups of developing countries. An absolute value of 1.65 for the test statistic in the normal distribution corresponds to a probability of 95 percent.

V Fixed Effects Empirical Test

A reasonable explanation for the empirical results above may be that the magnitude of environmental expenditures incurred by the industrialized countries in the late 1960s and early 1970s was not sufficiently large to cause a noticeable effect on trade patterns between countries with and without environmental protection programs. The cross-section HOV model may not be sufficiently precise to identify these small changes in factor abundances and comparative advantage. Thus, the effect of domestic environmental policy on trade may be getting lost in the "noise." By examining the change in trade patterns before and after the introduction of environmental measures in the industrialized countries, one might be able to detect the hypothesized shifts in trade patterns in response to environmental policies that do not show up in the equations using data from a specific point in time. Such a methodology would also be effective in capturing the effect of environmental policy even if there was a significant lag in the impact of pollution controls on international competitiveness.

Although endowment data are only available for the year 1975, most resource endowments change little over time. At least for the most polluting industries, one might argue that the most important endowment change over the period 1970 to 1984 was the increase in environmental regulations. Consider then a HOV

Table 6. Equations (D.F. = 22)

Variable Name	Mining ($R^2 = 0.03$)	Paper ($R^2 = 0.0+$)	Chems ($R^2 = 0.05$)	Steel ($R^2 = 0.0+$)	NFMetals ($R^2 = 0.04$)
E	−54155 (1.1)	−2298 (0.1)	78007 (1.9)	49437 (0.4)	−65593 (1.1)

model where the change in net exports over 1970–84 is linearly related to the change in factor endowments over the same period. Under a "fixed-effects" specification, assume that, except for the environmental endowment, the change in factor endowments equals zero. In this case, one is left with the following equations:

$$\Delta N_{it} = E_t + \mu_{it} \tag{6}$$

where ΔN_{it} is 1984 minus 1970 net exports of commodity i by country t. E_t is the Walter and Ugelow (1979) measure of the degree of the stringency of environmental policy in 23 countries in 1977. Since these countries generally did not have significant and enforced environmental programs in place by 1970, the level of environmental policy given by this index is a reasonable proxy for the change in environmental policy. Finally, μ_{it} is the random error terms.

The results of the OLS estimation of this model are shown in Table 6. If environmental policies reduce countries' international comparative advantage in the most pollution-intensive commodities, then the sign on the environmental endowment coefficient should be negative and significant. Only in the chemicals group does the significance of the coefficient approach a conventionally accepted level of confidence. The sign, however, is positive, and once again does not support the hypothesized impact of pollution control measures on trade patterns.

VI Alternative Structural Forms

Another possibility for the above results may be that the commodity groups studied flagrantly violate the assumptions of the HOV model. The HOV model assumes that commodities move internationally at zero cost of transportation, and that there are no other impediments to trade. However, transportation costs and tariffs are important elements in these industries and may significantly affect an individual country's composition of trade. This would not present a problem for the tests undertaken above if it is the case that these trade impediments are not distributed across countries in the same pattern as environmental controls. In the absence of empirical evidence (trade impediments are very difficult to measure for large sets of countries) there is no reason to believe that their distribution would be closely correlated with the stringency of countries' environmental controls.

Perhaps more worrisome is the HOV assumption of identical homothetic tastes – meaning that individuals facing identical commodity prices will consume commodities in the same proportions. In this cross-section study, with countries at widely different levels of development, this assumption may not be reasonable. To allow for nonhomothetic preferences, consumption across countries is assumed to be a linear function of population and national income. In this case, per capita net exports, n_{it}, become a linear function of per capita resource endowments, v_{kt}, as given by the following equation:

$$n_{it} = b_{i0}^{*} + \left(\sum_{k=1}^{K} b_{ik} v_{kt}\right) \tag{7}$$

where $b_{i0}^{*} = -c_{i0}$, and c_{i0} is a parameter that relates consumption of commodity i in country t to country t's population. As before, b_{ik} indicates the total effect of an increase in a resource on net trade of a specific commodity.

The HOV model also assumes that production functions exhibit constant returns to scale. However, Hufbauer (1970) has found the production of paper products to be subject to large economies of scale and the production of nonferrous metals to be subject to diseconomies of scale. To allow for scale economies, I use a model that Murrell (1990) derives and that follows Helpman and Krugman (1986) closely. It is assumed that each good can be produced in an infinite number of varieties and each variety exhibits economies of scale, at least at low levels of output. In this case, the exports of good i by country t, x_{it}, are specified as follows:

$$x_{it} = \sum_{k=1}^{K} b_{ik}^{*} v_{kt}(1 - G_t/G_w) \tag{8}$$

where G_t is the national income of country t and G_w is total world income. Equation (8) cannot be derived from the Heckscher-Ohlin theory and the asterisks on the coefficients of the equation are a reminder that these coefficients are not equivalent to b_{ik} in the previous HOV models.

The HOV model was tested under two sets of equations that allow for economies of scale and nonhomothetic preferences. Again, the tests did *not* support the hypothesis under review.

VII Interpretation of the Empirical Results

The empirical results found in this paper support other similar efforts that find that environmental management has had relatively little effect on trade. As Oates and Cropper (1990) observe, this is a comforting finding from an environmental perspective, for it means that there is little force to the argument that we need to relax environmental policies to preserve international competitiveness. The primary reason seems to be that the costs of pollution control have not been very large even in heavily polluting industries and countries with stringent pollution control policies. Existing estimates (Table 1) suggest that control costs in the United States have run on the order of only 2 to 2.5 percent of total costs in most pollution-intensive industries. The HOV model is probably not sufficiently precise to capture these small increments to costs; their impact on international trade is likely to be swamped by other considerations such as swings in exchange rates, for example. Moreover, international comparisons of environmental regulations show that nearly all the industrialized countries have introduced similar environmental measures, and at roughly the same time, so that such measures have not been the source of significant cost differentials among major competitors (Kopp et al., 1990; Walter and Ugelow, 1979; Tobey, 1989). Nor has there been a discernible movement in investment in these industries to the developing countries because other political and economic forces have tended to play much greater roles in location decisions than the modest savings from less stringent environmental controls have (Leonard, 1988).

VIII Future Effects

It is generally acknowledged that the marginal costs of pollution abatement increase slowly at first, but that increasingly greater levels of environmental quality can only be achieved at increasingly greater costs. The small impacts so far on competitiveness and trade seem to suggest that, for the present, the United States and other industrialized countries find themselves on the relatively flat portion of the marginal abatement cost curve, where additional increments in environmental quality are achieved at little extra cost.

There is some evidence that there are fewer opportunities for inexpensive increments to the level of environmental quality than there have been in the past. Oates et al. (1989) have estimated marginal abatement cost curves for controlling a common air pollutant (total suspended particulates) in Baltimore under the command-and-control and an incentive-based approach. In both cases, the marginal abatement cost curves are fairly flat over a low range of environmental quality levels, but eventually begin to rise steeply as emissions are increasingly reduced to achieve greater levels of environmental quality. Further, the intersection of marginal benefits and marginal costs of pollution abatement is located at the base of the steep portion of the marginal cost curve, implying that further shifts in the demand for environmental quality would entail large increases in control costs. One could speculate that more stringent environmental legislation might push industry to a new point on the marginal cost curve that would require significantly greater emissions control costs on the margin. This outcome is represented by the movement from point *a* to point *b* in Figure 1.

Predictions of economic catastrophe following the introduction of tougher environmental legislation may be flawed in the same way that the "limits to growth" arguments of the 1970s were flawed. The limits to growth literature predicted a collapse of the world system based on the following implicit assumptions: an iron law of resource use in which industrial production uses up resources in a fixed manner, no technical progress, and no substitution of inputs in production (Forrester and Meadows, 1972). Because of these unrealistic assumptions, the gloomy limits

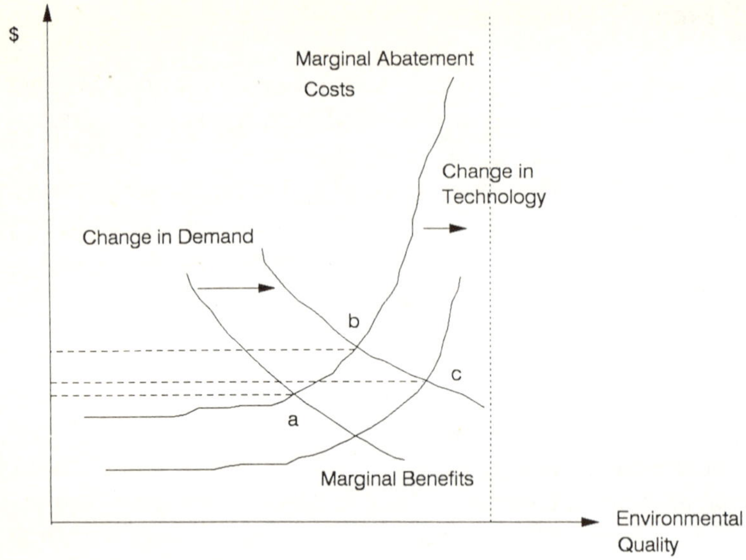

Fig. 1. Increase in demand for environmental quality with technological change in pollution abatement

to growth modeling exercises were never taken seriously by economists.

This literature made clear the importance of taking into consideration alternative production techniques, input substitutions, and technological change when assessing future impacts of environmental management. These economic responses could conceivably produce a movement from point *b* to point *c* in Figure 1. There is evidence that this type of movement has played an important role in the past. As Table 7 shows, environmental legislation in the United States induced a spurt of investment in pollution abatement equipment and plant modifications in the early and middle 1970s. Particularly in the pulp and paper industry, major plant modifications were introduced that led to significantly less polluting production practices. Following these modifications, pollution abatement capital costs fell dramatically. These same adaptations and technological advancements are likely to continue to be important considerations in determining the location and shape of industries' marginal abatement cost curves, and

Table 7. Pollution-Abatement Expenditures as a Percentage of Total New Plant and Capital Expenditures, 1973–84

	1973	1975	1977	1979	1981	1983
Mineral Processing	14.7	14.2	12.1	10.1	7.5	6.3
Chemicals	10.1	10.7	11.2	6.3	6.0	4.7
Pulp and Paper	15.6	16.0	10.6	8.2	7.4	6.3
All Manufacturing	4.5	8.7	6.4	5.0	4.2	3.7

Source: *Survey of Current Business* (1986, pp. 39–45).

the effect of environmental policy on the macroeconomy and international trade.

Bibliography

Asako, K. 1979. "Environmental Pollution in an Open Economy." *Economic Record* 55:359–367.

Balassa, B. 1965. "Trade Liberalization and Revealed Comparative Advantage." *Manchester School of Economics and Social Studies*, 33(5):99–123.

Baumol, W. and W. Oates. 1988. *The Theory of Environmental Policy*. Second Edition. Cambridge: Cambridge University Press.

Bowen, H. 1983. "Changes in the International Distribution of Resources and their Impact on U.S. Comparative Advantages." *Review of Economics and Statistics* 65:402–414.

D'Arge, R. 1974. "International Trade, Domestic Income, and Environmental Controls: Some Empirical Estimates." In: A. Kneese (ed.), *Managing the Environment: International Economic Cooperation for Pollution Control*, pp. 289–315.

Environmental Protection Agency. 1984. *The Cost of Clean Air and Water: Report to Congress, 1984*. Washington, D.C.

Forrester, J., and B. Meadows. 1972. *Limits to Growth*. Club of Rome.

Helpman, E. and P. Krugman. 1986. *Market Structure and Foreign Trade*. Cambridge: MIT Press.

Hufbauer, G. 1970. "The Impact of National Characteristics and Technology on the Commodity Composition of Trade in Manufactured Goods." In: R. Vernon (ed.), *The Technological Factor in International Trade*. New York: Columbia University Press.

Kalt, J. 1985. "The Impact of Domestic Environmental Regulatory Policies on U.S. International Competitiveness." Discussion Paper Series, Energy and Environmental Policy Center, John F. Kennedy School of Government, Harvard University.

Kopp, R., P. Portney and D. DeWitt. 1990. "International Comparisons of

Environmental Regulation." Discussion Paper, Resources for the Future, Washington, D.C.

Leamer, E. 1984. *Sources of International Comparative Advantage: Theory and Evidence*. Cambridge: MIT Press.

Leonard, H. 1988. *Pollution and the Struggle for the World Product*. Cambridge: Cambridge University Press.

McGuire, M. 1982. "Regulation, Factor Rewards, and International Trade." *Journal of Public Economics* 17:335–354.

Murrell, P. 1990. *The Nature of Socialist Economies: Lessons from East European Foreign Trade*. Princeton University Press.

Oates, W., P. Portney and A. McGartland. 1989. "The Benefits of Incentive-Based Regulations: A Case Study of Environmental Standard Setting." *American Economic Review* 79:1233–1242.

OECD. 1985. *The Macro-Economic Impact of Environmental Expenditures*. Organization for Economic Cooperation and Development, Paris.

Pearson, C., (ed). 1987. *Multinational Corporations, Environment, and the Third World*. Durham, NC: Duke University Press and World Resources Institute.

Pearson, C. 1985. *Down to Business: Multinational Corporations, the Environmental and Development*. Washington, D.C.: World Resources Institute.

Pethig, R. 1976. "Pollution, Welfare, and Environmental Policy in the Theory of Comparative Advantage." *Journal of Environmental Economics and Management* 2:160–169.

Portney, P., (ed). 1990. *Public Policies for Environmental Management*. Washington, D.C: Resources for the Future.

Robison, D. 1986. "Industrial Pollution Abatement: The Impact on Balance of Trade." Unpublished manuscript, University of Maryland, College Park, Maryland.

Siebert, H. 1974. "Environmental Protection and International Specialization." *Weltwirtschaftliches Archiv*. 110:494–508.

Survey of Current Business. 1986. " Plant and Equipment Expenditures by Business for Pollution Abatement," 66(2):39–45.

Tobey, J. 1989. "The Impact of Domestic Environmental Policy on International Trade." Ph.D. thesis, Department of Economics, University of Maryland, College Park, Maryland.

U.S. Department of Commerce. 1975. *Pollution Abatement Costs and Expenditures*. Bureau of the Census, Current Industrial Reports, Washington, D.C.

Walter, I. 1973. "The Pollution Content of American Trade." *Western Economic Journal* 11:61–70.

———. 1985, "Environmentally Induced Industrial Relocation to Developing Countries." In: S.J. Rubin and T.R. Graham (eds.), *Environment and Trade*, pp. 67–101. Allanheld, Osmum and Co. Publishers, Inc.,

Walter, I., and J. Ugelow. 1979. "Environmental Policies in Developing Countries." *Ambio* 8:02–109.

Yamane, T. 1967. *Statistics: An Introductory Analysis*. New York: Harper and Row.

Economics of the Trade in Endangered Species: Implications for Sustainable Management

Joanne C. Burgess*

Introduction

The extinction of key species and the decline of biodiversity in general has promoted interest in current levels of exploitation of endangered species and in the trade of these wild plants and animals and their products. Economic studies of the trade in endangered species and other resource products have an important role to play in:

- understanding the nature of the resource product trade and its impact on the supply and demand of species and species products;
- evaluating policies in both exporting and importing countries that affect the trade flow and the incentives for sustainable resource management; and
- developing appropriate trade and complementary domestic policy options to improve incentives for sustainable resource management (Barbier, 1991).

The following paper first examines the decline in endangered species and discusses the extent to which this is due to overexploitation. The international wildlife trade is a cause of concern because, when left uncontrolled, it can produce economic incen-

---

* I am grateful to Edward Barbier and Wilfred Beckerman for their constructive comments and Tim Swanson, Richard Luxmoore and Jorgen Thomsen for their helpful advice. All errors and omissions are of course mine alone.

tives that lead to overexploitation and species extinction.[1] Based on a brief review of the international trade in four key wildlife species, the major characteristics of the international wildlife trade are identified. These factors need to be taken into account by any policies designed to regulate the international trade.

Although control of the trade on the international level may be necessary, it is not always sufficient to ensure sustainable management of wildlife populations. So long as it remains in the direct economic interest of an individual to harvest endangered species, he/she will continue to do so. The market and government failures creating economic incentives for individuals to harvest endangered species need to be addressed through appropriate domestic policies, for example, community-based wildlife utilization projects. It is only through a combination of complementary international and domestic policies that wildlife exploitation and the trade in endangered species can be controlled and harnessed to encourage sustainable management.

I Endangered Species in Decline

While species extinctions have always been a biological fact of life, the stepwise increase in global species diversity over the last 600 million years appears to be over. Indeed, there is currently a dramatic reduction in the diversity of species (Trexler, 1989). Making reliable estimates of the number of endangered wildlife[2] and rates of species extinction is plagued with difficulties. Although the detailed ecological survey data that is required for such assessments prohibit precise figures, there have been some attempts to estimate

[1] In this paper overexploitation is taken to be a level of resource use that exceedes a "socially optimal" level of exploitation. The socially optimum level of exploitation is traditionally set at the point where the marginal costs equal the marginal benefits of resource use. However, as noted by Pearce, Barbier and Markandya (1990) this may need to be modified to account for the risk and uncertainty attached to the depletion of our natural capital stocks – due to a lack of substitutes, the irreversible loss of these stocks and the imperfect knowledge of the value of these resources.

[2] In this paper, wildlife is taken to include wild plants and animals but not commercial timber.

Table 1. Past Extinctions and Current Endangered Species

A. Recorded Extinctions, 1,600 to Present

	Mainland[1]	Island[2]	Ocean	Total	Approx. Number of Species
Mammals	30	51	2	83	4,000
Birds	21	92	0	113	9,000
Reptiles	1	20	0	21	6,300
Amphibians	2	0	0	2	4,200
Fish[3]	22	1	0	23	19,100
Invertebrates[3]	49	48	1	98	1,000,000+
Vascular Plants[4]	245	139	0	384	250,000

B. Endangered and Vulnerable Species

	Mainland[1]	Island[2]	Ocean	Total	% of Total Species
Mammals	159	48	9	216	5.4
Birds	91	87	0	178	1.9
Reptiles	41	21	6	68	1.1
Amphibians	14	0	–	14	0.3
Fish[3]	193	21	0	214	1.1
Invertebrates[3]	371	338	2	711	0.0
Vascular Plants[4]	3,985	2,706	0	6,691	2.6

[1] Landmasses greater than 1 million square kilometers.

[2] Landmasses less than 1 million square kilometers.

[3] Totals primarily representative of North America and Hawaii.

[4] Includes species, subspecies and varieties.

Source: Adapted from Reid and Miller (1989).

the number of species lost in the past and the current number of endangered species (see Table 1).

Estimations of future extinction rates are based on projected rates of habitat loss and the relationship between species richness and habitat area (see the "species area curve" in Figure 1). Using this approach, Reid and Miller estimated that if current tropical deforestation trends continue between 1990 and 2020, approximately 3–7% of species will be lost in Africa and Madagascar,

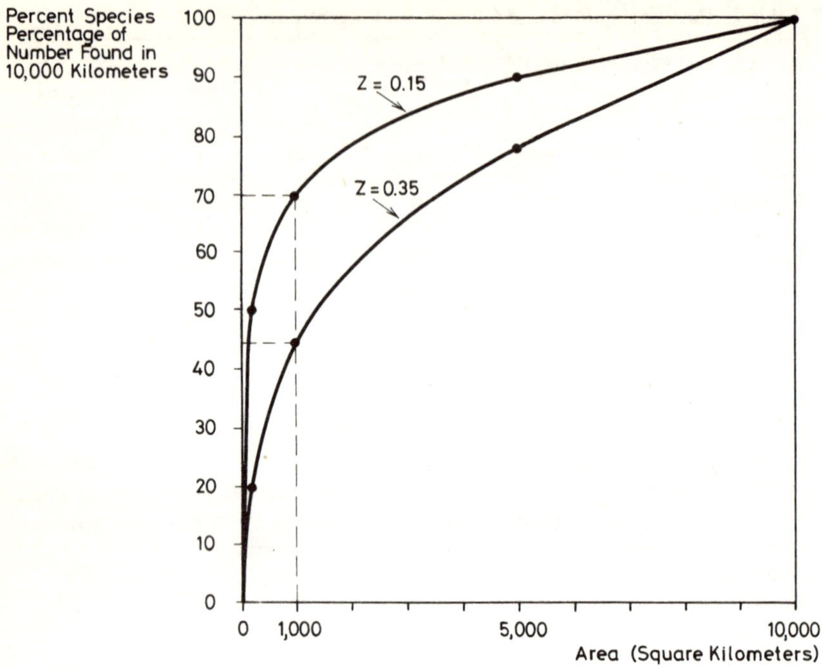

Fig. 1. Species area curve

The number of species found in a region increases with the area of habitat in a predictable manner. Consequently, it is possible to predict the effect of habitat loss on the number of species found in a region with use of a species-area curve such as this. A useful rule of thumb is that if a habitat is reduced by 90 percent in area, roughly one-half of its species will be lost. The two curves show the difference in the relationship found in island ($z = 0.35$) and continental ($z = 0.15$) habitats.

Source: Reid and Miller (1989).

7–17% in Asia and the Pacific, and 4–9% in Latin America and the Caribbean, respectively (Reid and Miller, 1989). The limited data that are available clearly indicate that many wild plants and animals are threatened with extinction, and that global biodiversity is declining.

Tropical countries are particularly important for protecting global biodiversity, because the moist forests in these regions contain more than half of all species. Past destruction and degradation of wildlife habitats has reduced the remaining habitat area to

Table 2. Wildlife Habitats

A. Wildlife Habitats in the Afrotropical Region,[1] 1986

	Original Area '000sq.km	Remaining Area '000sq.km	Percent Remaining
Dry Forests	8,217	3,416	41.6
Moist Forests	4,700	1,868	39.7
Savannah/Grassland	6,955	2,835	40.8
Scrub/Desert	177	172	97.8
Wetland/Marsh	62	44	70.9
Mangroves	88	39	44.6

B. Wildlife Habitats in the Indomalayan Region,[2] 1986

	Original Area '000sq.km	Remaining Area '000sq.km	Percent Remaining
Dry Forests	3,414	940	27.5
Moist Forests	3,362	1,227	36.5
Savannah/Grassland	46	12	36.0
Scrub/Desert	816	119	14.5
Wetland/Marsh	414	160	38.8
Mangroves	95	40	42.4

[1] Data from Angola, Benin, Botswana, Burkina Faso, Burundi, Cameroon, Central African Republic, Chad, Cote d'Ivoire, Djibouti, Equatorial Guinea, Ethiopia, Gabon, Gambia, Ghana, Guinea, Guinea Bissau, Kenya, Mozambique, Namibia, Niger, Nigeria, Rwanda, Senegal, Sierra Leone, Somalia, South Africa, Sudan, Swaziland, Tanzania, Togo, Uganda, Zaire, Zambia and Zimbabwe.

[2] Data from Bangladesh, Bhutan, Brunei, China, Hong Kong, India, Indonesia, Japan, Cambodia, Laos, Malaysia, Myanmar, Nepal, Pakistan, Phillipines, Sri Lanka, Taiwan, Thailand and Vietnam.

Source: *World Resources, 1990–91.*

40% of the original area in west-central Africa and to around 36% of the original habitat area in Indo-Malaysia (see Table 2). This has serious implications for the survival of many species.[3]

However, the threat of species extinction is not just confined to the tropical forests of Southeast Asia, Africa and Latin America. Figure 2 provides an overview of the percentage of threatened mammals, reptiles, birds, amphibians, fish and invertebrate species compared with total species contained in OECD countries. Many countries, especially those in Central and Eastern Europe, record over 40% of their wildlife species under threat.

Although the loss of natural habitats is widely considered to be a dominant cause of species extinction, the role of overexploitation and species introduction also has a significant impact on wildlife populations. Overuse of a species can reduce the population density and make the population more fragile and susceptible to extinction. Overexploitation can result from excessive local harvesting for subsistence use, sport hunting and commercial harvesting for domestic and international trade. Although the dominant demand for most wild plants and animals is from local use and domestic markets, the international trade in some key wild animals and plants and their products is putting considerable strain on the survival of many species.

Table 3 shows estimates of the impacts of habitat loss, overexploitation and other factors on species that have already become extinct and currently threaten species. Overexploitation was the primary cause of extinction of 23% of all mammal, 32% of all reptile, 11% of all bird and 4% of all fish species lost in the past (Table 3A).[4] Overexploitation continues to pose a significant threat to many wildlife species, especially mammals and reptiles (Table 3B). However, in most cases the cause of extinction of wildlife

---

[3] The hypothesis that competition from a population (in this case humans) for essential resources of food and habitat leads to the extinction of other species also dependent on the essential resources is based on Darwin's notion of the survival of the fittest. This is interpreted in Hardin's doctrine (1960).

[4] The data on the causes of extinction need to be revised, in particular the percentage of species extinct primarily due to species introduction needs to be revised upward. However, no statistics have yet been published containing this information (R. Luxmoore, WCMC, pers. comm.).

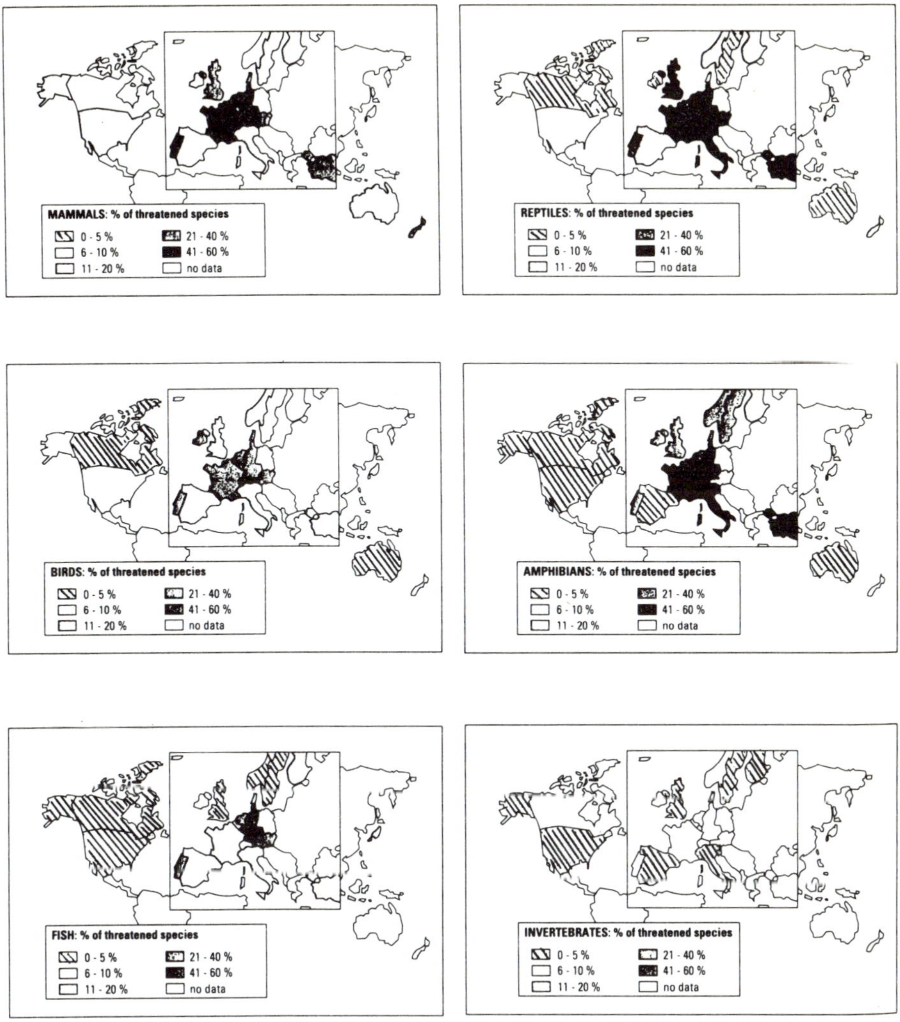

Fig. 2. State of wildlife – OECD countries, late 1980s
Source: OECD (1991).

cannot simply be attributed to a single factor, but is due to a complex interaction of several factors over a period of time. For example, although destruction or disruption of a species habitat may threaten the continued existence of 68% of all endangered mammal species, this threat may be further exacerbated by over-

Table 3. Causes of Extinction

A. Causes of Past Extinctions (percent due to each dominant cause)

	Habitat Loss	Over-Exploitation[1]	Species Introduction	Other[2]
Mammals[3]	19	23	20	38
Birds[3]	20	11	22	39
Reptiles[3]	5	32	42	21
Fish[4]	35	4	30	52

B. Current Threats to Species (percent due to each cause)

	Habitat Loss	Over-Exploitation[1]	Species Introduction	Other[2]
Mammals[4]	68	54	6	20
Birds[4]	58	30	28	2
Reptiles[4]	53	63	17	9
Amphibians[4]	77	29	14	3
Fish[4]	78	12	28	2

[1] Includes commercial, subsistence, sport hunting and live animal capture for pet, zoo and research trades.

[2] Includes unknown and predator control.

[3] Value reported represents the percentage of species whose extinction was caused primarily by the factor indicated.

[4] Value reported represents the percentage of species whose endangerment or extinction is influenced by each factor, thus row exceeds 100%.

Sources: Reid and Miller (1989, Tables 8 and 9).

exploitation, which threatens 54% of all endangered mammals species. The combined effect of habitat loss and overexploitation may drive some mammal species to extinction.

There have been attempts to reduce the threat of extinction by protecting the habitat of species from further destruction and degradation, and the number of protected areas have been rising steadily throughout the world (see Table 4). However, although the numbers and total area of protected areas have been increasing, they still only represent a small percentage of total wildlife habitat. In species-rich tropical Africa and the Indo-Malayan region, around 10–15% of wildlife habitat is protected (World Resources, 1991). Unfortunately, establishment of many of the pro-

Table 4. Parks and Protected Areas Designated

	1930–59		1960–98		Total Parks	
	No. Area	Area ('000ha)	No. Area	Area ('000ha)	No. Area	Area ('000ha)
World	689	60,151	2,671	363,580	4,320	486,400
Africa	123	29,443	282	53,910	486	95,491
N. & Central America	114	7,940	238	137,678	587	177,584
S. America	53	7,199	249	58,551	315	66,253
Asia	131	6,819	733	49,506	960	60,534
Europe	151	3,429	677	20,639	1,032	27,179
USSR	42	2,593	109	16,529	168	20,246
Oceania	75	2,728	388	26,570	767	38,918
Antarctic Treaty Territory	0	0	5	196	5	196

Notes: Areas included are those in IUCN management Categories I through V. The table only includes areas over 1,000 ha, and only those protected by the highest competent authority (i.e., state parks and reserves are not included).

Source: UNEP (1989/90).

tected areas has frequently worked against the direct economic interest of local communities and their incentives to conserve wildlife. As noted by Barbier, the "preservation" of areas has often led to the displacement or enforced relocation of rural communities. Although subsequent use of the land and the wild resources of these areas is prohibited, local communities have received very little real compensation for the loss of traditional livelihoods and resources. What is more, local communities often suffer economic costs from crop loss and other damages resulting from marauding wildlife or wildlife migration. The "protection" of wild areas has meant that local communities have lost their traditional management and use rights of local wild resources, and perceive little incentive, and often a major cost, to conserving these resources.[5]

The response on the international level to the threat of extinction of traded wildlife resources has been similar to the domestic

[5] See Chapter 4 by E.B. Barbier, "Community Based Development in Africa," in a forthcoming book by T.M. Swanson and E.B. Barbier (eds), (1992).

"protectionist" approach to habitat loss. Based on a perception that the international trade is encouraging overexploitation and threatens the survival of a species, the traditional policy response has been to control, or ban, the trade. Although the success of the level of adoption of such trade controls crucially depends upon the incentives given to the various nations to cooperate, there is little evidence that such incentive requirements have been implemented. In the cases where nations have accepted trade controls, the level of enforcement has generally been inadequate to successfully implement the controls and prevent the emergence of illegal trade. However, a further concern of trade controls is their effect on the economic incentives to conserve wildlife and their impact on national and community-based wildlife utilization projects.

II The Role of the Wildlife Trade

Wild plants and animals are harvested to yield important products (e.g., meat, skins, tusks, horns, feathers, etc.) or captured live for pets, for zoos and research activities. An additional, albeit much smaller, demand for wild animals is for sport hunting. Wildlife resources are exploited for:

- subsistence use;
- domestic commercial use (domestic trade); and
- commercial export (international trade).

It is extremely difficult to estimate levels of domestic wildlife use, as there are few records of subsistence use and domestic trade. The studies that do exist are usually site specific, and cannot be aggregated up to country level. However, the case studies do indicate that the domestic demand for wildlife is a major cause of most species exploitation. The extent to which the in-country use of these species effects the wildlife populations and poses a threat to the continued existence of the species is generally not well documented.[6]

[6] However, a recent book does provide a wide collection of examples; see Robinson and Redford (1991).

The exploitation of wildlife for international trade is less important for the vast majority of wildlife species. However, it does play an important role in the demand for a few key species. In the late 1980s, the annual international trade in exotic wildlife was worth well over US$5 billion, derived from around 40,000 primates, ivory from at least 90,000 African elephants, over 1 million orchids, 4 million live birds, 10 million reptile skins, 15 million fur pelts, over 350,000 tropical fish and a diverse range of other products (S. Fitzgerald, 1989). The international wildlife trade is a cause of concern because, when left uncontrolled, it can produce economic incentives that lead to overexploitation and species extinction.

There is little reliable information on the international trade in wildlife. One source of data is customs import and export statistics, although they rarely give detailed statistics on the trade in wildlife. This is partly because the volume and value of the trade is low compared to other internationally traded goods and services, but also because it is often extremely difficult to categorize many of the transactions of individual species and the products of species.[7] Where it is possible to obtain trade data from customs statistics, the information is often limited to the volume of trade (e.g., number of birds, cat skins and live primates), with little data on the value of the trade. Few attempts have been made to extract information from import and export statistics to assess the international trade in wildlife species.

The Wildlife Conservation Monitoring Centre (WCMC) compiles data on wildlife trade based on information that member countries submit to the Convention on Trade in Endangered Species of Wild Fauna and Flora (CITES). CITES was established in the early 1970s and provides the most important regulatory body controlling the international trade in wildlife and wildlife products. There are currently 111 countries who are members of CITES (TRAFFIC Bulletin, 1991). CITES trade restrictions are based on their biological status and the extent to which they are threatened by trade. The member countries prohibit commercial international trade in currently endangered species that are listed

[7] See Appendix 3.1 in Barbier et al. (1990).

Table 5. Trade in Wildlife and Wildlife Products, 1986

	Live Primates (number)	Cat Skins (number)	Raw Ivory (kg)	Live Parrots (number)	Reptile Skins (number)
World					
imports	51,256	192,402	429,549	696,002	10,480,798
exports	51,256	192,402	429,558	618,539	10,480,798
Africa					
imports	423	753	2,254	14,255	65,980
exports	8,879	2,272	130,391	169,237	399,256
North and Central America					
imports	23,588	38,683	5,051	318,162	1,388,169
exports	6,756	89,590	126	26,550	600,161
South America					
imports	82	11	3	2,811	47,191
exports	6,135	6,150	NA	256,634	1,403,942
Asia					
imports	7,921	16,093	355,782	60,365	4,682,360
exports	24,622	72,969	269,655	126,538	6,878,809
Europe					
imports	16,063	136,736	53,197	298,973	4,070,201
exports	4,781	18,335	28,394	37,234	1,193,904

Notes: NA – not available

Source: *World Resource, 1990–91.*

under Appendix I (approximately 600 species) and monitor closely trade in species that may become endangered listed under Appendix II (around 30,000 species). Appendix III allows countries to prohibit trade in nationally protected species. However, countries are permitted to take out "reservations" against the Appendix listing, which allows them to continue trading in any species, even those threatened with extinction.

Table 5 provides details on the volume of imports and exports of key wildlife resources – live primates, cat skins, raw ivory, live parrots and reptile skins – based on CITES data compiled by the Wildlife Conservation Monitoring Center (WCMC). The total volumes may overestimate the actual number of species supplied to the international market, as the figures are not adjusted for re-exports (i.e., double-counting may be present). However, the impact of the international trade on wildlife populations may be underrepresented by the data because of additional mortalities (of dependants, during capture and transportation), illegal trade and trade between countries not members of CITES. The trade in a few key species is briefly examined below, outlining the economic factors characterizing the trade and the implications of the trade for the wildlife populations.

A Parrots

Whilst it is acknowledged that habitat destruction has historically posed the major threat to parrot populations (and continues to be a problem), the trade in parrots is increasingly significant and may be the primary factor threatening the survival of some species today.[8] A large domestic demand for parrots has existed for centuries, with parrots being sought after as pets and for subsistence purposes (e.g. meat and feathers for traditional rituals and ornamental purposes). In contrast, a strong international interest in caged birds has only emerged over the past thirty years.

The change in the international demand for parrots is reflected in an increase in the world trade in parrots from over 80,957 in 1980 to 618,539 in 1986 (Table 6). This figure is based on CITES data and is expected to seriously underestimate the actual level of world trade due to substantial parrot smuggling. For example, in order to avoid trade restrictions, approximately 150,000 parrots are smuggled across the Mexican boarder into the United States each year (Thomsen and Hemley, 1987).

Around half of the recorded international trade in live parrots is destined for the pet market in the U.S.A. (see Figure 3), who imported a minimum of 703,000 neotropical parrots between 1981 and 1985. The major supplies of parrots to the USA come from Latin America, in particular Argentina, who exported more than 660,000 parrots during the period 1982–86 (Thomsen and Brautigam, 1991). The European market draws most of its supply

[8] See Chapter 24 by J.B. Thomsen and A. Brautigam in Robinson and Redford (1991).

Table 6. Major Importers and Exporters of Live Parrots (1981–86)

A. Imports ('000)

Country	1981	1982	1983	1984	1985	1986
USA	199	281	301	312	311	305
Germany	35	58	56	54	55	60
UK	9	17	24	16	22	34
Japan	21	45	39	39	23	28

B. Exports ('000)

Country	1981	1982	1983	1984	1985	1986
Argentina	73	89	114	109	179	178
Tanzania	22	74	52	45	70	84
Indonesia	26	33	78	79	44	59
Guyana	29	27	25	38	27	30
Uruguay	8	19	33	39	18	21
Peru	16	39	19	52	34	17
Senegal	7	25	21	27	20	28
World (gross total)	362	536	555	593	615	619

Source: UNEP (1989).

of parrots from Africa, whilst Japan imports parrots from Asia and Africa (Fitzgerald, 1989).

The financial incentive to trap and trade in parrots is high. Trappers receive an estimated minimum gross income of $25 per parrot, the middlemen $84 per parrot and the retailer $1,200 per parrot (Thomsen and Brautigam, 1991). Given that the costs of trapping and domestically trading in parrots are low, there are lucrative profits to be made by the trappers, and especially the middlemen, in the parrot trade. Although the costs of transporting the parrot to the consuming country and quarantine requirements are substantial, the economic return from retailing parrots is still highly attractive. Whilst the value of the parrot trade is important for some individuals, the value of the trade to the majority of exporting countries is often relatively insignificant (with the exception of Argentina, the largest exporter, whose total retail value of parrot exports is approximately $800 million).

Attempts to control the parrot trade through piecemeal regulations have not been successful in reducing the demand for par-

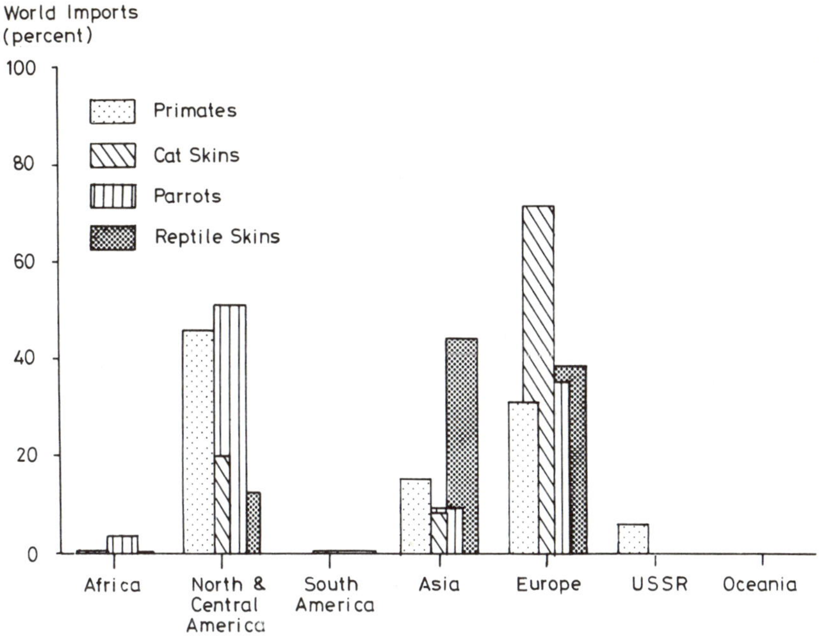

Fig. 3. Major importers of wild animals and skins
Source: *World Resource, 1990–91.*

rots. These policies have simply resulted in changes in the composition of exporting countries and species involved in the trade. In addition, the illegal trade in parrots has emerged as a serious problem. Although the laws protecting illegal parrot trading are being more heavily enforced, parrot smuggling remains an extensive and lucrative business.

B Cat Skins

In contrast to the expanding parrot trade, the trade in cat skins has been in decline throughout the 1980s. Total gross exports of cat skins dropped from 380,210 in 1981 to 192,402 in 1986 (see Table 7), reflecting changing market conditions – new trade controls, changes in consumer tastes, and the increasing difficulty of hunting prized species due to dwindling cat populations. Al-

Table 7. Major Importers and Exporters of Cat Skins (1981–86)

A. Imports ('000)

Country	1981	1982	1983	1984	1985	1986
USA	26	23	23	19	20	17
Germany	198	148	308	88	77	82
UK	7	2	10	16	11	16
France	3	2	15	46	4	8

B. Exports ('000)

Country	1981	1982	1983	1984	1985	1986
China	8	8	3	43	60	68
Paraguay	126	70	34	3	0	0
Bolivia	0	0	3	30	3	6
Argentina	6	0	0	12	NA	NA
World (gross total)	380	244	445	227	190	192

Source: UNEP (1989).

though there are no reliable figures on the financial returns from trading in cat skins, it is expected to be a financially rewarding activity. The majority of the fur trade supplies are used in the fashion clothes and accessory industry of the European markets (especially W. Germany and France), although Japan and Hong Kong are also important markets.

Following recognition of the threat of extinction of many big cats (e.g., tigers, leopards, jaguars and cheetahs) in the late 1960s, a mixture of CITES and national trade controls were implemented in the 1970s to ban the trade in big cat skins. Although these policies were relatively successful in reducing the pressure on the big cats, the demand for small cat skins increased. The composition of the cat skin trade shifted away from being dominated by big cat skins and moved towards the smaller cats (e.g., bobcats, lynx, ocelots, little spotted cats and maragays) (Fitzgerald, 1989).

Trade regulations imposed on the supply of small cat skins have been implemented relatively successfully in North America, but in Latin America illegal cat trade has emerged as a serious problem. However, publicity campaigns to inform the public of the plight of cat populations and the implications of purchasing cat skin products have been relatively effective in changing consumer preferences and reducing the demand for these products. For example, in the fur coat industry, following strong publicity campaigns, consumers have generally moved away from demanding "real" cat skin coats, and have switched towards synthetic substitutes.

C Rhinoceros Horn

Trade in rhinoceros horn has had a devastating impact on the population, being largely responsible for the reduction from 73,000 rhinos in the late 1970s to less than 11,000 in the 1990s. In particular, the black rhino population has been reduced from over 65,000 in 1970 to less than 4,000 today. North Yeman has been a major consumer of the valuable rhino horn for dagger handles, with the remaining horn supplying the traditional medicine markets of the Far East (e.g., China, Hong Kong, Macao, S. Korea, Taiwan, Thailand) (Fitzgerald, 1989).

Rhino horn is highly valued and fetches a high price. For example, African rhino horn in the markets of the Far East is worth approximately $450/pound. Based on an average horn weight of 3.5 pounds an African rhino horn is worth around $1,500. However, Asian horn is even more highly valued, and wholesale prices reach over $4,000/pound in some markets. This gives an Asian rhino horn a value of around $14,000. The rhino horn trade throughout the world may be worth as much as $3 million annually (Fitzgerald, 1989).

Although the trade in rhino horn slowed in the 1980s through a combination of CITES and nation trade bans, the illegal international market in rhino horn continues to be a serious threat for the survival of the species (Milliken et al., 1991). Given the high value of the horn, the financial incentives to continue trading in rhino horn are significant.

D Elephant Ivory

During the 1980s the population of elephants in Africa halved in eight years from 1.2 million to just over 600,000. In only a few countries – South Africa, Botswana, Zimbabwe and Namibia –

are populations stabilizing or rising. The dramatic decline in elephant numbers in most of Africa has been largely attributed to the illegal harvesting (poaching) of elephants for their ivory. Total exports of unworked ivory leaving Africa between 1979 and 1988 amounted to over 7,500 tonnes. The volume of raw ivory exports fluctuated around 900,000 kg in the early 1980s, peaking at 1,031,934 kg in 1983, but then declined sharply thereafter (Table 8).

Although the decline in tonnage since the mid-1980s looks encouraging, the statistics hide the real impact of the trade on the elephant populations. In 1979 a tonne of ivory represented approximately 54 dead elephants. These were mainly the bull elephants, valued for their bigger tusks, with an average tusk weight per elephant of 9.3 kg. By 1987 most of the mature bull elephants had been shot, leaving the cows and calves to support the demand for ivory. They have a much lower average tusk size of 4.7 kg, such that one tonne of ivory directly represents about 113 dead elephants. In addition, the high female ratio of the harvested population leads to the death of a further 55 calves who are orphaned or die of starvation. As a consequence, almost the same number of elephants were harvested in 1987 as in 1979 to support the demand for ivory, but from a much reduced and more fragile population.

The price of raw ivory increased from around $60 per kilogram in 1979 to $150/kg in 1988. In early 1989 – in anticipation of an international ban on the ivory trade – the price rose to $300/kg. The annual value of ivory exports from Africa in the mid-1980s is estimated to be around $50–60 million. As this figure includes c.i.f. costs and marketing margins in international trade, an estimate of $35–45 million is probably a more realistic measure of the value of ivory exports accruing to Africa. This amount is a tiny fraction of all African export earnings, and although significant for a few individual countries, the loss of these ivory revenues would not seriously impair African development. In addition, the other nonconsumptive values of the African elephant, such as its importance to tourism in some countries may be considerably more significant in terms of foreign exchange earnings.

The flow of ivory in the international trade has traditionally been towards the hard currency consumers – the USA, Europe and, more recently, Japan. These three consumers have acquired about 75 % of all ivory worked in Hong Kong and Japan (who work approximately 70% of all ivory) this decade. The remainder of the ivory in international trade has gone to the carving industries within various developing countries – for example, India and China – and has then been re-exported or sold to foreign tourists. The same is true for much African worked ivory. Therefore, it is reasonable to assume that nearly all the ivory in the international trade has ultimately found its way to one of the three hard currency consumers: the United States, Europe and Japan (Barbier, et al. 1990).

An economic analysis of the demand for raw ivory in Japan and Hong Kong indicated high income elasticities of demand for this product, that is, ivory is considered as a luxury good and as real incomes grow the consumption of ivory grows even faster.[9] There appears to be a latent demand for elephant ivory in a number of other Asian states – such as Korea and Taiwan, where demand has increased by 1,000 per cent in the past decade. This demand pressure will remain high so long as rapid economic growth continues in this region.

Other rapidly developing countries, such as Singapore, Dubai, and Macau, have been playing an increasingly important role in the movement of raw ivory stocks in their processing and carving. This fluidity is one of the characteristics of both the legal and illegal trade: whenever one channel through which ivory is passing has been blocked by trade controls, another has opened up almost immediately.

At the Seventh Conference to the Parties to CITES in 1989, the African elephant was transferred from Appendix II listing to Appendix I listing. This effectively bans all trade in elephant products, although in future individual countries with healthy elephant populations, effective elephant conservation and management programme and effective ivory trade controls will be able to apply to a "technical committee" (yet to be established) to have their elephant populations transferred back to Appendix II listing. It was also agreed that the international trade ban should apply to

[9] See Chapter 4, E.B. Barbier et al. (1990).

Table 8. Trade in Raw Ivory, (1979–88)

Raw Ivory Exports by Major African Exporters, 1979–88
(tonnes)

	1979	1980	1981	1982	1983	1984	1985	1986*	1987*	1988*
Botswana	13	5	9	5	6	4	17	.4	.4	.1
Burundi	139	126	61	46	124	184	215	138	50	9
CAR	181	183	107	202	204	122	117	19	2	.3
Chad	27	4	13	28	34	4	.03	0	2	0
Congo	93	175	237	102	53	95	72	17	86	19
Gabon	4	1	1	.2	.9	.2	.4	.5	4	14
Kenya	46	31	6	12	4	13	19	2	.1	0
S. Africa	42	35	33	28	46	36	50	41	18	8
Sudan	124	206	269	278	337	68	22	78	70	0
Tanzania	33	45	27	18	15	45	114	302	56	43
Uganda	25	19	45	12	13	100	206	3	0	.2
Zaire	160	84	45	78	157	90	22	23	12	11
Zambia	16	22	28	34	18	2	14	11	4	2
Zimbabwe	3	2	1	14	14	21	23	8	8	7
All Africa Min. Total	944	952	905	890	1,032	798	912	719	331	142
All Africa Max. Total	950	1,164	912	900	1,040	798	912	805	331	142

Note: These are the "best estimates" of African exports, disaggregated by country of export, using import and export data from customs sources, and CITES data. Both *legal* and *illegal* exports are likely to be included. For starred years (*), because of the adoption of the management quota system by CITIES, there may have been an incentive to evade both customs and CITIES systems in some countries.

Net Imports of Raw Ivory by Major Consumers
(tonnes)

	1979	1980	1981	1982	1983	1984	1985	1986*	1987*	1988*	
USA	6	23	11	7	20	55	24	17	21	9	
FR Germany	74	181	32	35	43	−7	16	7	2	1	
UK	−5	−26	0	−3	2	3	28	−1	7	3	
Hong Kong	366	376	427	318	428	267	109	129	150	133	
India	17	19	19	24	23	30	21	8	6	4	
France	89	22	7	4	11	21	5	5	4	−2	
China	7	10	10	54	20	7	7	19	39	50	
Japan	270	240	256	205	174	179	206	29	103	75	
Thailand	1	1	2	4	−5	−12	−2	1	0	−3	
Begium	16	−90	−248	−123	−105	−116	0	0	−10	12	
Singapore	−7	−4	3	7	0	120	60	324	−148	−129	
Macau		0	0	5	16	38	32	57	8	11	
Taiwan	11	18	17	18	28	34	21	18	80	5	
Total Net Imports, Countries *(Min. estimate)	979	967	895	891	1,018	710	749	600	370	153	All

Note: These "best estimates" of final demand for raw ivory by the main consuming countries are based on customs trade statistics and CITES documentation.

Minus figures indicate that countries were *net exporters* in that year, most likely through destocking.

For starred years (*), because of the adoption of the management quota system by CITES, there may have been an incentive to evade both customs and CITES systems in some countries.

Source: Barbier, Burgess, Swanson and Pearce (1990, Table 1.3).

all existing ivory stocks, with no special exemptions for the large ivory stockpiles – in particular in Hong Kong and Burundi.

The CITES ban received support from the majority of African nations and consuming countries, some of whom had already banned ivory trading domestically – for example, Kenya, the USA and Europe. However, some elephant range states and ivory consuming countries voiced dissatisfaction at the proposal. Zimbabwe, Botswana, South Africa, Malawi and Zambia (some of whom have healthy elephant populations) refused to support the CITES resolution to move the African elephant from Appendix II to Appendix I. Of the major consuming countries, China and Hong Kong have also declared reservations against the ban and have continued trading in elephant ivory. The fact that not all countries have agreed to the ban leaves the elephant populations vulnerable to ongoing illegal trade.

Although the trade in wild plants and animals is far from homogeneous across species, four major factors characterize the wildlife trade in general. These important issues need to be tackled by any regime designed to regulate the international wildlife trade:

- The demand for wildlife and wildlife products appears to be *linked to rising income levels.* In particular, there is a substantial demand for wildlife species and their products emerging in many rapidly developing Asian countries (e.g., elephant ivory and rhino horn).
- Attempts to control the trade by regulating traditional trading routes has led to the entrance of new trading countries, highlighted the *fluidity of the wildlife trade* and often resulted in an expansion of the illegal trade. Flourishing black markets exist for trade in most highly valued, but banned wildlife species (e.g., parrots, rhino horn, elephant ivory, etc).
- Restricting the trade in one species often leads to the expansion in trade of a *close substitute species*, e.g., banning trade in large cat skins encouraged traders to switch towards marketing small cat skins. Trade controls directed at an individual wild plant or animal type have to take into account the impact on the alternative species.
- Publicity campaigns have been relatively successful in *changing consumer preferences* for products derived from endan-

gered species (e.g., cat skins and ivory). However, the success of such campaigns has been limited to the markets of Europe and the United States, and may not be so effective in the Far East.

III Economics of the Decline in Endangered Species and the Role of Trade

Although control of the trade on an international level is necessary, it is not sufficient to ensure sustainable management of wildlife populations. So long as it remains in the direct economic interest of an individual to harvest endangered species, she/he will continue to do so. Individuals harvest endangered species for trade in order to make money. By investing time and effort in harvesting wildlife resources, individuals are essentially comparing the returns from this activity to alternative sources of income. Individuals will continue to harvest and trade endangered species so long as they perceive that the relative returns to this activity remain high. Unfortunately, whilst endangered species may be regarded as an important source of income they are not necessarily treated as a valuable asset to be sustainably managed and maintained.

If the endangered species are considered to be a valuable asset, it may be in the interest of the individual to maintain these resources into the future as they increase in value over time. However, the decision to sustain wildlife resources depends on the relative returns from these assets compared with the returns from other assets in the economy (given by the rate of interest) and the individual's preference for receiving the returns today rather than in the future (reflected by the individual's time preference) (Barbier et al., 1990).

The relationship between the price of the traded wildlife resource, the costs of harvesting and the return on comparable investments (the discount rate) determines the rate at which individuals decide to use the resource. In terms of the theory of renewable resources, it is possible to suggest an economic interpretation of the extinction of many wild plants and animals. If there is a combination of:

(a) a high price of the resource relative to the cost of harvesting, and
(b) a high discount rate by users relative to the species growth rate,

then, from the standpoint of the exploiter, it is actually optimal to run the resource down, even to extinction.[10]

Given that the costs of harvesting the plants and animals from the wild are often extremely low in comparison to the price of the traded resource, lucrative profits can be derived from exploiting the resource. The price of the wildlife species or product may reflect the scarcity value of the species; for example, in the case of the rhino horn, elephant ivory and cat skins consumers are willing to pay a "scarcity premium" for goods they perceive to be unique or rare. High economic rents (the total value of selling a commodity minus the costs of supplying it) create an incentive for individuals to harvest endangered species.

The existence of economic rents alone does not necessarily imply overexploitation of wildlife species. However, if the net effective discount rate (actual discount rate adjusted for any real price increase) exceeds the growth rate of the harvested population then it will be in the interest of the individual to deplete the resource as quickly as possible, even to extinction, and reinvest the returns in a higher yielding asset.

The growth rate of a species population is chiefly determined by the species' biological reproductive capacity. Although all wildlife species are potentially renewable resources, some are much less capable of responding favorably to harvesting pressures than others. Of the extensive list of species threatened principally by trade, a great proportion are slow-maturing and produce only a few offspring per year (e.g., many primates, elephants, rhinos, larger cats, and other fur-bearing carnivores).[11]

The low reproductive rate of a parrot species, the hyacinth macaw, typifies the problem facing many wild species. Of the 500 hyacinth macaws in Pantanal in Brazil, only 15% to 30% of the

---

[10] A bioeconomic model of elephant decline, which is applicable to other wildlife species, is presented in Appendix 1.1 in Barbier et al. (1990).

[11] See Chapter 8 on international trade and endangered species in Oldfield (1989).

adult population attempts to breed in any one year. What is more, not all breeding pairs of macaws are successful in fledging young and those that are successful, rarely fledge more than one offspring. Thus, 100 mated pairs of breeding macaws may produce between seven and twenty-five young each year. This is a very low reproductive rate, and given the size of the current hyacinth macaw population in this region, it is doubtful whether any substantial, long-term harvesting of the population is viable (Thomsen and Brautigam, 1991).

There are two reasons why the harvester may have a high discount rate. First, if the harvester is located in a rural area of a developing country (the source of the majority of traded endangered species) then capital is likely to be scarce. Where it is available, the cost may be extremely high, with informal lending rates typically around 50–100 percent. In addition, the harvester is likely to prefer to receive income today rather than waiting until the future (i.e., high rate of time preference) because of uncertainty over the future, poverty and risk of death. The prevalence of high economic rents and the combination of low species growth rates and high discount rates characterizes the situation facing many threatened and endangered species today.

IV Market and Government Failures Affecting the Trade

Declines in populations of wild plants and animals, or even extinction of species, may be socially acceptable assuming there are no *market or government failures* affecting the trade. However, there are several major market and policy failures that may distort the incentives for conserving wildlife.

A Market Fails to Reflect the Full Costs of Resource Use

Although the price of a wildlife resource reflects the direct harvesting costs, it is unlikely to reflect the *wider social values* of the wild plant or animal. These wider social values may include forgone direct use values (e.g., tourism), indirect use values (e.g., ecological values) and nonuse/preservation values (e.g., option, bequest and existence values).[12] Some of these values may be significant and reflect a large "willingness-to-pay" for conservation. For example, a travel cost study estimated the viewing value of elephants in Kenya to be approximately $25 million per year, based on survey questionnaires filled in by safari tourists and tour operators in Kenya. This nonconsumptive direct use value of elephants may be as much as ten times the value of harvesting elephants for ivory in Kenya (Brown and Henry, 1990).

Although the study reviewed above provides an estimate of the direct use value from viewing elephants, there is no attempt to estimate: (a) the *option value* of individuals who wish to preserve the elephants in order to have the option of elephant viewing in the future; (b) the *bequest value* of individuals who have no intention of viewing the elephants but value the opportunity of future generations viewing them; nor (c) the *existence value* of individuals who just derive satisfaction from knowing that the elephants will be preserved. Given the widespread public concern over the plight of the African elephants, it is reasonable to suggest that these nonuse and preservation values are highly significant.

The elephant also has an important *indirect use value* which is derived from its natural ecological functions and role as a "keystone species" (Western, 1989). The elephant plays a major part in diversifying savanna and forest ecosystems, acting as seed disperser, reducing bushlands, expanding grasslands and so on. The ecological benefits of elephants are dependent on their population density being neither too low nor too high. For example, in the protected areas of Amboseli National Park in Kenya where elephants crowd in, or in the areas of nonprotected lands that are abandoned, impoverishment results. The most equitable mix, and high relative abundance, of species occurs at the park boundaries where elephant densities are moderate.

Although it is extremely difficult to place a monetary value on these "other" values of the African elephant, it is important to recognize that these other values exist and are often highly significant. The failure of the market to reflect these values provides an

[12] E.B. Barbier (1989) provides a comprehensive discussion of total economic value, which encompasses direct use value, indirect use value and nonuse/preservation values.

economic rationale for intervention in the elephant ivory trade and investments in elephant conservation.

B Open Access Exploitation

Although many wildlife resources have traditionally been sustainably managed through common property regimes, these may be undermined by increasing populations, policy failures and the expropriation of resource ownership and rights, for example, through state establishment of "protected areas." The breakdown of these systems can lead to *open access exploitation*, where it is difficult to exclude individuals from using the resources. This creates an incentive for an individual to harvest the wild resources now, rather than wait until the future, because they cannot prevent other individuals from exploiting the resource in the meantime. Each individual will therefore ignore any *user costs* of plant and animal exploitation, encouraging overuse of the wild resources.

C Rent Dispersion

There are often high economic rents to be made from wildlife exploitation. However, these rents are often dispersed across a wide range of individuals, including harvesters, local traders, domestic officials, foreign traders, etc. The individual who actually makes the harvesting decision typically receives a relatively insignificant proportion of the total revenue upon which to base his consumption/investment decision. Governments often fail to capture these excessive rents and direct them towards investments in sustainable management of the wildlife.

V Policy Options for Sustainable Management

The international wildlife trade has aroused concern because it is perceived to create incentives to overexploit wild plants and animals and threaten their continued existence. The policy options put forward to resolve the "conflict" between trade and wildlife use have traditionally been limited to the choice between development and preservation options. For example, when faced by rapidly declining African elephant populations, CITES responded by banning the trade in elephant ivory. Although such a response may be an effective short-term solution in order to protect the elephant population, this policy option does not address the more complex issues surrounding the ivory trade, nor does it allow sufficient flexibility across African countries or create adequate incentives for conservation. In the long run, unless the ban is adequately adopted and enforced, it may have a detrimental impact on the conservation of elephants.

A simple graph illustrates this situation (Figure 4). The ban initially causes demand D_0 to drop – as the primary consumers, the United States, European Community and Japan, leave the market. The initial impact could be a fall in price, until demand adjusts by the entrance of new consumers – such as South Korea, Taiwan and Saudi Arabia – or until the demand by the existing consumers picks up again. But while overall demand will fall, the illegal component of demand, D_i, could increase. Similarly, although the ban may cause initial supply, S_0, to decrease, a larger proportion of it will be illegal supplies, S_i. As a result, the price of ivory could end up rising, increasing the incentives of poachers and the illegal trade to supply the market. In sum, an ineffective ban might increase prices and incentives to smuggle, and it will definitely result in the loss of the capacity to monitor the trade or invest its returns in conservation programs.

This means that an ineffective ban may be worse for the survival of the African elephant than a policy aiming to establish a controlled trade based on a sustainable yield of ivory, however small. There are several reasons for this. First, a modest production of ivory offers some incentive to consuming nations to accept a controlled legal trade and enforce it, whereas they would lose all benefits from a banned trade. Secondly, legalizing trading might make it possible to set up a trade mechanism that would allow only those producer countries with healthy and sustainably managed elephant populations to sell ivory. Finally, a properly constructed trade mechanism could allow for a larger share of the ivory profits to be retained in the producers states, to be used for sustainably managing elephant populations.

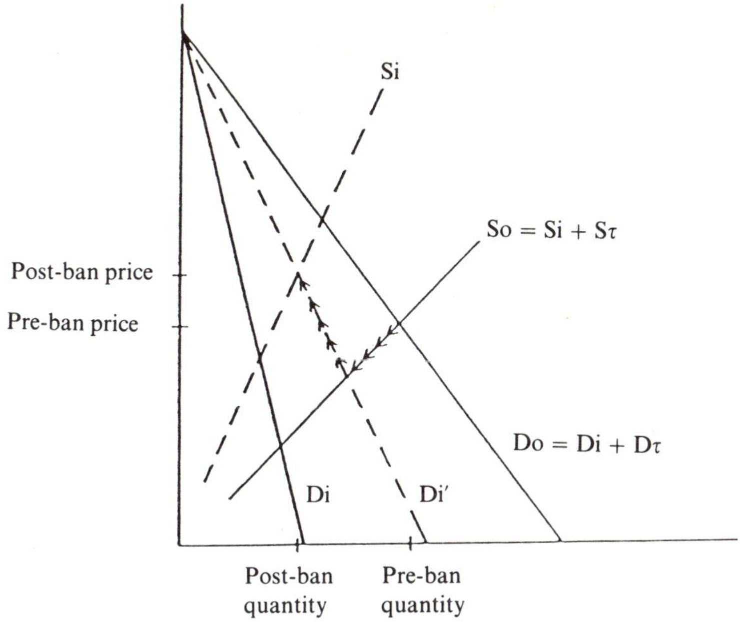

So = Supply curve before ban, illegal and legal supply (Si + Sτ)
Si = Supply curve after ban, illegal supply only
Do = Demand curve before ban, illegal and legal demand (Di + Dτ)
Di = Demand curve before ban, illegal demand only
Di′ = Demand curve after ban, illegal demand only

Fig. 4. The effects of an ivory ban
Source: Barbier, Burgess, Swanson and Pearce (1990).

There are a variety of alternative conservation or sustainable management options that enable maintenance of the natural resources combined with wildlife utilization, such as community-based wildlife development, tourism, recreation, commercial wildlife ranching and so on (Swanson and Barbier, 1992). In order to reconcile development and conservation in practice, the domestic market and policy failures, such as wider social values, open access exploitation and rent dispersion, need to be tackled through appropriate domestic policy responses. This needs to be combined with complementary international trade policies to improve incentives for sustainable wildlife management.

Bibliography

E.B. Barbier. 1991. "International Policies for Managing Key Tradeable Resources: The Case of the African Elephant." Workshop on Trade and the Environment, OECD, Paris.

E.B. Barbier. 1989. "The Economic Value of Ecosystems: 1 – Tropical Wetlands." *LEEC Gatekeeper* 89-02.

E.B. Barbier, J.C. Burgess, T.M. Swanson and D.W. Pearce. 1990. *Elephants Economics and Ivory*. London: Earthscan Publications.

G. Brown and W. Henry. 1989. "The Economic Value of Elephants." LEEC Discussion Paper 89-12. London: London Environmental Economics Centre.

S. Fitzgerald. 1989. *International Wildlife Trade: Whose Business Is It*? Washington D.C.: World Wildlife Fund.

G. Hardin. 1960 . "The Competitive Exclusion Principle." *Science* 131:1291–1297.

T. Milliken, E.B. Martin and K. Nowell, 1991. "Rhino Horn Trade Controls in East Asia." *Traffic Bulletin* 12(1/2):17–21.

OECD. 1991. *The State of the Environment*. Paris: Organisation for Economic Co-operation and Development.

M.L. Oldfield. 1989. *The Value of Conserving Genetic Resources*. Massachusets: Sinauer Associates.

D. Pearce, E. Barbier and A. Markandya. 1990. *Sustainable Development: Economics and Environment in the Third World*. London: Earthscan Publications.

W.V. Reid and K.R. Miller. 1989. *Keeping Options Alive: The Scientific Basis for Conserving Biodiversity*. Washington D.C.: World Resources Institute.

J.G. Robinson and K.H. Redford, (eds) 1991. *Neotropical Wildlife Use and Conservation*. Chicago and London: The University of Chicago Press.

T.M. Swanson and E.B. Barbier, (eds). 1992. *Economics for the Wild: Wildlife, Wildlands, Diversity and Development*. London: Earthscan Publications.

J.B. Thomsen and G. Hemley. 1987. "Bird Trade ... Bird Bans." *Traffic* (USA) 7(1):21–24.

TRAFFIC Bulletin. 1991. The Journal of the TRAFFIC Network, 12(1/2).

M. Trexler. 1989. *The Convention on International Trade in Endangered Species of Wild Flora and Fauna: Political or Conservation Success*? Berkeley: University of California.

United Nations Environment Program (UNEP). *Environmental Data Report 1989/90*. 1989. Blackwell.

World Resource. 1990–91. 1991. A report by the World Resources Institute in collaboration with the United Nations Environment Program and the United Nations Development Program, Oxford University Press.

Part IV
The Global Dimension

Tropical Deforestation as an International Economic Problem

Torsten Amelung*

Introduction

The destruction of the tropical forest ecosystem in general and of rain forests in particular not only impacts on the environment in tropical countries but incurs changes in the world climate by aggravating the greenhouse effect.[1] In addition to having effects on the global climate, rain forest ecosystems feature a variety of unknown biological species. This genetic diversity has been a major research input for natural scientists all over the world.[2] Hence, the destruction of the tropical forest ecosystem leads to negative ecological effects both in industrialized and in the respective tropical countries. These ecological effects cause negative externalities in tropical and industrialized nations:

- Due to the deforestation of tropical forests, the respective tropical countries face problems like changes in the microclimate, soil erosion and decline of the water endowment. These effects can lead to a decline in agricultural productivity. Moreover, native peoples engaging in economic activities that do not reduce the regenerative capacity of rain forest ecosystems are crowded out given the current speed of deforestation in tropical countries.
- The aggravation of the greenhouse effect is expected to destabilize the global climate and to cause fluctuations in climatic extrema like temperature and wind. At the present, the economic costs of the global warming cannot be quantitatively

* The author is gratefully indebted to Joanne C. Burgess for helpful comments and suggestions.

Footnotes appear on pp. 251–252

assessed. However, the resulting increase in the variations of temperature and wind are likely to reduce the productivity in sectors that are highly dependent on climatic conditions, i.e., tourism, transport, agriculture, forestry. Moreover, the expected increase in the sea level may threaten coastal zones, which are likely to be flooded, thus leading to a loss of land or expensive preventive measures (Simonis, v. Weizsäcker, Hauchler and Böll, 1989, pp. 11–13).[3]

- The extinction of a number of biological species is expected to affect the research input available for the pharmaceutical and chemical industries and the producers of agricultural inputs.[4]
- Finally, the mere existence of environmental goods like tropical forest areas, biological species or beautiful landscapes has a positive value in terms of consumer preferences. Thus, these environmental goods can be treated as ordinary consumer goods, as there is a positive demand for them. As the supply of these environmental goods is permanently declining, the welfare position of consumers all over the world is negatively affected (Pearce and Turner, 1990, p. 265).

Given these negative effects on the economic welfare in all countries, the conservation of tropical forests should be in the interest of both tropical and industrialized countries. However, the tropical countries have recognized that their forest areas are a major economic resource that can be exploited to foster economic growth and development. In these countries, costs cannot outweigh the economic benefits derived from destructive rain forest exploitation.[5]

Since nontropical countries suffer from negative externalities, there is a divergence of interest calling for international agreements leading to a coordination of policy measures. The recent literature on the conservation of tropical rain forests features a variety of international policy measures for the conservation of tropical rain forests, i.e., multilateral and bilateral development aid, debt-for-nature swaps, international funds providing compensation payments to countries conserving their tropical forests, international agreements on carbon dioxide reduction, import barriers for those goods that are produced by using tropical forest resources (e.g., Ruitenbeek, 1990; EK, 1990; Oberndörfer, 1988;

Amelung, 1989). These international policy measures have to be complemented by domestic policy measures in the tropical countries in order to be effective. This paper will attempt to give a short overview of the discussion on suitable international policy measures that can internalize international externalities and create incentives for rain forest protection in tropical countries. In the next section, the extent and causes of deforestation will be briefly discussed. Thereafter, Section 3 will provide a short conceptual discussion of compensation payments and trade barriers, since in theory both of these measures can help to internalize international externalities. Finally, Section 4 will briefly survey the policy measures that have been recently proposed or even implemented.

I Extent and Causes of Deforestation in Tropical Countries

Even though statistics on deforestation in tropical countries are seriously deficient, it can be concluded that deforestation has increased during the 1980s in almost all tropical countries. Table 1 shows the results of the 1980 estimates and the preliminary estimates of the 1990 forest inventories performed by the FAO. There is a high discrepancy between the rates of deforestation for the 1976–1980 period and the preliminary results for the 1981–1990

Table 1. Results of the 1980 and 1990 FAO/UNEP Tropical Forest Resources Assessment Projects

	Average Annual Deforestation 1976–80 (in %)	Average Annual Deforestation 1981–90 (in %)
West and Central Africa (15 countries)	0.5%	1.7%
Latin America (22 countries)	0.7%	0.9%
Asia & Oceania (15 countries)	0.6%	1.4%
Total	0.6%	1.2%

Source: FAO/UNEP (1981); FAO (1990); Amelung and Diehl (1991).

Table 2. Subcategories of Closed Tropical Forest 1980 (million ha)

	West and Central Africa (15 countries)	Latin America (23 countries)	Asia and Oceania (16 countries)
Forest Area	338	897	336
(incl. Fallow)	(426)	(1,066)	(409)
Closed Broad-leaved Forest	188	654	292
thereof:			
undisturbed	115	453	97
logged[a]	32	54	95
unproductive	42	147	100

[a] Managed forestry or exploitation.

Source: FAO/UNEP (1981); Amelung and Diehl (1991).

period. This discrepancy is due to two factors. On the one hand, tropical deforestation has accelerated especially in West and Central Africa. By contrast, rates of deforestation in Latin America have increased only slightly. On the other hand, deforestation in some large Asian countries was underestimated in the 1976–1980 data. Following the 1980 assessment, almost 60 percent of closed tropical forests were located in Latin America, which also accounted for almost 70 percent of undisturbed forests (Table 2). On the whole, the undisturbed forests comprise the majority of tropical forest areas, while logged forests are comparatively small.

Table A.1 in the Appendix shows that the bulk of tropical closed forests is located in Zaire, Brazil and Indonesia. Therefore, their absolute deforestation rates measured in sq. km range among the highest in the world. In relative terms, however, deforestation is much higher in countries like Thailand, Philippines, Nigeria, the Ivory Coast, Madagascar and Vietnam, as is indicated by the percentage annual deforestation rates calculated from the Myers' (1989) study. Relative rates are usually calculated by dividing the absolute rate of deforestation by the remaining forest area. For the latter countries relative deforestation rates range above 5 percent. Hence, these countries seem to deplete their forests much faster than the countries that have been at the center of interest in the debate about tropical deforestation, namely Brazil, Indonesia and Zaire.

As far as the sources of deforestation are concerned, there are a number of economic sectors that use the rain forest as an economic resource, thereby depleting the rain forests. The forestry sector and the related wood industry in tropical countries make use of the tropical wood in these forests. For the agricultural sector, the tropical forest areas constitute a huge land reserve that can be utilized to expand agricultural production. The mining sector and the related processing industries located in tropical forest areas engage in the exploitation of mineral resources and the hydropower potential, which facilitates large-scale electricity production and the establishment of highly energy-intensive industries. An assessment of the percentage share of these economic activities in the destruction of the rain forest ecosystem has to remain tentative, since in most tropical countries at least two of these sectors exploit rain forest resources jointly or successively. Therefore, it is difficult to blame one specific sector for deforestation when joint use is prevailing.

Table 3 shows the percentage share of various economic activities in deforestation which is a reduction of the crown cover to less than 10 percent. Accordingly, the agricultural sector recorded the highest share in all tropical countries, ranging between 80 and 100 percent. Within the agricultural sector the shifting cultivators accounted for the largest share of deforestation in Indonesia, Cameroon and on average for all tropical countries. It has to be noted, however, that the majority of these shifting cultivations result from small, market-oriented farmers producing cash crops and export crops. Only a small segment of the shifting cultivation sector is confined to subsistence production. Hence, the separation between shifting cultivations and permanent agriculture is somehow superficial. While shifting cultivators as a whole accounted for the largest share of deforestation in Indonesia and Cameroon, the shifting cultivators' share in deforestation was relatively small in Brazil. The major part of deforestation in this country was due to livestock production.

By contrast, the mining industry and their related processing facilities accounted for a very small share of total deforestation, as the analysis for Cameroon, Brazil and Indonesia shows. Only in Brazil, where a number of mining projects in tropical rain forests were established in the last decade, did the deforestation due to

Table 3. Sources of Deforestation in Tropical Countries, 1981–1988[a]

	Brazil	Indonesia[b]	Cameroon	All Major Tropical Countries
Forestry	2[d]	9	0	(10)[e]
Agriculture	89	80	100	(83)[f]
shifting	13	59	92	n.a.
cultivators[c]	(23)	(67)	(95)	(47)
permanent agriculture	76	21	8	36
of which:				
pastures	40	0	0	17
permanent crops	4	2	5	3
arable land	32	19	3	16
Mining (incl. related industries)	<3	<0.3	0	n.a.
Hydroelectricity production	4[b]	0	0	2[b]
Residual[g]	2	11	0	(13)[h]

[a] Percentage shares in deforestation refer to averages for the respective period.

[b] Data refer to the 1980–1990 period.

[c] Figures in parentheses show the results of the FAO for 1980 (see Table A.1). These data include also market-oriented farmers who produce cash and export crops and engage only partly in shifting cultivation.

[d] Deforestation due to logging is due to charcoal production.

[e] The figure in parentheses refers to the estimation of EK (1990). The calculation includes only Indonesia and Brazil, since these countries account for the largest share in clear cutting by the forestry sector.

[f] This percentage rate is based on the assumption that the percentage share calculated for shifting cultivators can be taken as an average for the 1981–1988 period.

[g] This includes other industries, housing, infrastructure services and fire loss.

[h] The residual has been calculated from the data in this column, which includes data from different periods.

Source: Amelung and Diehl (1991), p. 155.

the mining industries and the respective infrastructure requirements exceed 2 percent. In the same vein, large dam projects have not significantly added to worldwide deforestation in relative terms. Again, it was Brazil that recently built a number of dam reservoirs in the rain forest. The share of these dam reservoirs in deforestation was 4 percent, against an average of 2 percent for all major tropical countries.

The forestry sector recorded relatively low shares in terms of deforestation because in most tropical countries trees have been harvested through selective logging rather than total clearing. Selective logging does not add to deforestation according to the definition given above, even though the reduction of biomass and the modification of forests through selective logging may incur serious ecological damage and economic costs.

In order to take account of these damages caused by the forestry sector, other measures than deforestation have to be considered. Table 4 features two other indicators, namely percentage share in biomass reduction and percentage share in forest modification. Assuming that the ecological and economic damages can be measured by the degree of biomass reduction, this percentage rate can serve as a proxy for the sectoral share in forest degradation. As Table 4 shows, the forestry sector's share in forest degradation was much higher than its share in deforestation. Nevertheless, even in terms of biomass reduction the agricultural sector was responsible for the lion's share of forest degradation. Degradation is especially high in Indonesia, where the number of trees harvested per hectare is larger than in Africa and Latin America.

An alternative measure, namely forest modification, assesses the share of various economic activities in converting virgin forests into productive closed forests or other forms of land use. Hence, even minor disturbances are considered to constitute irreversible damage. The rationale behind this concept is the assumption that forest modification opens up virgin forests for other economic sectors. Hence, successive users of other tropical forest resources face lower costs of investment in infrastructure. If one takes the percentage rate of forest modification as a yardstick, the forestry sector accounted for nearly all forest modification, since agriculture and other sectors did not enter virgin forest formations. Hence, deforestation by other sectors is mainly confined to disturbed or modified forest areas.

However, the percentage shares of forest modification cannot be interpreted to indicate that the forestry sector accounts for the lion's share of the destruction of the tropical forest ecosystem and that a prohibition of logging would preserve virgin forests

Table 4. Sectoral Share in Forest Degradation and Forest Modification, 1981–1985[a]

	Percentage Share in Biomass Reduction (Degradation)				Percentage Share in Forest Modification			
Sector	Brazil	Indonesia	Cameroon	Total[b]	Brazil	Indonesia	Cameroon	Total[b]
Forestry	6	44	10	10	(100)[c]	(100)[c]	98	71
Agriculture[d]	85	49	90	76	0	0	2	26
Others[d]	9	7	0	13	0	0	0	4

[a] For the definition of modification and biomass reduction (degradation) see Lanly (1982).

[b] Total refers to all major rain forest countries.

[c] Following FAO statistics, deforestation in virgin forests is 0, since clearing by agriculture and other sectors concentrates on disturbed forests. Even though some clearing occurs in virgin forests, there is reason to assume that the bulk of deforestation is due to forests that have been logged over prior to the clearing of the respective areas.

[d] These figures are derived from Table 3 and reflect averages for the 1981–1988 period or, in the case of Indonesia, the 1980–1990 period.

Source: Amelung and Diehl (1991), p. 157.

and hinder other sectors from entering these forest areas. There are two reasons for this. Firstly, forest modification does not measure the degree of disturbance of the rain forest ecosystem. Though forest modification certainly incurs ecological damages, it does not necessarily destroy the entire regenerative capacity of the ecosystem. This is to say that deforestation in degradated and modified forest areas may incur more ecological damage than modification or degradation, since it is only clearing that results in the complete, irreversible destruction of the rain forests.

Secondly, the opening up of forests by the forestry sector could only be regarded as the main source of deforestation if it were clear that otherwise potential users would face prohibitive costs of entering virgin forests. This, however, is a strong assumption, which does not hold true for all forests and all economic sectors. Basically, mining activities, large-scale agricultural holdings and dam projects do not depend on infrastructure established by the forestry sector. Only in countries in which the share of shifting cultivators in deforestation is very high can loggers be considered the true source of destruction because they open up forest areas. Hence, a general prohibition of forestry activities cannot be considered a means of reducing deforestation to any large extent. However, further research is needed in order to find out to what extent logging actually facilitates successive economic activities.

All rain forest resources and the commodities produced by using these resources are of relatively minor importance to the world economy, since their share in world trade, world production or world reserves is comparatively low. Nevertheless, the sectors using forest resources record sizable shares in total exports, GDP and employment in tropical countries. There are a number of countries in which the exports of the forestry sector accounted for more than 5 percent of total export revenues in 1988.[6] If one includes processed wood, this share exceeded 10 percent for most countries in Africa and Asia. Moreover, in 1980 the processing of wood accounted for more than 10 percent of employment and more than 5 percent of value added in the manufacturing sector for the majority of tropical countries. Hence, both in terms of employment and exports the logging and processing of wood seems to be an important industry in most tropical countries.

As far as the *agricultural sector* is concerned, there are a number of countries in which the conversion of tropical forest areas adds a sizable area of land to total agricultural land. For instance, more than 5 percent of agricultural land in Indonesia, Brazil, Ecuador, Suriname, the Ivory Coast, Guatemala, Costa Rica, Thailand and Cameroon in 1988 consisted of tropical forest areas converted in the 1981–1988 period. Agricultural production on areas converted in the 1981–1988 period in Cameroon comprised approximately 6 percent of agricultural production in 1988, excluding livestock production. In Indonesia, this share was 5 percent of agricultural production, while in Brazil it was 7 percent. Whereas in Indonesia and Cameroon livestock production in tropical forest areas plays only a minor role, in Brazil 3.9 percent of production in 1988 took place on pastures cleared in the 1981–1988 period. Employment effects due to these cattle ranches were negligible, accounting for 0.04 percent of national employment in 1988. In the same vein, export shares of cattle production should be negligible, since production in tropical forest areas is mainly for the domestic market. On the whole, agricultural production on areas converted in the 1981–1988 period accounted for less than 2 percent of GDP in all three countries analyzed. In the same vein, the proportion of people depending primarily on shifting cultivation to total population was 2 percent in Asia in 1980. Though this figure looks very low, a government-enforced prohibition of these activities in tropical forests is likely to cause major economic, social and political problems.

II Policies for Internalizing International Externalities

As was shown in the preceding section, tropical countries derive economic benefits from the exploitation of rain forests. Since these activities involve international externalities, worldwide welfare can be increased through internalization of these externalities. In this respect, two basic concepts can be derived from economic theory, which will be illustrated in Figure 1. The horizontal axis depicts the amount of rain forests cleared, while the vertical axis shows the respective marginal net benefits of clearing for the tropi-

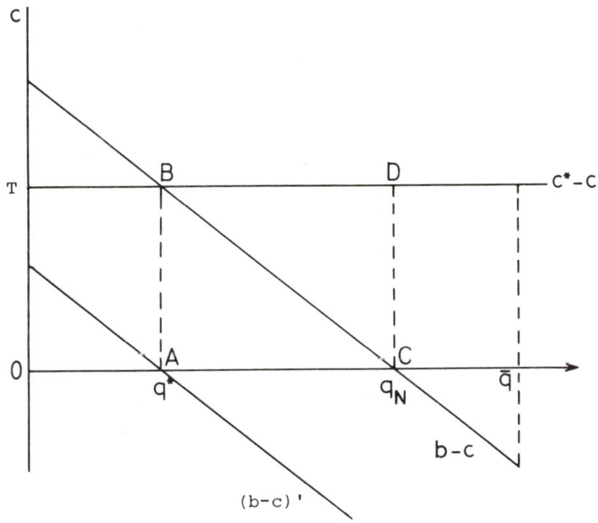

Fig. 1

cal countries as well as the marginal worldwide costs of clearing. The marginal net benefits, b–c, of clearing, which are the differential between marginal profits from forest exploitation, b, and marginal costs of environmental destruction, c, in the tropical country, are assumed to decrease with increasing quantity of clearing. This can be explained by the fact that economic activities tend to expand into increasingly less profitable rain forest areas. The national optimum for the tropical forest country is given in C, which corresponds to clearing of q_N. A rain forest area of $\bar{q} - q_N$ is not cleared because of the costs of environmental degradation in the tropical country.

This, however, is not a worldwide optimum. If one considers the worldwide marginal costs of rain forest depletion, c^*, and adds the marginal environmental costs of nontropical countries, $c^* - c$, to the analysis, the optimum amount of clearing is q^*, which refers to a worldwide optimum given in B. From the viewpoint of the nontropical countries, there are basically two ways to make the tropical country reduce its clearing from q_N to q^*. First, the nontropical countries can jointly implement an import barrier for all goods produced by using tropical forest resources. Given a tariff-equivalent of OT, the b–c curve shifts to the left. If all goods produced by using tropical forest resources are actually exported, the $b–c$ curve shifts to $(b–c)'$, so that the national optimum corresponds to the worldwide optimum. This, however, is a very strong assumption. In reality, only a minor share of goods produced by using tropical forest resources is actually exported. Even in the case of tropical hardwood at least two thirds of all trees are harvested for domestic demand, while only one third is exported in the form of hardwood or processed products (Amelung and Diehl, 1989, Chap. 3). Hence, trade barriers can hardly internalize externalities due to forest clearing. Moreover, trade barriers shift all costs of worldwide environmental protection towards tropical countries. Given the prevailing economic and social problems in many tropical countries, trade barriers against tropical countries are not likely to be politically acceptable.

Yet, there is another economic solution. The nontropical countries can compensate the tropical countries for the losses in terms of economic benefits if these countries deliberately decide to reduce rain forest clearing from q_N to q^*. The minimum amount that has be be offered comprises the triangle *ABC*, since this corresponds exactly to the lost net benefits of the tropical country in the case of a reduction of clearing of $q_N - q^*$. The amount of the compensation payment is the result of a bargaining process between tropical and nontropical countries. If the former are very weak relative to the latter in terms of bargaining power, the transfer covers only *ABC*. However, if tropical and nontropical countries are equally strong, the profit derived from negotiations has to be equally distributed among tropical and nontropical countries. The profit derived from a bargaining solution reaching point *B* in Figure 1 is the reduction of costs of clearing for nontropical countries. In *C*, nontropical countries face environmental costs of *OTDC*. These costs are reduced to *OTBA* in the worldwide optimum in *B*. Hence, for nontropical countries a reduction of clearing from q_N to q^* results in cost reduction of *ABDC*, of which a minimum of *ABC* is compensation to tropical countries. The triangle *BCD* is the worldwide welfare gain (reduction of worldwide costs) resulting from these negotiations. If tropical and nontropical countries reveal equal bargaining power, the compensation payment comprises *ABC* plus the half of *BDC*. Depending on the distribution of bargaining power of the compensation, payment ranges between ABC and *ABDC*. All of these bargaining solutions are Pareto optima, since they lead to a maximization of worldwide welfare.

Compensation payments are a better solution to the rain forest problem than trade barriers, as they are more likely to internalize international externalities, even if strategic behavior on part of tropical and nontropical countries is taken into account.[7] The implementation of compensation payments is due to a number of institutional requirements:

- In order to avoid free-riding among nontropical countries it could be useful to form an international rain forest fund as it has been proposed by UNEP. Nontropical countries, or at least all major industrial nations, could pay fresh money into this fund, while tropical countries would provide rain forest areas that are to be protected (Amelung, 1989).
- Compensation should be paid periodically instead of being paid in once-for-all lump-sum transfers. The former could possibly avoid principle-agent problems in the sense that countries that have already received a lump-sum transfer might have an interest in contract default and start clearing in forest reserves. In the same vein, periodical transfers can solve the obsolescing bargain issue: under periodical payments renegotiations are easier, for instance, when exploration activities in particular tropical forest areas discover new mineral deposits (which is equivalent to a shift of the *b–c* curve in Figure 1 to the right). Moreover, periodical payments correspond to the periodical benefits that nontropical countries derive from the mere existence of rain forests.
- Compensation payments have to be tied to conditionalities with respect to protecting rain forest reserves. Tropical countries that do not stick to these conditionalities and clear more forest land than they are allowed to must face a reduction of their compensation payments. In theory, other political conditionalities are not needed, since individual tropical countries may decide themselves how to protect their rain forest areas. However, this might lead to political and social tension in these countries if a large share of the transfers accrue to local elites, while less privileged people have to bear the costs of

adjustment. Moreover, such conditionalities and technical aid can be useful if the respective tropical countries lack the institutional and administrative capacity to implement protection policies. However, a general extension of conditionalities with regard to the use of compensation payments may be considered an interference in internal affairs, which, in turn, would complicate negotiations on compensations.

- Compensatory finance must be complemented by economic measures and adjustments in tropical countries aiming at protecting rain forests. As there are a number of sectors involved in the degradation of rain forests, the conservation of tropical forests can only be achieved by a bundle of policy measures including both the forestry sector and agriculture, which are the two main causes of deforestation.[8]
- Conditionalities should not exclude all economic activities in rain forests that are to be protected, but should implicitly foster economic activities that do not destroy the regenerative capacity of this ecosystem and the development of the necessary technologies.
- Compensation payments should not be administered and regarded as development aid. Since the mere existence of tropical rain forests incurs positive externalities, transfers should be rather regarded as a payment for exports of environmental services.
- The contribution of particular nontropical countries should be tied to the GNP of these countries. This can be justified for two reasons. Firstly, all people are affected more or less equally by the negative externalities of forest clearing. Hence, countries with a large population comprise more "consumers" than countries with a small population. Secondly, countries with a higher per capita GNP tend to have lower marginal utilities of consumption and thus lower discount rates. Since the preservation of rain forests provides long-term benefits, rich nations should have a higher consumer preference for rain forest protection.[9]

Compensation payments as they have been discussed above have not been institutionalized yet. However, there are a number of similar transfer systems that have already been implemented and will be briefly surveyed in the next section.

III Recent Programs for Rain Forest Protection

There are a number of rain forest protection programs that have been supported by multilateral institutions, nongovernment institutions and official bilateral development aid. One of the first initiatives in this area was taken by the UNESCO, which has established two funding programs aimed at establishing rain forest reserves. Under the Man and Biosphere Program, so-called biosphere reserves have been founded. With these reserves it is planned to foster applied research for sustainable production in tropical forest areas. Moreover, the UNESCO has created a World Heritage Trust offering financial support for the establishment of nature reserves in so-called World Heritage Sites, which are defined as landscapes and ecosystems with outstanding universal value. As of 1990 more than 90,000 sq.km of tropical forests in 16 countries were protected under these two programs. However, both programs are not suited for extensive protection of rain forest ecosystems. As far as the World Heritage Sites are concerned, UNESCO officials tend to be very selective. Hence, the program is not intended to save a large portion of the existing rain forests but rather a few unique ecosystems. Moreover, the delimitation of biosphere reserves has not prevented environmental degradation in the respective forest areas.

Another far-reaching concept, the Tropical Forest Action Plan (TFAP), was worked out by the FAO, the World Bank, the World Resource Institute and the United Nations Development Program in 1985. The TFAP is a framework including a list of recommended five-year programs and projects in order to coordinate both bilateral and multilateral development aimed at the protection and more efficient use of rain forest resources. The TFAP stresses the following five main areas: fuelwood and agroforestry, land use on upland watersheds, forest management for industrial uses, conservation of tropical forest ecosystems and strenghthening institutions for forest management. Nevertheless, the TFAP has been criticized on the grounds that the financial support of the TFAP reveals a bias towards financing sections like fuelwood and agroforestry as well as forest management for industrial uses. By contrast, conservation of tropical forest ecosystems plays a negligible role. Hence, the TFAP cannot be regarded as a coherent concept for the protection of tropical rain forests, though TFAP projects may foster a more efficient use of tropical forest resources.

In addition to these official programs, nongovernment organizations have undertaken actions for rain forest protection. Especially the so-called debt-for-nature swaps (DNSs) initiated by the World Wildlife Fund for Nature (WWF) have been successfully implemented. Usually DNSs work as follows: A nongovernment organization (NGO) acquires foreign debt obligations of a tropical country on so-called secondary markets, where private banks from industrialized countries sell their claims against these countries at high discounts featuring the debt default risk; thereafter the NGO engages in negotiation with the government of the tropical country concerning the establishment of nature reserves and their financing; the NGO transfers the debt obligation to the central bank of the tropical country, which changes the debt obligation into a debt obligation denominated in the domestic currency of the tropical country; the respective debt service payments are used to finance the establishment and maintenance of nature reserves. Between 1987 and 1990, 14 DNSs were implemented in 7 tropical countries (Bolivia, Ecuador, Costa Rica, the Philippines, Madagascar, Zambia) totaling more than US$96 million in terms of external debt obligations (Amelung, 1991, p. 4). Nevertheless, the financial support due to the DNS has not been sufficient to evoke a change of incentives and the subsequent restructuring of the economies in the respective tropical countries in favor of rain forest conservation. Moreover, this concept seems to be suited only to highly indebted countries, while tropical countries without a sizable external debt are neglected.

Summing up, it seems that all of these programs have not been effective in the past. None of these arrangements can be regarded as transfers compensating the tropical countries for the protection of their rain forests. A coherent approach to saving tropical forest areas requires a tropical forest fund financed by the industrialized countries as it has been partly discussed in the preceding section.

If it is not possible to form an international fund under the UN system, one should also think of bilateral compensation payments or transfers implemented by groups of industrialized countries.

IV Summary

As the above discussion has shown, the clearing of rain forests incurs negative externalities for industrialized countries which have an interest in rain forest conservation. Tropical countries, however, view their rain forest resources as an input for their economic development and continue to clear their rain forests despite the negative environmental impacts. In theory, both trade barriers and compensation payments can internalize these international externalities. However, since a high proportion of tropical forest resources are consumed in tropical forest countries, trade barriers can be regarded as a less effective measure compared with compensation payments. Such compensation payments can be provided by an international tropical forest fund financed by all major nontropical countries. This fund can be used to compensate those tropical countries that are prepared to save their rain forest ecosystems. The compensation is for the economic benefits foregone if a country deliberately decides to save its tropical rain forests and expose its economy to the necessary costly adjustments. All compensation payments have to be tied to strict conditionalities referring to the use of the compensatory finance and the specification of environmental protection. In order to prevent the governments of tropical countries from defaulting, compensation payments have to be given periodically and not once-for-all. This is to say that countries not willing to stick to the conditionalities have to face a reduction of their compensation payments. It has to be noted that such compensatory finance cannot be regarded as development aid but rather as a payment for environmental services that accrue to all countries of the world. Transfer schemes resembling compensation payments have already been implemented by nongovernment organizations and multilateral institutions. However, due to financial constraints and institutional deficiencies, these transfer schemes have not been in a position to protect sizable shares of the rain forest ecosystem.

Appendix

Table A.1: Tropical Moist Forests: Present Status and Deforestation in Selected Countries (1,000 sq.km)

Country	Extent of Closed Forests FAO (1980)	Extent of Closed Forests Myers (1989)	Annual Rates of Deforestation Myers (1976–1980)	Annual Rates of Deforestation FAO (1981–1985)	Annual Rates of Deforestation Myers (1989)
Bolivia	440.10	70.0	0.75	0.87	1.5
Brazil	3,562.80	2,200.0	14.50	13.60	50.0
Burma	311.93	245.0	1.80	1.00	8.0
Cameroon	179.20	164.0	1.20	0.80	2.0
Central America (excl. Caribbean States)	169.71	90.0	4.60	3.40	3.3
Colombia	464.00	278.5	4.60	8.20	6.5
Congo	213.40	90.0	0.20	0.22	0.7
Ecuador	142.30	76.0	2.20	3.40	3.0
Gabon	205.00	200.0	0.20	0.15	0.6
Guyanas (French Guiana, Guyana and Suriname)	422.05	410.0	0.35	0.06	0.5
Ivory Coast	44.58	16.0	3.80	2.90	2.5
India	460.44	165.0	2.60	1.32	4.0
Indonesia	1,135.75	860.0	6.60	6.00	12.0
Kampuchea	71.50	67.0	0.60	0.25	0.5
Laos	75.60	68.0	0.80	1.00	1.0
Madagascar	103.00	24.0	2.00	1.50	2.0
Malaysia	209.96	157.0	2.90	2.55	4.8
Mexico	265.70	166.0	6.10	4.70	7.0
Nigeria	59.50	28.0	3.10	3.00	4.0
Papua New Guinea	337.10	360.0	0.70	0.22	3.5
Peru	693.10	515.0	2.90	2.60	3.5
Philippines	93.20	50.0	4.60	0.90	2.7
Thailand	81.35	74.0	3.40	2.44	6.0
Venezuela	318.70	350.0	1.10	1.25	1.5
Vietnam	74.00	60.0	1.80	0.60	3.5
Zaire	1,056.50	1,000.0	2.60	1.80	4.0

Note: FAO figures refer to "closed broadleaved forest" (excl. fallow areas). Myers's figures refer to "tropical moist forest" (primary and secondary); his definition of deforestation includes "severe cases of over-logging."

Source: FAO/UNEP (1981); Molofsky, Hall and Myers (1986); Myers (1989); Amelung and Diehl (1991).

Notes

[1] According to Crutzen et al. (1989) and Houghton et al. (1987), the estimated share of carbon dioxide emissions resulting from tropical deforestation in global carbon dioxide emissions was between 10–30 percent in 1980. Following a more recent study by Myers (1989) this share was 30 percent for 1989. In the following, all countries with major rain forest reserves will be termed as "tropical countries."

[2] According to Lovejoy, 33–55 percent of the 750,000 to 2,500,000 biological species in tropical rain forests will be extinguished in the 1980–2000 period, depending on the trends in deforestation (EK, 1990, pp. 285–300).

[3] Though the climatic effects due to global warming are still disputed among scientists, insurance companies have started to adjust their risk charts showing the regional intensity and frequency of storms and floods. For instance, the Münchner Rückversicherungsgesellschaft AG prepared a revision of its meteorological charts already in 1989 (see *Welternährung*, Vol. 19, No. 3, 1989, p. 3).

[4] It has been reported that a third of all medical drugs used in the European Community include a main ingredient that has been derived from wild plants or animals living in tropical rain forests (EK, 1990, p. 321). Moreover, the development of cash crops that are resistant to particular diseases is highly dependent on wild crops in tropical rain forests. As a result, costs of research and development can be expected to increase in these sectors (Oberndörfer, 1988, p. 4).

[5] Even when benefits are smaller than the costs of environmental degradation, there can be an economic rationale for rain forest depletion. There are mainly two reasons for this. Firstly, the costs of environmental degradation become effective in the long run, while benefits accrue immediately after the economic exploitation. Given the developmental problems and the poverty prevailing in some parts of the population in many tropical countries, governments, consumers and producers have an interest in short-run improvements in their welfare position. Secondly, the economic costs of environmental degradation and the economic benefits of exploitation may accrue to different people. If the beneficiaries are politically more powerful, the degradation of forest areas can be viewed as a consequence of the political process in these countries.

[6] The percentage shares in GDP, employment and total exports, as they are presented in the following, were estimated in a fact-finding study by Amelung and Diehl (1991).

[7] The simple model presented above assumes perfect symmetric information. As a result, tropical and nontropical countries cannot adopt a strategic behavior in the sense that they pretend to show lower costs of environmental and destruction, and in the case of tropical countries higher net benefits of clearing. However, an alteration of these assumptions does not change the results of the model, though the range of possible solutions increases. Moreover, it is assumed that tropical countries clear a forest area corresponding to the national

optimum. Due to administrative deficiencies, subsidization of clearing activities and ignorance of environmental costs, tropical countries may clear even larger quantities. In such a case, negotiations would not start off from a national optimum but from a nonoptimal situation.

[8] As far as the forestry sector is concerned, long-term concessions should be introduced in order to create incentives for long-term sustainable management (Pearce, Barbier and Markandya, 1990). Moreover, a resource use tax could be a useful policy instrument incentive for an optimal use of wood resources. In order to enforce these policy measures, an improvement of the administrative capacity in tropical countries is needed. These measures aimed at the forestry sector have to be supplemented by agricultural policy reforms, since agriculture is the main source of deforestation. In order to achieve an efficient use of land, land reserves outside tropical forest areas have to be allocated to potential farmers, while special incentives for migration into tropical forest areas and production in these areas have to be reduced. Moreover, the present system of land titling in many tropical forest areas has to be improved in order to guarantee property rights, reduce extensive expansion of land and increase incentives for long-term use of agricultural holdings.

[9] At the present, it is not possible to calculate the amount of compensation payments necessary to save a sizable share of the remaining rain forests. However, calculations have been made for the transformation of rain forest areas into protected forest. For instance, Ruitenbeek has calculated the compensation payments necessary to save the Korup Park in Cameroon. Accordingly, the conservation of this 200 sq.km of rain forest would require 212,000 ECU per year or 1,060 ECU per sq.km per year. The author concedes that the cost of protection for this rain forest reserve is comparatively high.

Bibliography

Amelung, T. 1989. "Zur Rettung der tropischen Regenwälder: Eine kritische Bestandsaufnahme der wirtschaftspolitischen Lösungsvorschläge." *Die Weltwirtschaft* 2:152–165.

———. 1991. "Debt-for-Nature Swaps als Instrument zum Umweltschutz und zur Entschuldung der Dritten Welt – Zwei Fliegen mit einer Klappe?" Arbeitspapier Nr. 476. Kiel: Institut für Weitwirtschaft (Mai).

Amelung, T. and M. Diehl. 1991. *Deforestation of Tropical Rain Forests: Causes and Impact on Development* Report commissioned by Greenpeace, Hamburg. Kiel: Kiel Institute of World Economics (August).

Crutzen, P.J., W.M. Hao and M.H. Liu. 1989. *Estimates of Annual and Regional Releases of CO_2 and other Trace Gases to the Atmosphere from Fires in the Tropics, Proceedings of the University*, Freiburg, 16–20 May. Berlin, Heidelberg, New York.

Enquete-Kommission (EK) zum Schutz der Erdatmosphäre. 1990. *Schutz der tropischen Wälder*. Deutscher Bundestag, 11. Wahlperiode, Drucksache 11/7220. Bonn (24.05.).

Food and Agriculture Organization of the United Nations (FAO). 1990. *Interim Report on Forest Resources Assessment, 1990 Project* Rome (September).

Food and Agriculture Organization of the United Nations/United Nations Environment Programme (FAO/UNEP). 1981. "Tropical Forest Resources Assessment Project." Technical Report 1–3. Rome.

Houghton, R.A. et al. 1987. "The Flux of Carbon from Terrestrial Ecosystems to the Atmosphere in 1980 due to Changes in Land Use; Geographic Distribution of the Global Flux." *Tellus* 39(2):122–139.

Molofsky, J., C.A.J. Hall and N. Myers. 1986. "A Comparison of Tropical Forest Surveys." Report prepared for the U.S. Department of Energy, Washington, D.C.

Myers, N. 1989. "Deforestation Rates in Tropical Countries and their Climatic Implications. A Friends of the Earth Report." London (December).

Oberndörfer, D. 1988. *Schutz der tropischen Regenwälder durch Entschuldung. Perspektiven und Orientierungen* Schriften reihe des Bundeskanzleramtes, Bd. 5. Munich.

Pearce, D.W. and R.K. Turner. 1990. *Economics of Natural Resources and the Environment* London.

Pearce, D.W., E. Barbier and A. Markandya. 1990. *Sustainable Development* Aldershot, Hants: Edward Elgar Publishing.

Ruitenbeek, H.J. 1990. "The Rain Forest Supply Price: A Step Towards Estimating a Cost Curve for Rain Forest Conservation." Discussion Paper No. 29. London: Development Economics Research Programme, London School of Economics (September).

Simonis, U.E., E.U. von Weizsäcker, I. Hauchler and W. Böll. 1989. "The Crisis of Global Environment Demands for Global Politics." Working Paper No. 3/1989. Bonn: Stiftung Entwicklung und Frieden.

How Much Should We Invest In Preserving Our Current Climate?

William D. Nordhaus

Introduction

Over the last decade, scientists have studied extensively the greenhouse effect, which holds that the accumulation of carbon dioxide (CO_2) and other greenhouse gases (GHGs) is expected to produce global warming and other significant climatic changes over the next century. Along with the scientific research have come growing alarm and calls for drastic curbs on the emissions of greenhouse gases, as, for example, the reports of the Intergovernmental Panel on Climate Change (IPCC, 1990) and the Second World Climate Conference (October 1990). To date, these calls to arms for forceful measures to slow greenhouse warming have been made without any serious attempt to weigh the costs and benefits of climatic change or alternative control strategies.

The need to address the potential issues raised by future climate change is daunting for those who take policy analysis seriously. It raises formidable issues of data, modeling, uncertainty, international coordination, and institutional design. In addition, as I suggest in the empirical part of this paper, the economic stakes are enormous, involving investments on the order of hundreds of billions of dollars a year to slow or prevent climate change.

In earlier studies, I developed a simple cost-benefit framework for determining the optimal "steady-state" control of CO_2 and other greenhouse gases.[1] This earlier study came to a middle-of-

[1] The latest version appears in abbreviated form in Nordhaus (1991a) and in greater detail in Nordhaus (1991b).

the-road conclusion that the threat of greenhouse warming was sufficient to justify modest steps to slow the pace of climate change, but I found that the calls for draconian cuts in GHG emissions by 50 percent or more were not warranted by the current scientific and economic evidence on costs and impacts.

The earlier study had a number of shortcomings, but one of the most significant from an analytical point of view was the inadequate treatment of the dynamics of the economy and the climate. The earlier work examined a "resource steady state," one in which all physical flows are constant (e.g., in which population, emissions, concentrations, climate change have all stabilized in their steady state) although there might be improvements in real incomes because of technological change. It then went on to examine the optimal control strategy in the resource steady state.

The previous approach is unsatisfactory primarily because of the extraordinarily long time lags involved in the reaction of the climate and economy to greenhouse gas emissions. For example, current scientific estimates indicate that the major GHGs have an atmospheric residence time over 100 years; moreover, because of the great thermal inertia of the oceans, the climate appears to have a lag in the order of 50 years behind the changes in GHG concentrations; and there are long lags in introduction of new technologies in human economies to changing economic conditions. It would appear, therefore, that the dynamics are of the essence and that an examination of the steady state may provide misleading conclusions for the steps that we should take at the dawn of the age of greenhouse warming.

The plan of the present study is twofold. In the first section, we lay out the framework of an optimal growth model in which to analyze the issue of the optimal response to the threat of climate change under conditions of certainty. This part shows that the optimal policy will depend upon a number of different parameters of both the climate system and the economy.

In the second section, I provide a sketch of an empirical model that embodies the principles of the theoretical model. The empirical model estimates the major relationships in the economy and climate system that will determine the optimal investment policy. This new model is an advance over earlier studies in that it allows for different policies in the transition path from those in the ultimate steady state. It does this through the extension of the standard tools of modern optimal economic growth theory, adding to this analysis both a climate sector and a closed-loop interaction between the climate and the economy. The model is sufficiently small as to be transparent (or at least translucent), to allow a range of sensitivity analyses, and to be available for a number of further extensions.

I Optimal Growth with Climate Change

In weighing the different options for slowing climate change, the first factor that becomes immediately apparent is the long time lags between actions or policies and responses. We must take steps now (in effect, invest in emissions reductions) in order to slow climate change over the coming centuries. Few societal decisions, and no personal ones except those involving Pascal's wager or the afterlife, have comparable time horizons.

A useful way to view decisions involving such long time horizons is with the apparatus of optimal growth theory. This approach was developed by F. Ramsey in the 1920s, made rigorous by T.C. Koopmans and others in the 1960s, and is summarized nicely by R.M. Solow in his masterful exposition of economic growth. In the neoclassical growth model, society invests in tangible capital goods, thereby abstaining from consumption today, in order to increase consumption in the future.

The issue of climate change is the exact analog with respect to emissions reductions: society must take steps today, reducing consumption by devoting resources to reducing greenhouse gas emissions, in order to prevent economically harmful climate change and therefore to increase consumption possibilities in the future. At the unlikely extreme, we might suppose that food production would be curbed sharply and starvation increase if global temperatures were to rise by x degrees. Devoting resources today to prevent the x-degree rise would then allow greater food production and consumption in the future.

A A Simple Model of Economic Activity and Climate Change

We noted above that policies to slow greenhouse warming involve investing today to reduce costs in the future. In this section, I lay out the issues of intertemporal choice in a stylized model of the relationship between economic growth and climate modification. It must be emphasized that the purpose of the model used here is not complete realism but to uncover the elements necessary for intelligent policy choices; the subsequent section applies this model to empirical estimates of the major relationships in the analysis.

1 The Emissions-Climate Model

In the model that follows, we analyze the climate dynamics in terms of the CO_2-equivalent of GHG emissions. We assume that there are only two reservoirs for GHGs – those that are linked to emissions with a short lag (atmosphere, biosphere, and the mixed layer of the ocean) and a large reservoir where deposition is very slow (deep ocean, perhaps trees). The larger reservoir is assumed to have an infinite capacity for absorbing carbon. Let us consider then only the GHGs in the atmosphere, M. If β is the fraction of the increase of GHGs in short-lived reservoirs that resides in the atmosphere, we have:

$$\dot{M} = \beta E - \delta_M M \tag{1}$$

where M = increase of mass of atmospheric GHG from pre-industrial levels; E = rate of emissions of GHGs in the atmosphere; and β and δ_M = parameters of process. Dots over variables indicate time derivatives.

For purposes of later analysis, we assume that damage to the economy comes from climate change, which is represented by an increase in temperature, $T(t)$. For simplicity, with an inessential change in units, we assume in Part I that the temperature increase is equal to the change in GHG concentrations. Finally, it is assumed that there is a delay of years in the reaction of the climate and the accompanying economic effects to changes in GHG concentrations. Hence, $T(t) = M(t - \theta)$. Note that this simplifying assumption will be modified in the direction of greater realism in the empirical section.

2 *The Economic Model*

The economic model used here is also highly simplified. Economic activity will be affected by the level of GHG *emissions* because abatement is costly; and in addition there will be economic costs or benefits associated with different levels of *climate change*, which is a function of GHG accumulations.

First, starting with emissions, I assume that we are examining a market economy in which capital, labor, land, and resources are combined in productive activities. The outputs of these activities are consumption goods, new capital goods, and GHG emissions. However, GHG emissions and concentrations are not properly "priced." As a result, GHG emissions are produced and consumed up to the point where the marginal cost of reductions is zero.

Next, turn to the impacts of GHGs on economic activity. Emissions themselves are not harmful; rather it is the effect of climate change (which is determined by changes in concentrations) which leads to economic harm or good. The economic effects are on agriculture, energy consumption, and ocean levels. Thus the costs of GHG buildup are assumed to be a function of the lagged concentration.

The macroeconomic environment will also be treated in a highly stylized way in the theoretical section. At the beginning, we assume that the economy has no technological progress or population growth. Moreover, we reduce the system by solving out the capital accumulation equations. Thus real income equals real output equals consumption. In this simplest case, real consumption per capita is constant over time unless effects of climate change intervene. (An extension to include technological progress will be included later.) Under these assumptions we will represent our stylized economy very simply as:

$$c(t) = f[E(t)] - h(M(t - \theta)] \tag{2}$$

where c = per capita consumption; while E (emissions) and M

(concentrations) were defined above. One further simplification in the present model is that we assume that both sinks and sources of GHGs are inexhaustible. Thus the deep ocean is assumed to be an infinite sink, as discussed above. Similarly, there is assumed to be an inexhaustible source of carbon, perhaps high, cost shales. Again, omission of the realistic features of depletion of fossil carbon or of the absorptive capacity of the deal oceans is necessary to simplify the analysis. As has been shown elsewhere, (Nordhaus, 1979), it is possible to incorporate exhaustion of both types in a growth model, but the complications take the analysis beyond the intuitive comprehension we are seeking here.

3 *Choice Among Consumption Paths*

To complete our analysis, we need a description of how society chooses between alternative CO_2 paths or control strategies. In what follows, I propose that CO_2 control strategies be weighed by examining their implications for the consumption (or real income) possibilities of different generations. I will briefly describe the issues involved in such an analysis: (a) what is meant by consumption; (b) how do we weigh present against future generations; (c) how do we weigh different levels of consumption; (d) is the actual political process of making choices (b) and (c) consistent or defective?

(a) In the analysis that follows, we assume that the goal of economic activity is *consumption.* Consumption consists of a "bundle" of goods and services and should be interpreted in a very broad way – including not only conventional items such as food, clothing, and shelter, but also services and intangibles such as culture, recreation, leisure, and enjoying the environment. We make the key judgment that higher levels of consumption are more desirable; more or better food or shelter and cleaner air are preferable to less or poorer quality goods and services. In this view, the purpose of economic policy – and GHG control – is to enhance to the greatest extent the total consumption bundle.

Unfortunately, even if we agree that consumption is the central goal of economic activity, we have not gotten very far. More difficult is to know how we should weight the consumption of different groups – different generations in the same nation or different groups in today's world. In our simplified economic model, we see that the climate externality will force a reduction in consumption at some point – either because of damages from increased concentrations or because of the lower output due to GHG abatement. How should the consumption reductions be spread over time and space?

A reasonable way to start would be to begin by assuming that the economic costs of slowing climate change should be equally spread over space and time. This would be a plausible outcome if all generations and countries were equally well off to begin with and had equal voting power or ethical value. In any analysis of how to spread consumption over time, however, we must recognize the possibility that the costs will be differentially spread because of (b) time, (c) differences in consumption levels, or (d) unequal representation in political choice.

(b) The first reason why we might want to spread the costs of CO_2 control unequally over time might be that we have different levels of concern about consumption of different generations. We call this phenomenon *time discounting*. For example, if, as between equally well-off generations, society is indifferent between an increment of real income today and $(1 + \rho)^{100}$ increments in 100 years, we say that the "social rate of time preference" is ρ per year. Most economists and political philosophers find it hard to defend a pure rate of time preference above zero in the abstract, although the contingency of future generations has been used as a justification for discounting the distant future.

(c) A second and much more compelling reason why we might want to spread consumption or GHG control costs unequally comes from the fact that different generations have different levels of consumption. Industrial countries have witnessed more or less continual growth in living standards for more than a century; thus the per capita real consumption in the U.S. has grown by a factor of seven over the twentieth century. Society might well feel less urgency about the GHG control costs being levied upon a richer than a poorer generation. We might then discount future costs if average living standards were improving – a phenomenon we call *growth discounting*.

A more precise analytical representation would run as follows. Individuals and society may feel a greater urgency of delivering real consumption to poorer over richer generations. Thus, if c is per capita consumption, $u(c)$ is the social valuation (or "utility") of consumption; then $u''(c) < 0$. In other words, society might make the judgment that it is indifferent between delivering 1 unit of consumption today and delivering $(1 + k/100)$ units for a generation which is 1 percent poorer. In this case, the redistributive parameter $\alpha[= -u''(c)c/u'(c)$, or the elasticity of the marginal utility of consumption with respect to consumption] has value $\alpha = k$.

In considering growth it is important to distinguish whether growth is a result of population growth or growth in per capita income. The growth discount is probably different in these two cases. The analysis presented here is strictly applicable to the case where population is constant and growth occurs through an increase in per capita consumption. If real income is growing over time, society will discount future consumption if it values incremental consumption of poorer groups more than that of richer groups. If real consumption is growing at g percent annually, then the growth discount will be αg, where α was the distributional parameter defined above.

One must take into account both time and growth discounting to understand the phenomenon of *goods discounting*. Goods discounting is the familiar concept of the relative value of a unit of GNP or consumption at different points of time; if the goods discount rate is 10 percent per annum, this implies that we will forego a unit of consumption, or make an investment, today if the investment will yield at least 1.1 units of consumption next year. Ignoring taxes and risk, a goods discount rate can be observed as a real (inflation-corrected) market interest rate. When we observe a real return on capital, r (say around 6 percent per annum after taxes in the U.S. today), this refers to how society can transform consumption today into consumption tomorrow. In an optimal growth framework, with no population growth and in steady state, the discount rate on goods is related to the other concepts as follows:

$$\begin{array}{lccccc} & \text{goods discount} & & \text{time discount} & & \text{growth discount} \\ (*) & r & = & \rho & + & \alpha g \end{array}$$

where r = real return and discount rate on goods;

ρ = pure social rate of time preference;

α = redistributive parameter (elasticity of marginal utility of income);

g = growth rate of real income.

In the standard equation ρ is the *time* discount rate while αg is the *growth* discount rate. If, for example, ρ is .03, $g = .03$, $\alpha = 1$ – parameters which might reflect today's conditions – the real interest rate on goods would be 6 percent. However, if economic growth ceases and the growth discount evaporates, the discount rate on goods should fall toward 3 percent. Note that a high discount rate can be generated either by a high rate of time preference or by high aversion to inequality in a growing economy.

(d) The final question is whether the allocation of consumption over time (or setting the discount rate on goods) is determined in the rational and consistent fashion that is described above. Many people feel that there is a systematic bias in decision making in favor of the current generation, and there can be little doubt that national decision processes place much higher weight on the nation's citizens than on the rest of the world. Should we accept the current discount rate on goods as the appropriate one to use in making central allocational decisions across generations?

This question is theoretically difficult, perhaps unanswerable. Kenneth Arrow and other political theorists have shown that there is no general democratic process which will translate individual preferences into overall social decisions without inconsistencies (sometimes known as voting paradoxes). In addition, the decision processes that operate do so with no representation from future generations other than today's altruists. Moreover, the key institutions for determining interest rates – central banks – appear more concerned with inflation and trade balances than with ethical judgments about the consumption tradeoffs between current and future generations. And elected officials who compete in periodic elections may find that reallocating consumption from the future to the period before the next election will increase their chance of reelection. Both from a theoretical and institutional viewpoint, then, we may observe that the process by which social investment decisions are made will lead to an inappropriate balance between the present and future and to too high a revealed social discount rate. Ultimately, we must (and later will) fall back on home-baked value judgments about whether the current market discount rates appear reasonable.

I have collected our different discount concepts together in Table I-1. This shows how different discount rates relate to different technological parameters or value judgments. In addition, I have indicated some possible numerical values for a set of assumptions. To reiterate the fundamental point about discounting, we see that a high goods discount rate can arise in a growing economy when there is aversion to inequality. Put differently, the more that the future is better off than we are, the more justifiable it is to leave the future with less capital or more climate change to cope with.

Coming to our climate-change problem, we investigate the following criterion for choosing between alternative carbon strategies: society should choose GHG controls so as to maximize the

Table I-1. Alternative Discount Concepts in Steady State, with Illustrative Values in Parentheses

Item	Without Growth	With Growth in per capita Consumption	Application
Discount Rate on Utility, Human Life	ρ (3%)	ρ (3%)	To compare overall welfare of different generations
Discount Rate on Goods	ρ (3%)	$\rho + \alpha g$ (6%)	To compare alternative consumption paths; to make investment decisions
Discount Rate on GHGs.	$\rho + \delta_M$ (3.8%)	$\rho + \alpha g + \delta_M$ (6.8%)	To compare the value of postponement or the weighting on GHGs with different lifetimes

Note: The definition of the parameters and illustrative values are as follows:

ρ = pure rate of social time preference (e.g., .03 per annum);
α = redistributive parameter (e.g., 1 for logarithmic utility);
g = rate of growth of per capita consumption (e.g., .03 per annum);
δ_M = disappearance rate of GHGs from the atmosphere (e.g., .008 annum).

discounted expected utility of consumption. More precisely, we should maximize:

$$\max_{c(t)} W = \int_0^\infty e^{-\rho t} u[c(t)]\, dt \tag{3}$$

where W = welfare functional to be maximized; ρ = pure rate of social time preference (per annum); $c(t)$ = real consumption; and $u[c(t)]$ = utility of real consumption.

B Optimal Controls on Greenhouse Gases

We next turn to solution paths for our simple optimal growth problem. We will discuss two alternative models – one without technological change at some length and then a brief extension to include technological progress.

1 Strategies without Growth

Recapitulating our model without growth, we have:

$$\max_{c(t)} W = \int_0^\infty e^{-\rho t} u[c(t)]\, dt$$

$$c(t) = f[E(t)] - h[M(t-\theta)]$$

$$\dot{M}(t) = \beta E(t) - \delta M(t).$$

Solving such a system explicitly is straightforward using principles of optimal control, but a more intuitive approach will be used here. We first assume that $u(c)$ and $f(E)$ are concave while $h(M)$ is convex. These assumptions are probably warranted except for that about $h(M)$: we have little precise information about the $h(M)$ function but it is likely to be nonlinear, perhaps even concave. Next, we separate the future into two parts – the transition period (phase I), and a steady state (phase II). I assume that the system will tend toward a steady state, so it is useful to begin with an analysis of that. We make one important oversimplification by assuming that discount rates are constant in the two phases; this assumption makes the analysis much more tractable but will generally not hold in an optimal path.

Phase II (*steady state*). In the steady state, the atmospheric concentrations of GHGs have stabilized, so $M(t)$ is constant at M^*. This implies:

$$\beta E^* = \delta M^*$$

and

$$c^* = f(E^*) - h(M^*).$$

The easiest way to find the optimal steady state is by a simple variational technique, illustrated in Figure I-1. In the optimum, a small increment of emissions will leave welfare, W, unchanged. An increase in E by Δ at time 0 raises consumption by $f'(E^*)\Delta$. In addition, however, it raises GHG concentrations by $\beta e^{-\delta t}\Delta$, causes climatic damages θ years in the future, and lowers consumption in the future by $h'(M^*)\beta e^{-\delta(t-\theta)}\Delta (t \geq \theta)$.

Thus the present value of the change in W is:

$$u'(c^*)f'(E^*)\Delta - \int_{\theta}^{\infty} \beta e^{-\rho v} u'(c^*)h'(M^*)e^{-\delta(v-\theta)}\Delta dv,$$

which will equal zero when:

$$f'(E^*) = h'(M^*)\left[\frac{\beta}{\rho + \delta}\right]e^{-\rho\theta}. \tag{4}$$

The left-hand side is the increment to current consumption, while the right hand side is the present value of the decrement to future consumption, each with respect to a unit increase in emissions of GHGs.

We have illustrated the optimal control strategy in Figure I-2. We have first drawn the marginal cost of reducing emissions – $f'(E^*)$. The upward sloping lines show the marginal damage of increased atmospheric concentration of GHGs. At the bottom is $h'(M^*) = h'(\beta E^*/\delta)$ – the one-year marginal cost of increasing atmospheric concentrations. The curve above that – $h'(\beta E^*/\delta)[\beta/(\rho + \delta)]\exp(-\rho\theta)$ – is the discounted value of total future marginal costs of increased emissions.

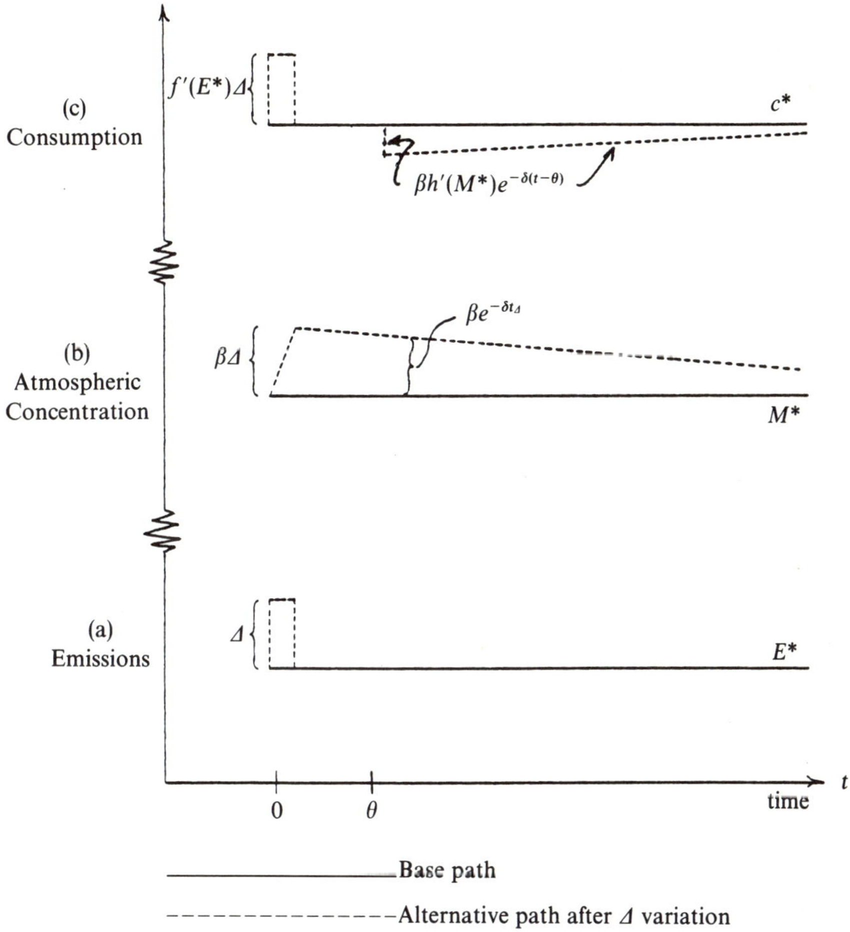

Fig. I-1. Figure shows the fundamental variational derivation of optimum. In panel (*a*) an increase of Δ in emissions is allowed in period $t = 0$. This results in an increase in atmospheric concentrations as shown in panel (*b*). In panel (*c*) the effect on consumption is illustrated. An optimum path is one in which the discounted value of changes in consumption path is zero.

The optimal control strategy comes where the two marginal cost curves intersect at point A. Note that at point A the marginal abatement cost $f'(E^*)$ equals the present value of incremental emissions, $h'(M^*)[\beta/(\rho + \delta)]\exp(-\rho\theta)$.

We are particularly interested in the "price of GHG" in our optimal solution. Let us define q as the shadow price of GHG

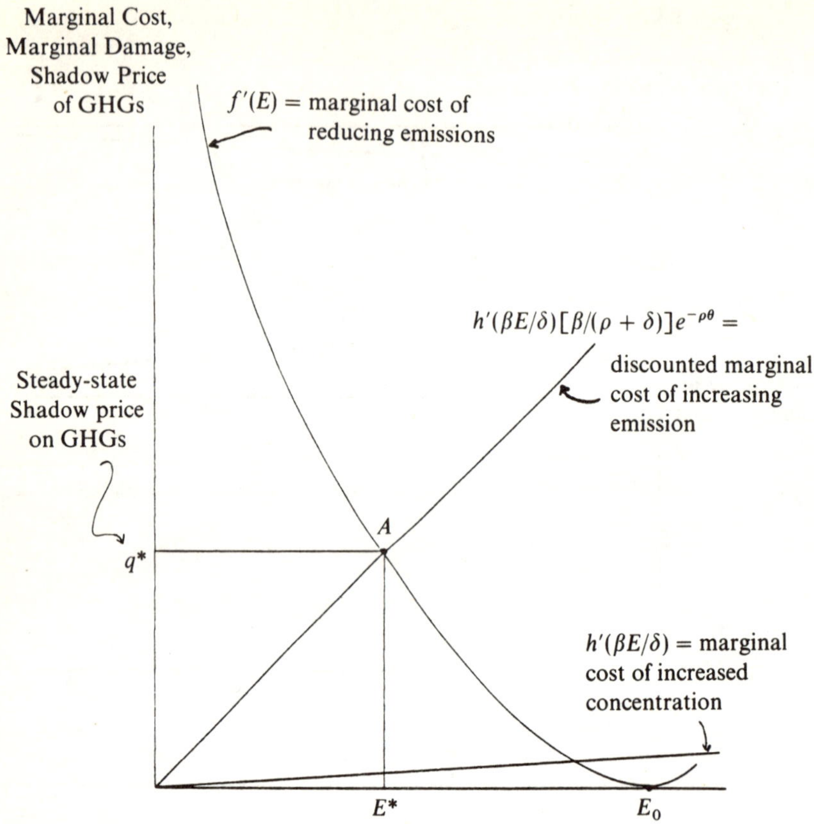

Fig. I-2. Diagram shows marginal abatement cost and discounted cost of abatement. Optimal strategy described in text.

emissions. That is, $q(t)$ represents the incremental cost in terms of consumption, $c(t)$, of increasing GHG emissions, $E(t)$. Along our optimal path we can calculate our shadow price q in two different ways because the marginal emission benefits equal the marginal concentration costs. Thus in a steady state:

$$q^* = f'(E^*) = h'(M^*)\left[\frac{\beta}{\rho + \delta}\right]e^{-\rho\theta} \tag{5}$$

where q^* is steady-state shadow price of GHG. Equation (5) states that the shadow price is equal to both the marginal cost of reducing emissions as well as the discounted cost of the atmospheric concentration from one unit of emission. The shadow price is an absolutely essential part of any rational calculation of efficient control of CO_2. It is even more important a part of an efficient decentralized control strategy for it allows individual decisions to be made as to the optimal CO_2 emissions.

Phase I (transition). Because the world economy is not in steady state, we must examine transition paths toward some potential future steady state. Using the same variational calculation as before, we find that an optimal path is the solution to the following equation for all values of $E(t)$:

$$0 = u'[c(t)]f'[E(t)] - \int_{\theta}^{\infty} \beta e^{\delta\theta} e^{-(\rho+\delta)v} u'[c(t+v)]h'[M(t+v-\theta)]\,dv. \qquad (6)$$

We can also provide a condition for our shadow price during the transition. Here again the shadow price, $q(t)$, must equal costs and benefits of future GHG reduction in terms of current period consumption:

$$q(t) = f'[E(t)] = \int_{\theta}^{\infty} \beta e^{-(\rho+\delta)v+\delta\theta} \frac{u'[c(t+v)]}{u'[c(t)]} h'[M(t+v-\theta)]\,dv. \qquad (7)$$

Equation (7) is identical to equation (6) except that it has been divided by $u'[c(t)]$, which is the marginal utility of consumption in period t. It states that the shadow price on GHG is (i) the consumption cost of reducing GHG by one unit – $f'[E(t)]$ – and (ii) the consumption cost of increasing atmospheric concentration by β units discounted as that unit of concentration gradually dissipates.

Two interesting special cases for the transition path can be described. In both we assume that the marginal utility of consumption is constant, so that without loss of generality we can take $u(c) = c$.

Case 1. Threshold level of M. Assume that there is a threshold level of GHG concentration, $M^{\otimes}$, such that for GHG concentrations up to $M^{\otimes}$ there is no damage from increases in GHG, but that when M passes $M^{\otimes}$ the costs become catastrophic. (There is no evidence that this is a likely outcome, but it is very useful analytically.) Further, assume that the marginal cost of reducing GHG emissions is constant at a fixed level, λ.

Clearly the steady state equilibrium is for $\beta E^{\otimes} = \delta M^{\otimes}$, and the steady-state shadow price is $q^{\otimes} = f'(E^{\otimes}) = f'(\delta M^{\otimes}/\beta) = \lambda$. We can also determine the shadow price in the transition. Denote time $T^{\otimes}$ as the year in which concentrations reach the fateful level, $M^{\otimes}$. Because costs are constant, it will pay to do no abatement until time $T^{\otimes}$. In this case, the shadow price of CO_2 along the

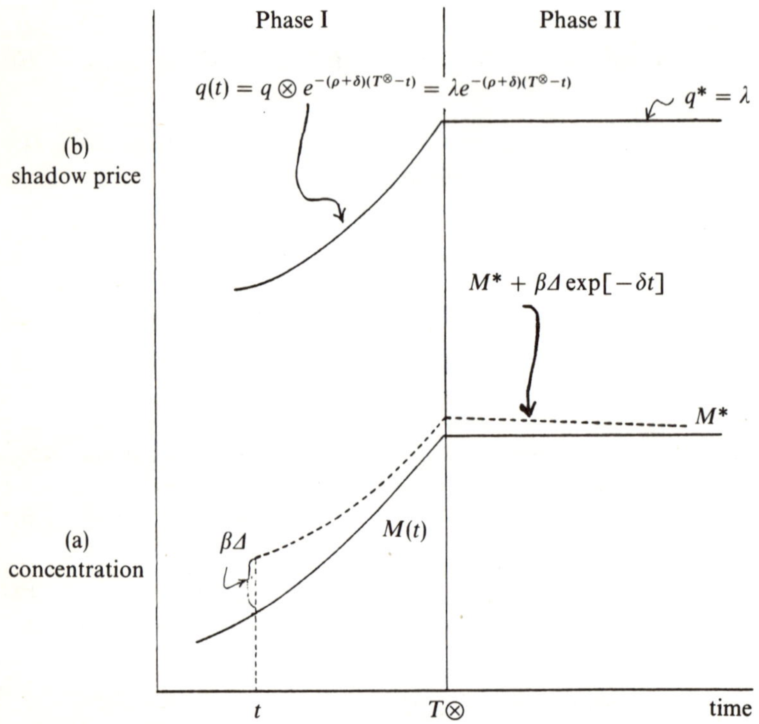

Fig. I-3. Illustration of the optimal trajectory for the case of catastrophic damage whenever M exceeds $M^{\otimes}$, with no cost of climate change up to that concentration level. The time path of concentrations after an increase of emissions of Δ is shown in panel (*a*). Shadow price must equal the constant marginal cost of GHG reduction (λ) at the time concentrations hit the maximum. Before that period, the GHG shadow price rises at the discount rate on GHGs.

transition path from (7) is:

$$q(t) = q^{\otimes} e^{-(\rho+\delta)(T^{\otimes}-t)} = \lambda e^{-(\rho+\delta)(T^{\otimes}-t)}. \tag{8}$$

This case is illustrated in Figure I-3. In words, the current shadow price of GHGs in this special case is equal to the steady-state value discounted at the GHG discount rate for the period of time until the steady state is reached. The interesting and counterintuitive result here is that the optimal carbon tax will rise very sharply over time in the case of the threshold.

Case 2. Constant costs. A second interesting case for investigating the transition is where the marginal cost of the damage of increased GHGs is constant, so that $h'(M) \equiv Z$. In this case, we can integrate the right-hand side of equation (7). Again assuming that $u'(c)$ is constant, we obtain:

$$q(t) = \int_{\theta}^{\infty} \beta e^{-(\rho+\delta)v+\delta\theta} Z\, dv = \beta Z e^{-\rho\theta}/(\rho+\delta) = q^*. \tag{9}$$

In this extreme case, the shadow price is equal to the steady-state shadow price even in the transition period. Therefore, the optimal control strategy will be invariant over time – that is, the strategy will be to go immediately to the steady-state control level, E^*.

2 *Strategies with Technological Change*

The model described in Section 1 above is unrealistic in assuming that there are no improvements in technology over time. Technological change alters the outcome in two fundamental ways. First, whereas the no-growth model above projects a gradual decline in consumption over the future, a growth model builds an upward trajectory into consumption. Second, in the earlier model, no growth meant that steady-state emissions would be stable and no progressive buildup in atmospheric concentrations of GHGs would occur; with growth, on the other hand, the only limitations to GHG buildup are resource limitations (such as the limits on fossil fuels and deforestation).

In analyzing the impact of technological change, we assume that economic growth is "unbiased" with respect to both GHG emissions and the climate-intensiveness of consumption. These assumptions imply that a doubling of output will lead to both a doubling of GHGs and to a doubling of the impact of climate change upon consumption. Under these assumptions, we can write the production and consumption relation as $c(t) = \exp(gt)\{f[E(t)/\exp(gt)] - h(M)\}$. We further simplify by an assumption concerning the transition from today's growth to a future steady state. We assume that economic growth proceeds at rate g for a period of τ years and then ceases. In addition, we assume that there is no population growth.

For analytical convenience, we introduce two new variables. $x(t)$ represents the growth of potential consumption (or consumption with no climatic constraints) from the initial period. In other words, if the impacts of climate change were magically to disappear, then $x(t) = c(t)/c(0)$. Our assumptions about economic growth are equivalent to assuming that potential consumption, $x(t)$, grows at a steady annual rate of g for τ years, reaching a new steady state, x^*, at time τ, where $x^* = x(0)\exp(gT)$.

The second variable is Φ, which is the ratio of controlled emissions to uncontrolled emissions. Clearly $\Phi = 1$ in a laissez-faire policy and $\Phi < 1$ with carbon taxes. Using the new variables, our consumption possibilities become $c(t) = x(t)\{f[\Phi(t)] - h(M)\}$.

Phase II (steady state). Using the assumption about technological change, we can then simply modify our earlier analysis to indicate the optimal path. Note that – because after τ years the growth process has stopped – we can draw upon our earlier steady-state analysis. Our steady-state level of consumption is given by $c^* = x^*\{f(\Phi^*) - h(M^*)\}$, where $M^* = \beta E^*/\delta$ and Φ^* is the steady-state level of controls. Using the same analysis as for phase II above, the optimal levels of emissions, concentrations, and the GHG shadow price are the same as equation (5) when E^* is replaced by Φ^*. For conventionally shaped cost and damage functions, the effect of growth is to raise the optimal control rate and GHG shadow price.

We can work out the impact of growth for the special cases described above. In the interesting case of the outcome with a

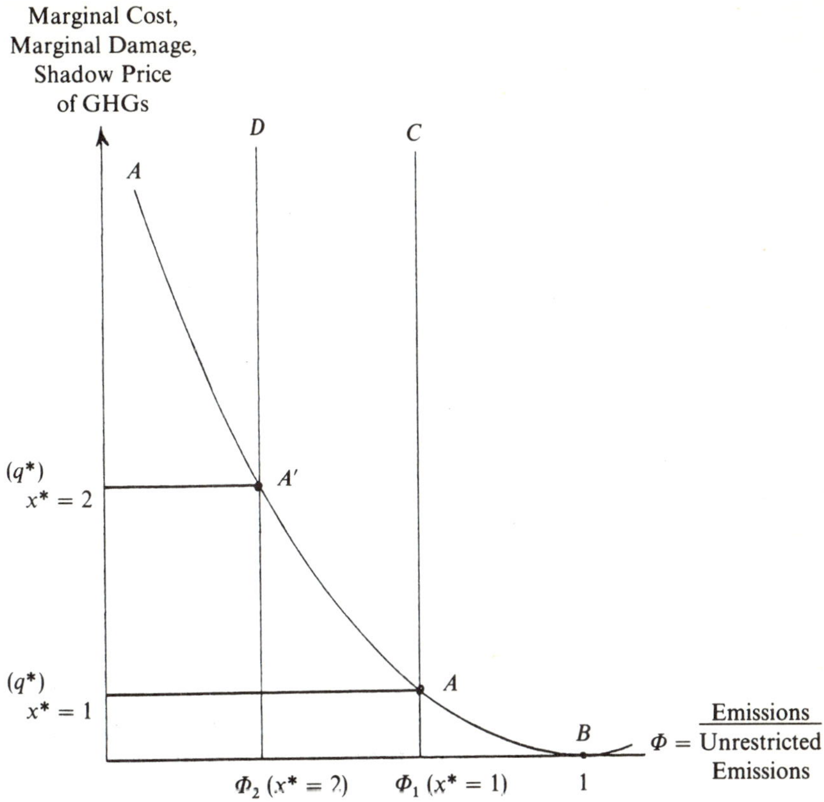

Fig. I-4. With economic growth factor of $x^* = 2$, the catastropic threshold requires controls to A' rather than A With concave costs, this raises the GHG shadow price at A' more than proportionately to x^*.

threshold or catastrophic level of concentration, the ultimate steady-state emissions are fixed and determined by the level of the threshold. For concave marginal cost function, the shadow price on emissions rises more than proportionately with x^*. The effect of higher x^* (i.e., of more growth) on the shadow price of controls is shown in Figure I-4. The case of constant marginal damage costs is shown in Figure I-5.

What can be concluded about the impact of economic growth on the optimal control of greenhouse gases? In the normal case of rising marginal abatement costs and rising marginal damage costs, the optimal steady-state policy will show higher control

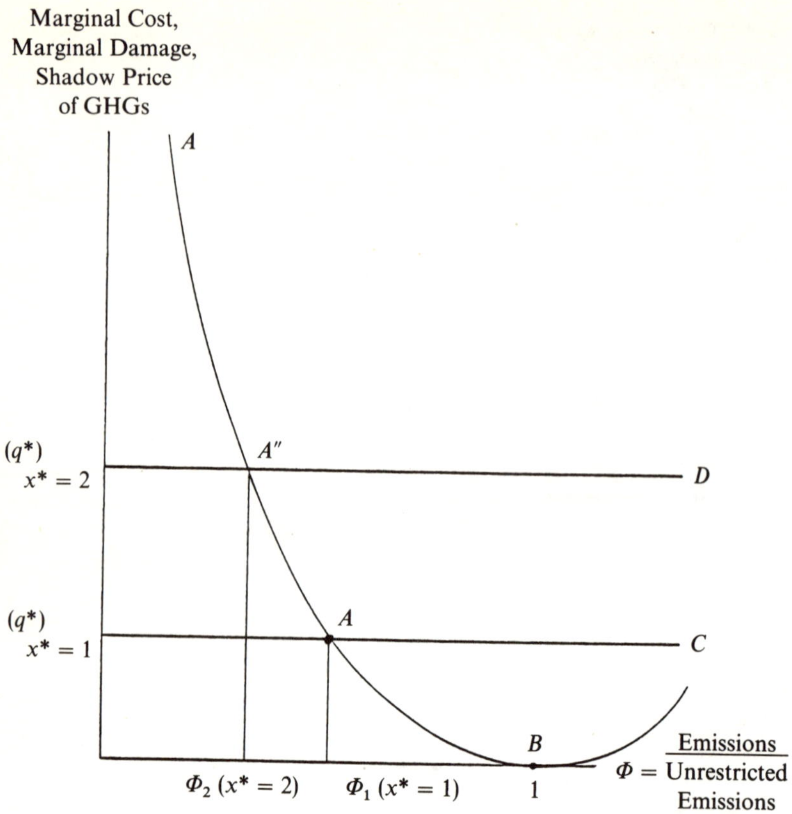

Fig. I-5. With case of constant marginal damage from climate change, the discounted value of future damages rises proportionally to the growth factor x^*. Hence the shadow price with $x^* = 2$ is twice that of no growth with $x^* = 1$. With a concave cost function, the control rate rises less than proportionately with x^*.

rates (Φ^*) for higher levels of potential consumption because the damage per unit emissions is higher. (This case is illustrated in Figure I–6.) Total emissions and atmospheric concentrations will be higher, however, because an optimal plan will allow some compromise between the higher costs from abatement and the higher damages from increased atmospheric concentrations. The increased economic and environmental stress will be reflected in a higher steady-state shadow price of greenhouse gases.

Phase I (transition path). The principles which lie behind the transition path with economic growth are virtually identical to those for the no growth path. The only difference is that the discount rate may differ because of the presence of the phenomena of "growth discounting" discussed above.

Recall that, in the presence of growth in average living standards, the discount rate on goods will be higher if there is a desire to redistribute consumption from richer to poorer generations. We again assume no population growth for simplicity. Denote $r(t)$ as the discount rate on goods. Then, assuming that the impact of climate change on consumption is second-order, the discount rate on goods during the transition period will be $r^\star = \rho + \alpha g$, while the discount rate on goods in the steady state is $r^{\star\star} = \rho$. (Again, we are oversimplifying the optimal discount rate slightly by assuming that it corresponds exactly to the equilibrium discount rate in each phase.) We can write our choice equation for the transition period as:

$$\begin{aligned} q(t) &= f'[E(t)] \\ &= \int_\theta^{\tau - t} \beta e^{-(r^\star+\delta)v} e^{\theta\delta} h'[M(t+v-\theta)]\, dv \\ &\quad + e^{-(r^\star+\delta)(\tau-t)+\delta\theta} \int_\tau^\infty \beta e^{-(r^{\star\star}+\delta)v} h'[M(v-\theta)]\, dv. \end{aligned} \tag{7'}$$

We can easily solve (7′) for our polar extremes. In the case of the catastrophic threshold, assume the threshold date $T^\otimes > \tau$. Then we have:

$$\begin{aligned} q(t) &= q * e^{-(\delta+r^\star)(\tau-t)} e^{-(\delta+r^{\star\star})(T^\otimes-\tau)} \\ &= q * e^{-(\delta+\rho)(T\otimes-t)} e^{-\alpha g(\tau-t)}. \end{aligned} \tag{8'}$$

At time 0, this becomes:

$$q(0) = q^* e^{-(\delta+\rho)T\otimes} (x^*)^{-\alpha}. \tag{8''}$$

Equation (8″) shows that the shadow price is calculated in the same way as in (8) except that the growth term – $(x^*)^{-\alpha}$ – is tagged onto the end to allow for the discounting that occurs to reflect growth in living standards.

Equation (8″) shows very handily why growth in living standards reduces the shadow price on GHGs, the carbon tax, and the control rate. For example, if the growth of living standards

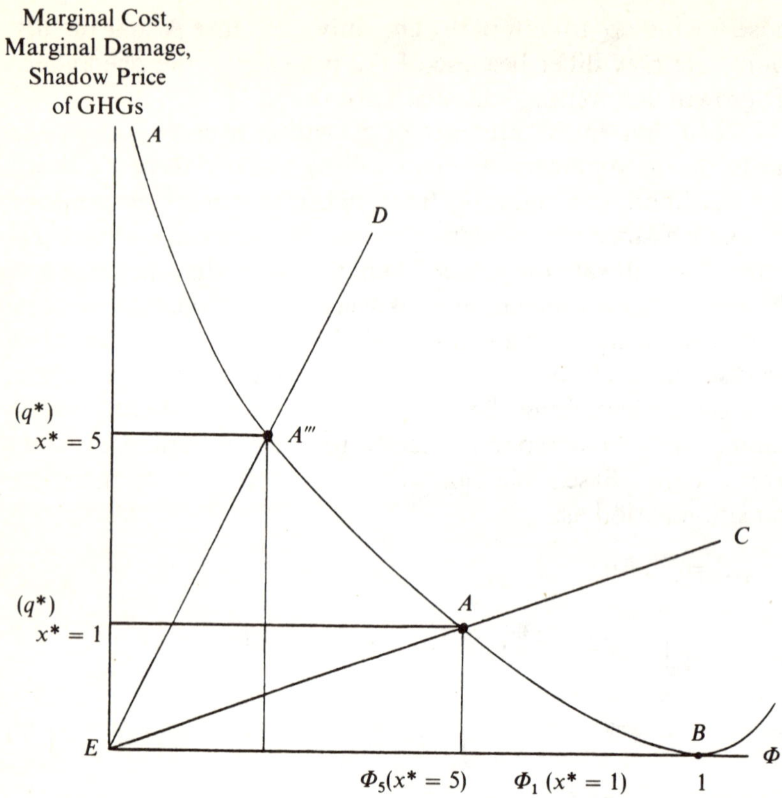

Fig. I-6. In normal case of rising marginal costs of climate damage and convex costs, growth leads to a higher control rate for GHGs and a higher GHG shadow price at A''' as compared to no-growth optimum at A'.

is a factor of five and the elasticity of marginal utility is -1, this implies that the shadow price on GHGs will be reduced to 20 percent of its steady-state value at the beginning of the growth era.

3 *Discussion of the Optimal Control Path*

Equation (7′) presents a rather forbidding answer to the issue of the optimal path for controlling greenhouse gases, so we conclude with an interpretation and some general remarks. The first point to note about (7′) is that it differs from the simple steady-state result in equation (5) only by the discount rate used. More precisely, note that equation (7′) includes the term r^* in the discount rate for the transition period. If r^* is close to r^{**}, then the optimal control paths are similar in the presence of growth and without growth.

On the other hand, observations of realistic returns on capital suggest that the transitional return on capital is likely to be well above zero and perhaps well above some ethical presumption that the long-run r^{**} should also be zero. In this view, the divergence of the transitional discount rate from zero is primarily a reflection of economic growth and the aversion to inequality that is reflected is relatively low present savings and investment rates. Put differently, a high discount rate during the transition path implies that society is averse to inequality and that most of economic growth is due to productivity growth.

What are the implications of economic growth for control of greenhouse gases? The major point to note is that the optimal shadow price of GHGs may be initially low and rising rapidly during periods of rapid economic growth. This implies that the level of control of GHGs will rise over time. The logic behind this result is that the current generation (including notably those living in developing countries) should not make large sacrifices to slow climate change today if future generations are richer and can slow climate change themselves.

This concludes our theoretical analysis of optimal strategies for the control of greenhouse gases. We have shown that it is possible to put the greenhouse problem into a general framework involving questions of the pace of economic growth and the value judgments about the allocation of costs of control strategies between current and future generations. The advantage of such a framework is that it allows a comparison of programs for the abatement of greenhouse gases with investment decisions and rates of return on investment, rather than treating GHG in isolation of other economic problems and constraints.

The framework used for the analysis is highly simplified to allow comprehension of the effects of major variables. Yet even in this highly simplified world, it is clear that there are no simple rules for deciding the timing and stringency of GHG control strategies. One key question is the ultimate level of GHG control. As is shown, the level will depend upon the appropriate discount rate (which in turn depends upon time preference, inequality aversion, and growth rates), the costs of GHG control and damage, the rate of economic growth, and the parameters of climate change.

These conclusions are, however, only qualitative. To go beyond these to quantitative findings concerning the trajectory of the optimal GHG control rate as well as the implication for carbon taxes requires actual estimates of the major empirical relationships linking climate and economic activity. That is the purpose of the preliminary model sketched in the second half of this paper.

II Empirical Application of the Optimal-Growth Approach

A Methodology

In this section, we use the framework sketched in the first part of this paper to develop an empirical model of optimal investments in the presence of the greenhouse effect. The basic approach is to use a Ramsey model of optimal economic growth with certain adjustments and to estimate the optimal path for both capital accumulation and GHG-emission reductions. The resulting trajectory can be interpreted as either the most efficient path for slowing climate change given initial endowments or as the competitive equilibrium among market economies where the externalities are internalized using the appropriate social shadow prices for GHGs.

The model is very similar in spirit to the simple version developed in the last section. In order to incorporate certain realistic features, however, it is somewhat more complicated. We describe the model verbally, reserving the equations for the appendix, and then present the results.

First, begin with the "traditional" sector of the economy, that is, the economy without any incorporation of climate change. The global economy is assumed to produce a composite commodity. It is not necessary that the countries actually be identical. Rather the goods produced must be perfect substitutes and the production functions must be identical except for multiplicative differences in productivity. This means that countries can differ in their quantitative attributes, but there cannot be large differences in the composition or relative proportions of different commodities.

Our composite economy is endowed with an initial stock of capital and labor and an initial level of technology, and all industries behave competitively. Each country maximizes an intertemporal objective function, identical in each region, which is the sum of discounted utilities of per capita consumption times population. We assume that the utility function is logarithmic or Bernoullian. Output is produced by a Cobb-Douglas production function in capital, labor, and technology. Population growth and technological change are exogenous, while capital accumulation is determined by optimizing the flow of consumption over time. There is no need for international trade, since the outputs of the different countries are perfect substitutes.

Turning to the "nontraditional" part of the model, we introduce a number of relationships that attempt to capture the major features of the forces affecting climate change. This part includes an emissions equation, a concentrations equation, a climate equation, a damage relationship, and a cost function for reducing emissions. Emissions represent all GHG emissions, although they are most easily viewed as CO_2. Uncontrolled emissions are a slowly changing fraction of gross output, which is consistent with a complex set of assumptions about the underlying production functions. GHG emissions can be controlled by increasing the prices of factors or outputs that are GHG-intensive.

Atmospheric concentrations are increased with emissions, with concentrations reduced with an atmospheric residence time of 120 years. Climate change is represented by realized global mean surface temperature, which uses an equilibrium relationship drawn from a model run close to the consensus of climate modelers and a lag given by a recent coupled ocean-atmospheric model. The economic impacts of climate change are assumed to be increasing in the realized temperature increase.

We note that this model has one major shortcoming as a representation of reality. It assumes that the public goods nature of climate change is somehow overcome. That is, it assumes that, through some mechanism, countries internalize in their decision making the *global* costs of their emissions decisions. This seems unlikely, but the current solution has the virtue of calculating the equilibrium that would emerge were each country to behave in such a farsighted and altruistic fashion. In addition, the model assumes that the objectives are efficiently attained; this requires a degree of effectiveness in implementing environmental policies that is rarely observed in practice.

B Data and Calibration

This section describes briefly the sources of the data used for the model and the calibration of the model to the data. Data on the major variables are collected for three years, 1965, 1975, and 1985, while future periods are estimated by the calculations described above and in the Appendix. Data on population, GNP, consumption, and investment are obtained from existing data sources of the World Bank, the United Nations, the OECD, and U.S. government sources. The capital stock is obtained by applying capital-output ratios from A. Maddison to our GNP data.

The parameters of the Cobb-Douglas production function are obtained by assuming that the output-elasticity of capital is 0.25 and then by estimating the level and rate of Hicks-neutral technological change directly as a residual. The utility function is assumed to be logarithmic, and the rate of social time preference is taken to be three percent per year. This preference function leads to rates of return on capital that are in the neighborhood of the observed levels in industrial countries (e.g., 6 to 7 percent per year in the 1970–89 period).

Assumptions about future growth trends are as follows: The rate of growth of population is assumed to decrease slowly, stabilizing at 11 billion people in the 22nd century. The rate of growth of world total factor productivity is calculated to be 2.0 percent per annum in the 1965–87 period. This rate is assumed to decline slowly over the coming decades.

The model has been run using the 386 version of the GAMS algorithm on various 386 compatible machines. The canonical runs presented below use a 30-period (300 year) calculation with terminal valuations on GHG concentrations, capital, and atmospheric temperature; these terminal valuations were obtained from a 50-period run and are sufficient to stabilize the solution for the first 20 periods. The canonical 30-period run can be solved in about three minutes on an Intel 486/33 processor.

C Policy Experiments

We now describe the different scenarios or policy experiments to which the model is applied.

1 Laissez-Faire, No Controls

The baseline run is one in which there are no controls or policies; i.e., no steps are taken to slow or reverse greenhouse warming. Individuals would, of course, adapt to the changing climate, but there would be no attempt to take policies that would curb greenhouse gas emissions or to "internalize" the greenhouse externality. This policy is one which has been followed for the most part by nations through 1989.

2 Optimal Policy

The next run is a calculation of the optimal policy. This run maximizes the discounted value of utility subject to the economic and climatic constraints described above and in the Appendix. This policy can be thought of as one in which the nations of the world get together and set the efficient policy for "internalizing" the greenhouse externality. It is assumed that the policy is efficiently implemented, say through uniform carbon taxation. The policy is implemented in the decade beginning 1990.

3 Ten-Year Delay of Optimal Policy

This policy is one which delays implementing the optimal policy for ten years. This policy examines the costs and benefits of delaying implementing policies until our knowledge about the greenhouse effect, along with its costs and benefits, is more secure. Hence in this scenario, the optimal policy is implemented beginning in the decade beginning in 2000.

4 *Environmentalist Policy: Constrain Temperature Growth*

Environmental groups are concerned to slow climate change to a pace that will prevent major ecological damage. One proposal is to slow the rate of temperature increase to 0.1 degrees C per decade from 1950. This policy is, by our calculation, infeasible given the current buildup of GHGs. An alternative and ambitious policy is to slow the rate to 0.1 degrees C from 1910 and to limit the ultimate temperature rise to 1.5 degrees C from the middle of the last century. This program requires very heavy controls for the indefinite future.

5 *Geoengineering*

A final policy would be to determine the benefit of a technology which would provide costless mitigation. This could occur, for example, if some of the geoengineering options, such as fertilizing the oceans or placing dust in the stratosphere, proved technically feasible and environmentally benign.[2] An alternative interpretation would be that the greenhouse effect has no harmful economic effects. This scenario is useful as a baseline to determine the overall economic impact of greenhouse warming and of policies to combat warming.

D Results and Conclusions

Because this is a highly preliminary model, designed mainly to illustrate the application of optimal growth theory to issues of

[2] The issues of geoengineering are discussed in NAS (1991).

Table II-1. Impact of Alternative Policies on Discounted Consumption

Case Policy	Discounted Value of Consumption, 1990 on Base Value [trillions of 1989 US$]	Impact of Program $ difference [billions]	Percent difference
1 No Controls	$978.70	$0	0.000%
2 Optimal Policy	979.08	385	0.039%
3 10-Year Delay	978.78	354	0.036%
4 Environmental	968.64	−45575	−4.657%
5 Geoengineering	980.13	6504	0.665%

climate change, we must emphasize that the results are only illustrative at this stage.

1 *Overall Results*

Table II-1 shows the overall evaluation of the different policies. The first column shows the discounted value of consumption for the five paths (where each path is discounted at the pure social rate of time preference). The optimal path has greater value than the three other policies in rows 1, 3, and 4. The optimal policy has a net benefit of $385 billion relative to a laissez-faire policy of no controls. This number is absolutely large, although it is only .039 percent of the discounted value of consumption.

The environmental policy of limiting global temperatures to a rise of 1.5 degrees C is enormously costly. I estimate that this policy has a discounted cost of $45.6 trillion relative to the optimal policy; this amounts to 4.7 percent of the discounted value of consumption.

The last row shows the value of a geoengineering option which arrests all climate change at zero cost; alternatively, this can be interpreted as the estimated cost of the climate changes. I estimate that the value of a geoengineering option to be $6.5 trillion relative to the policy of no mitigation. This represents .67 percent of the discounted value of consumption.

The cost of a 10–year delay in implementing policies is relatively small. Globally the cost is $31 billion or .003 percent of the discounted value of global consumption relative to the optimal policy.

In general, these numbers are mind-numbing in absolute size – largely because we are considering global output over the indefinite future. On the other hand, the numbers are modest relative to the total size of the global economy.

2 *Emissions Control Rates*

Figures II-1 and II-2 show the emissions control rates in different scenarios. These show the extent to which GHG emissions are reduced below their uncontrolled levels. In the optimal path, the rate of emissions reduction is approximately 10 percent of GHG emissions in the near future, rising to 16 percent late in the next century. The environmental case shows steeply rising control rates, with the rate of control reaching 100 percent by the end of the next century.

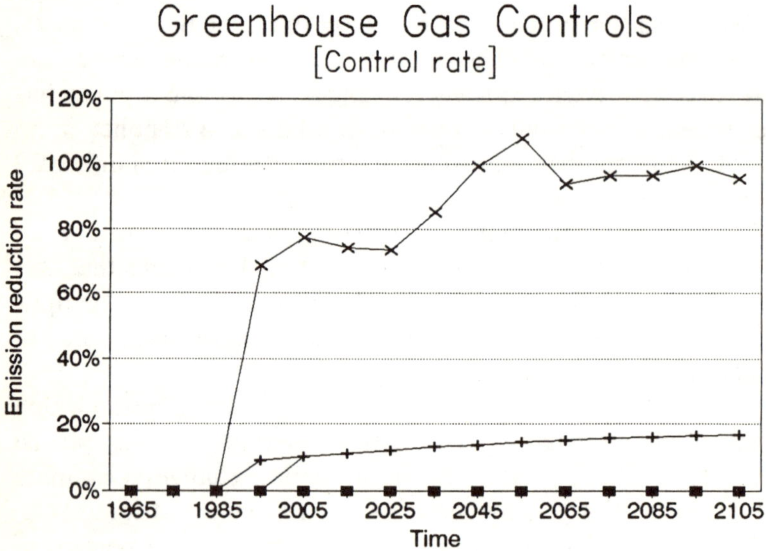

Fig. II-1

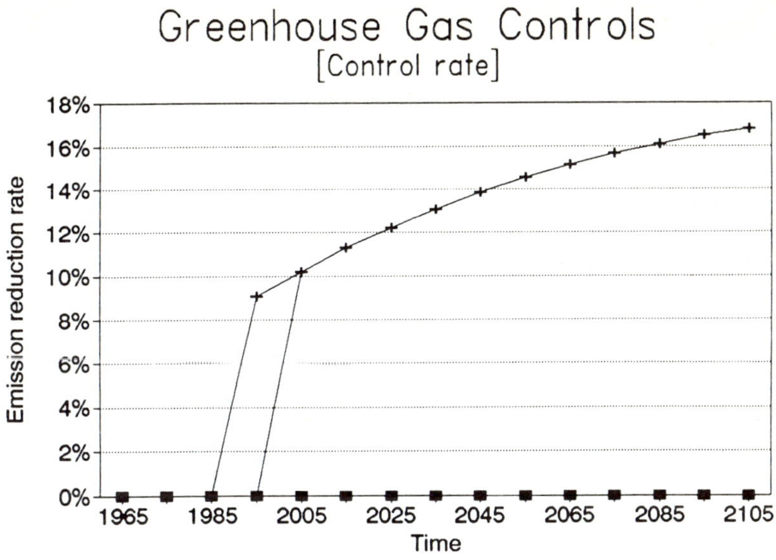

Fig. II-2

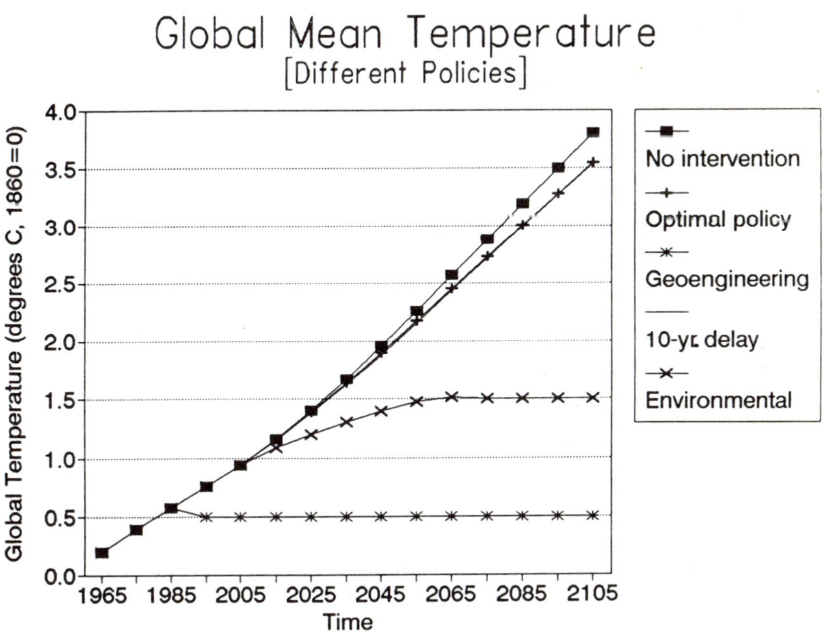

Fig. II-3

3 *Global Temperature*

Figure II-3 shows the resulting projected increase in realized mean global surface temperatures (relative to temperatures in the mid-19th century). This projection shows an initial increase of around 0.5 degrees C today, rising to slightly above $3\frac{1}{2}$ degrees C by 2100 for the uncontrolled path.

The optimal path shows a modest decline in the growth rate of global temperatures, with a rise of about one-quarter degree C less than the uncontrolled path by the end of the next century. Clearly, the optimal policy has only a minor effect on slowing climate change.

By contrast, the environmental policy succeeds in slowing climate change dramatically, with the temperature leveling off at 1.5 degrees C above the 19th century level by the middle of the next century.

4 *Carbon Taxes*

Figures II-4 and II-5 show the carbon tax that would be necessary to implement each of the policies. The carbon tax should be thought of as the tax (or its regulatory equivalent) that would be necessary to raise fossil fuel and other prices sufficiently to induce economic agents to substitute other goods and services for carbon-intensive ones.

Figure II-4 shows a carbon tax for the optimal path of around \$5 per ton carbon (or the equivalent in other GHGs) for the first control period, 1990–99. The carbon tax increases gradually over time to around \$20 per ton carbon in the middle of the next century and to about \$30 per ton by the end of the next century. The rising tax reflects the rising global output rather than increasingly stringent control efforts. These tax rates are the incentives necessary to bring about the reductions in CO_2 emissions shown in Figure II-1. The 10-year delay has a zero-tax in the fourth period, but then is virtually indistinguishable from the optimal policy. The policy of no mitigation not surprisingly has a zero carbon tax.

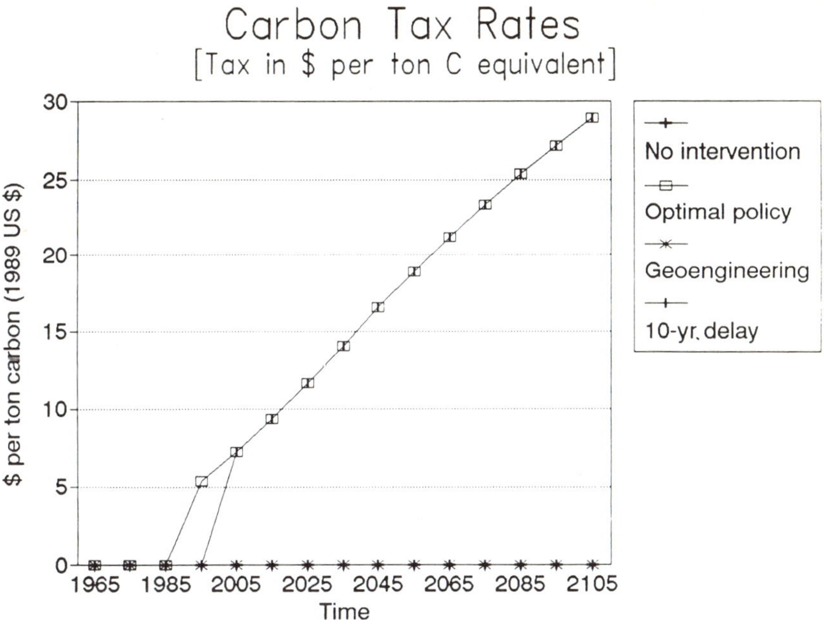

Fig. II-4

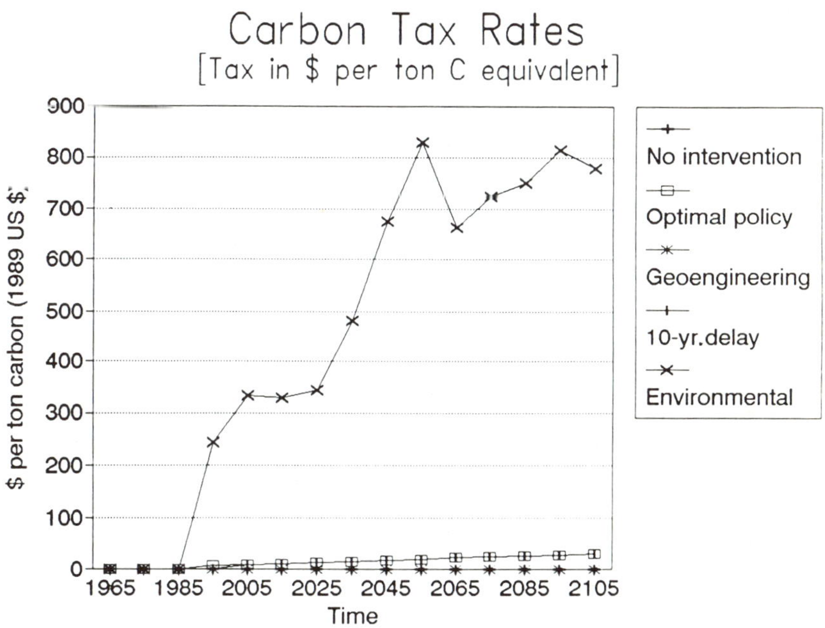

Fig. II-5

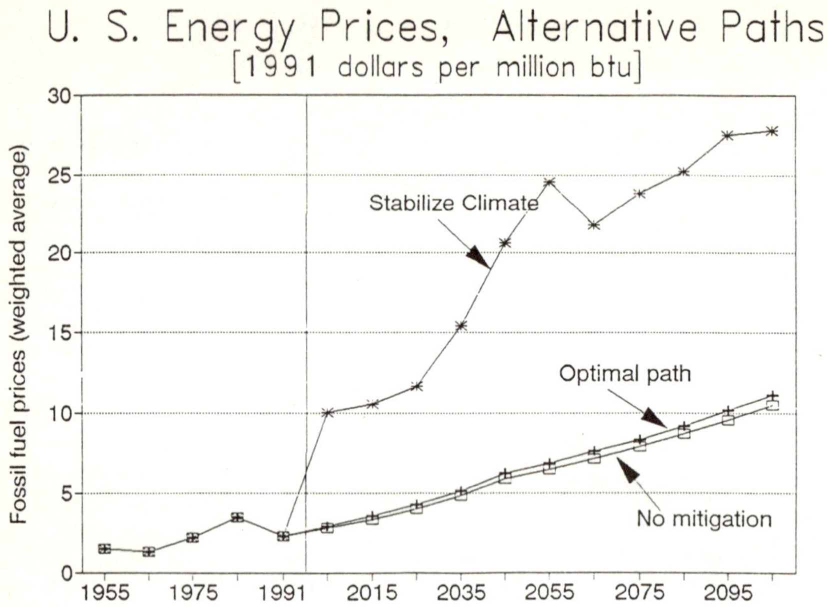

Prices represent wholesale prices of crude oil, natural gas, and bituminous coal in the United States, deflated by the GNP deflator. (Source: U.S. Energy Information Agency, Annual Energy Review, various issues and U.S. Department of Labor, producer price index for period before 1965.) Data run through 1991. For future values, I assume that real oil and natural gas prices rise by 2 percent per year from 1991 to 2045 and by 1 percent a year thereafter. Real coal prices are assumed to rise 0.5 percent per year after 1991. The index of prices uses Btu weights of fossil fues for 1987. The carbon content of fuels is assumed to be 21.9 kg of carbon per mmBtu of oil, 14 kg carbon per mmBtu of natural gas, and 27.6 kg of carbon per ton of coal. The future prices then add onto the fuel price a term that reflects 100 percent passthrough of the carbon tax into the wholesale price.

Fig. II-6

Figure II-5 shows the trajectory for the environmental policy, which requires very high taxes to implement the virtual cessation of GHG emissions. The tax starts at about $300 per ton early in the 21st century and climbs to around $800 per ton by the end of the next century. Clearly, very substantial fiscal incentives are necessary to bring about a trajectory which stabilizes climate.

Figure II-6 shows the impact of the different control strategies on energy prices. This figure shows graphically how the optimal policies have but a modest impact upon prices while the restrictive policies send average prices up by a factor of 10 over the next century.

5 *Saving*

We have emphasized that policies to abate the emissions of GHGs are investments in the prevention of future damages from climate change. Just how much, we might want to know, are we investing in our environmental program? In calculating the rate of saving, we define the "true saving" as net capital formation plus the decrement to consumption from greenhouse gas abatement. The true savings rate is true saving divided by net output for the no-controls case.

Figure II-7 shows the true net savings rates for our different cases. These cases begin with relatively high net saving (in the order of 11 percent of net output) in the historical period. For all

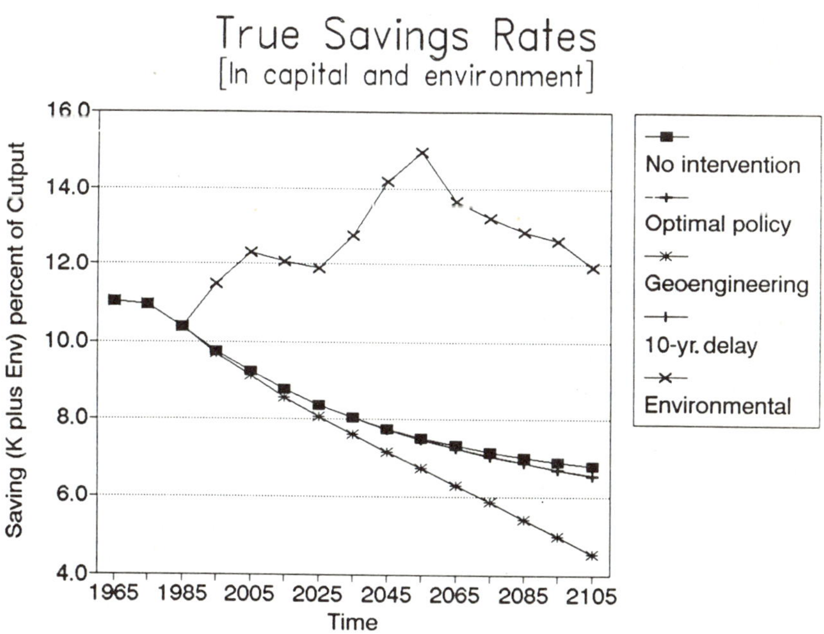

Fig. II-7

but the environmental case, the rate of net saving declines as output and population growth decline; this behavior is consistent with the presumption that as economic growth slows, the net savings rate (which is the rate of growth times the capital-output ratio) would tend toward zero.

The major surprise concerns the savings rate for the environmental case. The environmental case requires that net true savings rise from slightly above 10 percent in the third period to a peak of 15 percent in the middle of the next century. Put differently, by the middle of the next century, the world saving rate must be about twice as much in the environmental case as in the other cases. This rise in the savings rate is not due to an increase in capital formation; rather it represents a decrease in both measured output and consumption that comes from very large resources devoted to GHG emissions controls.

Figure II-7 shows graphically the dilemma of those who would take an aggressive approach to slowing climate change. Either the abatement programs to slow climate change are at the expense of productive tangible capital, in effect starving nonenvironmental programs in the name of ecology; or the world's savings rate must rise sharply, and the consumption rate decline, in order to slow the pace of climate change.

6 *Output*

Figures II-8 through II-10 show the impact of different policies on annual real output. The first shows the dollar difference from the no-control path in the early years, while the second shows the dollar effect for the period through 2105. The third shows the percentage impact.

For these calculations, the value of output is gross world output corrected for damages from climate change. Conceptually, it equals consumption plus capital formation less the flow of damages from climate change. The surprising result of these figures is that the impact of a policy of no mitigation is relatively small through the next century. The flow impact, relative to the optimum, is somewhat less than $\frac{1}{2}$ percent of real output at the maximum. Of course, the actual damage (equal to the difference be-

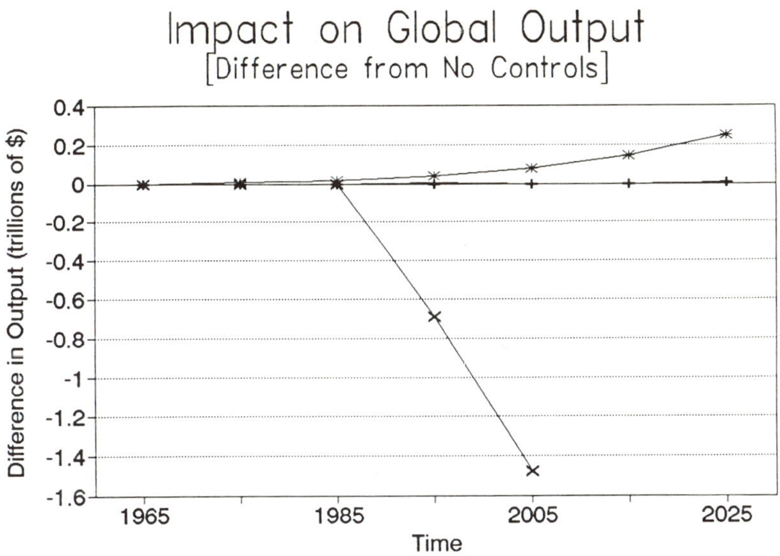

Fig. II-8

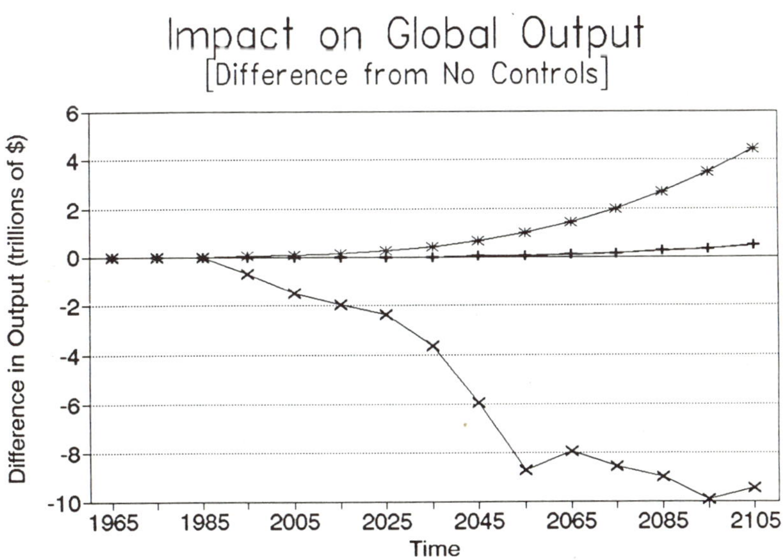

Fig. II-9

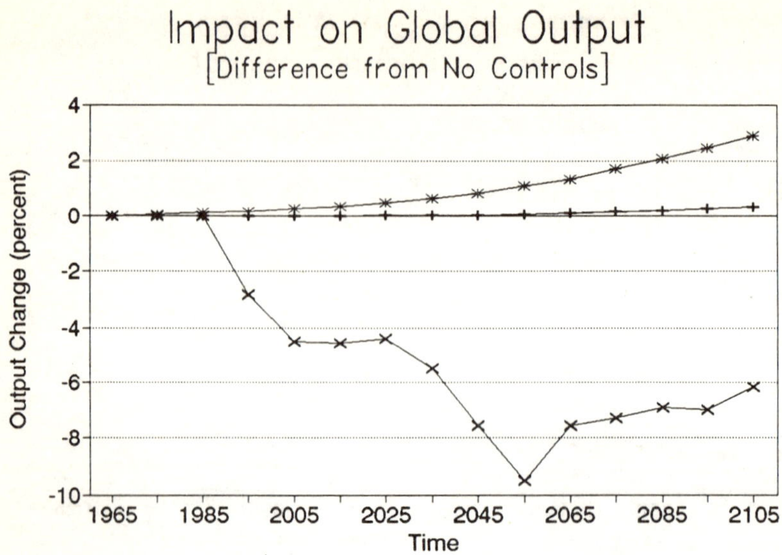

Fig. II-10

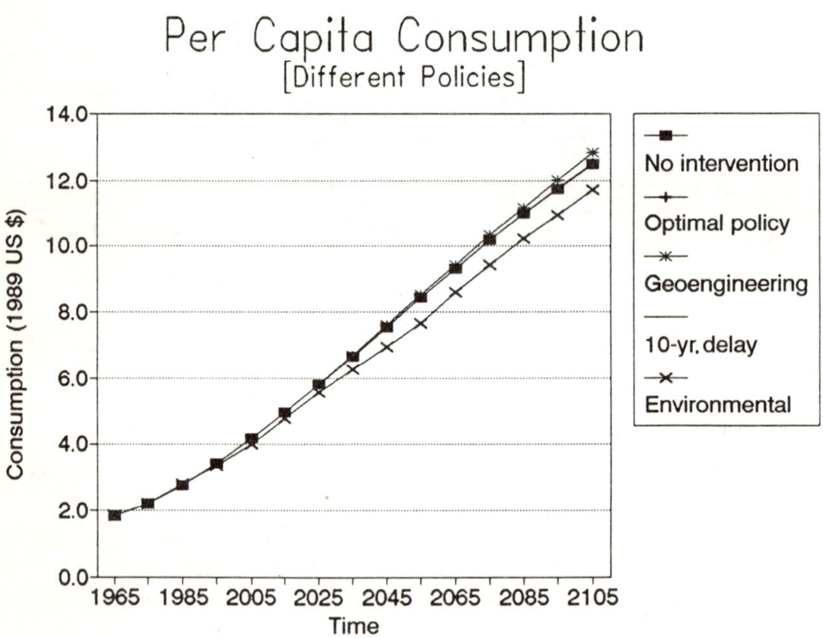

Fig. II-11

tween the "no mitigation" and the "geoengineering" options) is much larger than the cost of no mitigation relative to the optimum. The latter difference appears small because a fair amount of economic cost would occur even in the optimal trajectory.

Finally, Figure II-11 shows the trajectory of real consumption per capita in the five cases. The striking feature of this figure is that, even though there are differences among the five cases studied here, the overall economic growth projected over the coming years swamps the projected impacts of climate change or of the policies to offset climate change. In these scenarios, future generations may be worse off as a result of climate change, but they are still likely to be much better off than current generations. In looking at this graph, I was reminded of Tom Schelling's remark that the difference between a climate-change and a no-climate-change scenario would be thinner than the pencil line needed to draw the curves. Thanks to the improved resolution of computerized graphics, we can now barely spot the difference!

Appendix. Detailed Equations of the Model

1 *Objective Function*

We treat the world as a single economic entity. The different regions of the world are aggregated together and we analyze the optimal policy for the mythical "representative" country.

The model operates in steps of 10 years centered on 1965, 1975, 1985,... 2095,.... The model is "tuned" by fitting the solution for the first three decades to the actual data for 1965, 1975, and 1985 and then optimizing for capital accumulation and GHG emissions in the future. This approach assumes that it is desirable to maximize a social welfare function that is the discounted sum of the utilities of per capita consumption. In technical language, we desire to maximize the objective function:

$$\max_{\{c(t)\}} \sum_t U[c(t), P(t)](1 + \rho)^{-t}, \tag{A-0}$$

which is the discounted sum of the utilities of consumption, $U[c(t), P(t)]$, summed over the relevant time horizon. Here U is the level of utility or social well-being, $c(t)$ is the flow of consumption per capita at time t, $P(t)$ is the level of population at time t, and p is the pure rate of social time preference.

The maximization is subject to a number of constraints. The first set is the usual economic constraints, while the second is the novel climate-emissions set of constraints.

2 *Economic Constraints*

The first set of relationships concern the growth of output. The first equation is the definition of utility, which is equal to the size of population $[P(t)]$ times the utility of per capita consumption $u[c(t)]$. We take a power function to represent the form of the utility function:

$$U[c(t)] = P(t)\{[c(t)]^{1-\alpha}\}/(1-\alpha). \tag{A-1}$$

In this equation, the parameter α is a measure of the social valuation of different levels of consumption, which we call the "rate of inequality aversion." In the experiments reported here, we take (the limit of) $\alpha = 1$, which is the logarithmic or Bernoullian utility function.

Output $[Q(t)]$ is given by a standard Cobb-Douglas production function in capital in technology $[A(t)]$, capital $[K(t)]$, and labor, which is proportional to population. The term $\Omega(t)$ relates to climatic impacts and will be described in equation (A-11).

$$Q(t) = \Omega(t)A(t)K(t)^{\gamma}P(t)^{1-\gamma} \tag{A-2}$$

where γ is the elasticity of output with respect to capital. We assume constant returns to scale in capital and labor.

The next equation shows the disposition of output between consumption $[C(t)]$ and gross investment $[I(t)]$:

$$C(t) = Q(t) - I(t). \tag{A-3}$$

This simply notes that output can be devoted either to investment in capital goods or to consumption.

The next equation is the definition of per capita consumption:

$$c(t) = C(t)/P(t). \tag{A-4}$$

Finally, we have the capital balance equation for the capital stock:

$$K(t) = (1 - \delta_K)K(t - 1) + I(t) \tag{A-5}$$

where δ_K is the rate of depreciation of the capital stock.

3 Climate-Emissions-Damage Equations

The next set of constraints will be unfamiliar to most economists and consists of a simple representation of the relationship among economic activity, emissions, concentrations, and climate change, and then links up the climate change with the rest of the economy. As with the economic relationships, these equations are highly stylized.

The first equation links greenhouse-gas emissions to economic activity. In the analysis that follows, we translate each of the GHGs into its CO_2 equivalent. To aggregate the different GHGs, we use a measure of the total warming potential, which is the contribution of a GHG to global warming summed over the indefinite future. Approximately 80 percent of the total warming potential is due to CO_2, and we therefore devote most of our attention to that gas.

In modeling GHG emissions, I assume that the ratio of GHG emissions to gross output is a slowing moving constant. We represent the uncontrolled ratio of GHG emissions to output by the parameter $\sigma(t)$. In what follows, we assume that the exogenous decline in σ is 1.25 percent per annum.

GHG emissions can be reduced through a wide range of policies. We represent the rate of emissions reduction by an "emissions control factor," $1 - \Phi(t)$. This is the fractional reduction of emissions relative to the uncontrolled level. The emissions equation is given as:

$$E(t) = \Phi(t)\sigma(t)Q(t). \tag{A-6}$$

In this equation, $\sigma(t)$ is determined from historical data, and it is assumed that GHG emissions were uncontrolled through 1990. The variable $\Phi(t)$ is determined by the optimization.

The next relationship in the economy-climate nexus represents the accumulation of GHGs in the atmosphere. We assume that emissions of methane and N_2O are exogenous and take the IPCC values for those. Our estimates of the cost of control and emissions are for the CO_2-equivalent of CO_2 and CFCs. I assume that CO_2 accumulation and transportation can be represented by the following equation:

$$M(t) = \beta E(t) + (1 - \delta_M)M(t-1) \tag{A-7}$$

where β is the marginal atmospheric retention ratio and δ_M is the rate of transfer from the quickly mixing reservoirs to the deep ocean. This equation is estimated by fitting to historical data.

The next and the most difficult step concerns the relationship between the accumulation of greenhouse gases and climate change. Climate modelers have developed a wide variety of approaches for estimating the impact of rising GHGs on climatic variables. On the whole, existing models are much too complex to be included in economic models. The basic approach is to develop a small model that captures the summary relationship between GHG concentrations and the dynamics of climate change. In what follows, we represent the climate system by a multilayer system; more precisely, there are three layers – the atmosphere, the mixed layer of the oceans, and the deep oceans – each of which is assumed to be well mixed. The accumulation of GHGs warms the atmospheric layer, which then warms the mixed ocean, which in turn diffuses into the deep oceans. The lags in the system are primarily due to the thermal inertia of the three layers.

We can write the model as follows:

$$\begin{aligned} T_{1,t} &= T_{1,t-1} + (1/R_1)[F_t - \lambda T_{1,t-1} - (R_2/\tau_2) \\ &\qquad \times (T_{1,t-1} - T_{2,t-1})] \\ T_{2,t} &= T_{2,t-1} + (1/R_2)[(R_2/\tau_2)(T_{1,t-1} - T_{2,t-1})] \end{aligned} \tag{A-8}$$

where $T_{i,t}$ = temperature of layer i in period t (relative to the preindustrial period, degrees C); $i = 1$ for the atmosphere and upper oceans (rapidly mixed layer) and $=2$ for the deep oceans (slowly mixed layer); F_t = radiative forcing in the atmosphere in W/m^2; R_i = the thermal capacity of the different layers; τ_2 = the transfer rate from the upper layer to the lower layer; and λ = feedback parameter. We estimate the parameters in (A-8) by calibrating the smaller model to transient runs from larger general circulation models using the runs of Schlesinger and Jiang (1990) for calibration purposes. This study has a temperature-CO_2 sensitivity of 3 degrees C for CO_2 doubling and an e-fold time (that is, the time required to reach $1 - e^{-1}$ of the distance to equilibrium) of 19 years.

The next link in the chain is the impact of climate change on human and natural systems. Estimating the damages from greenhouse warming has proven extremely elusive, and I have reviewed some of the issues in Nordhaus (1991b). The overall assessment of the cost of greenhouse warming in the U.S. is that the net economic damage from a 3-degree warming is likely to be around $\frac{1}{4}$ percent of national income for the United States in terms of those variables we have been able to quantify. This figure is clearly incomplete, for it neglects a number of areas that are either inadequately studied or inherently unquantifiable. As a rough adjustment, I increased this number to around 1 percent of total U.S. output to allow for these unmeasured and unquantifiable factors. Making adjustments for output composition in different countries, I further raised the estimated impact to 1.3 percent of global output for all countries. In addition, there is evidence that the impact increases sharply as the temperature increases, and we assume that the relationship is quadratic. Therefore, the final relationship between global temperature increase and income loss is:

$$d(t) = .0014T(t)^2 \qquad \text{(A-9)}$$

where $d(t)$ is the loss of global output.

The last major link in the chain is the costs of reduction of greenhouse gases. This is the one area that has been extensively studied and, while not without controversy, the general shape and extent of the cost function has been sketched on a number of occasions. There are numerous estimates, particularly for CO_2, of the cost of reducing GHGs (see the extensive survey in EPA, 1989, and the survey in Nordhaus, 1991). Using current annual emissions of 8 billion tons of CO_2 equivalent, my survey suggested that a modest reduction of GHG emissions can be obtained at low cost. After 10 percent reduction, however, the curve rises as more costly measures are required. A 50 percent reduction in GHG emissions is estimated to cost almost $200 billion per year in today's global economy, or around 1 percent of world output. This estimate is understated to the extent that policies are inefficient or are implemented in a crash program. The final form of the equation used in the model is:

$$\mathrm{TC/GNP} = b_1(1 - \Phi)^{b2} = .0686(1 - \Phi)^{2.9} \qquad \text{(A-10)}$$

where $1 - \Phi$ is the fractional reduction in GHG emissions and TC/GNP is the total cost of the reduction as a fraction of world output.

Combining the cost and damage relationships, we have the Ω relationship in the production function as follows:

$$\begin{aligned} \Omega &= (1 - b_1(1 - \Phi)^{b2})/[1 + d(t)] \\ &= (1 - .0686(1 - \Phi)^{2.9})/[1 + .00144T(t)^2]. \qquad \text{(A-11)} \end{aligned}$$

Equations (A-0) through (A-11) form the mathematical model that is optimized and whose results are described in the text.

Bibliography

Edmunds, J.A. and J.M. Reilly 1983 "Global Energy and CO_2 to the Year 2050." *The Energy Journal* 4:21–47.

Intergovernmental Panel on Climate Change (IPCC). 1990. *Climate Change: The IPCC Scientific Assessment*. Cambridge: Cambridge University Press.

Jorgenson, D.W. and P.J. Wilcoxen. 1990. "The Cost of Controlling U.S. Carbon Dioxide Emissions." Paper presented at a Workshop on Economic/Energy/Environmental Modeling for Climate Policy Analysis, Washington, D.C., October 1990.

Manne, A. and R. Richels. 1990. "CO_2 Emissions Limitations: An Economic Cost Analysis for the United States," *The Energy Journal* (April).

NAS. 1991. *Policy Implications of Greenhouse Warming*. Washington, D.C.: National Academy Press.

National Research Council. 1983 *Changing Climate*. Washington, D.C.: National Academy Press.

Nordhaus, W.D. 1979. *The Efficient Use of Energy Resources*, New Haven, Ct.: Yale University Press.

———. 1991. "A Survey of the Costs of Reduction of Greenhouse Gases." *The Energy Journal* (March).

———. 1991a. "A Sketch of the Economics of the Greenhouse Effect." *American Economic Review* (May).

———. 1991b. "To Slow or Not to Slow: The Economics of the Greenhouse Effect." *Economic Journal* (July).

Schelling, T.C. 1983. "Climatic Change: Implications for Welfare and Policy." In: National Research Council, 1983, pp. 449–82.

Schlesinger, M.E. and X. Jiang. 1990. "Simple Model Representation of Atmosphere-Ocean GCMs and Estimation of the Timescale of CO_2-Induced Climate Change." *Journal of Climate* (October).

Stouffer, R.J., S. Manabe and K. Bryan. 1989. "Interhemispheric Asymmetry in Climate Response to a Gradual Increase of Atmospheric CO_2." *Nature* 7 December: 660–662.

U.S. Environmental Protection Agency (EPA). 1989a. *The Potential Effects of Global Climate Change on the United States: Report to Congress.* EPA-230-05-89-050, December.

U.S. Environmental Protection Agency (EPA). 1989 *Policy Options for Stabilizing Global Climate.* Draft Report to Congress, February.

Wagonner, Paul E., (ed). 1989. *Climate Change and U.S. Water Resources.* Wiley, New York.

List of Contributors

Torsten Amelung
Pubukohle AG, Essen

Edward B. Barbier
London Environmental Economics Centre

Wilfred Beckerman
Balliol College, Oxford

Joanne C. Burgess
London Environmental Economics Centre

Georg Erdmann
ETH Zürich

Herbert Giersch
Universität Kiel

Johannes Heister
Kiel Institute of World Economics

Peter Michaelis
Kiel Institute of World Economics

William D. Nordhaus
Yale University

Wallace E. Oates
University of Maryland and Resources for the Future, Washington, D.C.

Joanna Pasek
University of Warsaw

Friedrich Schneider
Universität Linz

James A. Tobey
U.S. Council on Environmental Quality, Washington, D.C.